Taking Oneself Playfully

Taking Oneself Playfully is a fascinating journey into the life and work of Marta Badoni, a highly respected adult and child training analyst in Italy and France.

The book is mainly formed of a collection of essays written in different moments of her life, skilfully woven together to recount Badoni's life in parallel with the evolution of her thinking and her clinical work. Drawing on influences from Winnicott and Bion, we explore the importance of the body and of the dialogue between analyst and patient in Badoni's theoretical and clinical development. The book offers a remarkable interplay of personal reflection and confidence with theoretical insight and illuminating clinical material. This is the first book in English to explore Badoni's full contribution to psychoanalysis.

Offering a playful yet deep exploration of the making, life and work of a psychoanalyst, this is key reading for all psychoanalysts.

Marta Badoni (1938–2024) was a child and adolescent neuropsychiatrist, child analyst, full member and training analyst of the Italian Psychoanalytical Society, of which she had been national secretary and vice-president, and a member of the International Psychoanalytical Association.

THE NEW LIBRARY OF PSYCHOANALYSIS
General Editor: Anne Patterson

The *New Library of Psychoanalysis* is published by Routledge Mental Health in association with the *Institute of Psychoanalysis*, London.

The purpose of the book series is:

- to advance and disseminate ideas in psychoanalysis amongst those working in psychoanalysis, psychotherapy and related fields
- to facilitate a greater and more widespread appreciation of psychoanalysis in the general book-reading public
- to provide a forum for increasing mutual understanding between psychoanalysts and those in other disciplines
- to facilitate communication between different traditions and cultures within psychoanalysis, making some of the work of continental and other non-English speaking analysts more readily available to English-speaking readers, and increasing the interchange of ideas between British and American analysts.

The *New Library of Psychoanalysis* published its first book in 1987 under the editorship of David Tuckett, who was followed by Elizabeth Bott Spillius, Susan Budd, Dana Birksted-Breen and Alessandra Lemma. The Editors, including the current Editor, Anne Patterson, have been assisted by a considerable number of Associate Editors and readers from a range of countries and psychoanalytic traditions. The present Associate Editors are Susanne Calice, Katalin Lanczi and Anna Streeruwitz.

Under the guidance of Foreign Rights Editors, a considerable number of the *New Library* books have been published abroad, particularly in Brazil, Germany, France, Italy, Peru, Spain and Japan. The *New Library of Psychoanalysis* has also translated and published several books by continental psychoanalysts and plans to continue the policy of publishing books that express as clearly as possible a variety of psychoanalytic points of view. The *New Library of Psychoanalysis* has published books representing all three schools of thought in British psychoanalysis, including a particularly important

'Marta Badoni's book communicates all the vitality, originality and maturity, at once confident and courageous, of contemporary Italian psychoanalysis: speaking of children, adolescents, adults and institutions, her voice as an innovative, competent, unprejudiced and playful analyst accompanies us towards an integrative vision of our discipline. This volume conveys, in a very personal and harmonious way, something new and substantial that was missing in our specialistic literature.'

Stefano Bolognini, *Past-President of the International Psychoanalytical Association*

'The Author tells different stories of psychoanalytic work with children and parents: theories are used as elements of an interactive play in session, which each time generates solutions of the technique tailor-made to each little patient. The different chapters are like pieces of a puzzle that generates a vivid and unified image of the psychoanalytic treatment in developmental age, that is, always. Special attention is given to the dimension of time, as a silent ally in the process of growth of the body and psyche.'

Anna Ferruta, *psychoanalyst, Full Member IPA, co-author* of Extending the Psychoanalytic Listening Paradigm, *Routledge, 2025*

'It is to these pages that Marta Badoni has entrusted her illuminating experience of discovery and knowledge under the sign of the lived experience of astonished wonder in discovering, crossing the Simplon Pass, the Rhone valley, illuminated by the luminous blade of the sun.'

From a story that Marta told me, I find the other essential element of her work, independence. In the evenings, after the days of study meetings with psychoanalysts from Eastern Europe, in which Marta participated with great interest and much success, the participants spontaneously settled into small groups characterized by affiliations to schools and currents. And Marta, who was not in any group, was the curiosity of everyone. Marta was a very clear example of the psychoanalyst for whom the definition of psychoanalyst is sufficient. She knows and shares all the contributions of Authors and Schools but does not exhaust herself in the streams of affiliations and does not deviate from the essence of psychoanalysis, maintaining both the ability to illuminate and independence.

Giuseppe Di Chiara, *Past-President of the Italian Psychoanalytical Society; former training analyst at the Training institute of the Italian Psychoanalytical Society*

'An original, independent, thoughtful book that stays with and transforms the reader. It recounts what it means to listen to oneself while listening to a patient, to feel one's own body while feeling the other's, to question one's own and the other's subjectivity. Badoni's movingly written clinical reports highlight the contribution of child analysis to psychoanalysis. The book weaves the personal and professional life and commitment to transmitting psychoanalysis of a passionate psychoanalyst, eager to learn from her patient.'

Chiara Cattelan, *child psychiatrist, SPI and IPA full member and training analyst, child analyst*

'A truly fascinating book that seems to capture the essence of the psychoanalytic experience, expertly mixing theory and personal experience. Marta Badoni's approach seems to invite the reader to a journey of introspection, pushing him to reflect on his own existence and his inner path. The tension towards complexity and the 'unsaturated' suggests a dynamic and open perspective of psychoanalysis, capable of embracing the nuances of the human condition. The idea of 'unexpected guests' and unexpected meanings further enriches the narrative, making it not only a theoretical work, but also a deeply human and relational work.'

Cristina Saottini, *Membro Ordinario Società Psicoanalitica Italiana*

'A book to be savored slowly, also to not blur the many precise references to psychoanalysts, both classical and contemporary, who have provided significant theoretical and technical contributions to the themes developed in the text. A book that also has the merit of introducing the non-Italian reader to the richness of the polyphonic character of Italian psychoanalysis. A personal travel notebook, dense with a vital, curious mental attitude, capable of inducing vital curiosity, that makes one think.'

Laura Colombi, *Supervising and Training Analyst for Child Adolescent and Adult Psychoanalysis (SPI IPA)* work edited by Pearl King and Riccardo Steiner, *'The Freud-Klein Controversies 1941–45'*, expounding the intellectual and organisational controversies that developed in the British psychoanalytical Society between Kleinian, Viennese and 'middle group' analysts during the Second World War.

The *New Library of Psychoanalysis* aims for excellence in psychoanalytic publishing. Submitted manuscripts are rigorously peer-reviewed in order to ensure high standards of scholarship, clinical communications, and writing.

For a full list of all the titles in the New Library of Psychoanalysis main series as well as both the New Library of Psychoanalysis 'Teaching Series' and 'Beyond the Couch' subseries, please visit the Routledge website.

Taking Oneself Playfully

Narrative of a Psychoanalyst

Marta Badoni

Routledge
Taylor & Francis Group

LONDON AND NEW YORK

Designed cover image: © Marta Badoni

First English edition published 2026
by Routledge
4 Park Square, Milton Park, Abingdon, Oxon, OX14 4RN

and by Routledge
605 Third Avenue, New York, NY 10158

Routledge is an imprint of the Taylor & Francis Group, an informa business

English translation by Peter Henderson
© 2026 Marta Badoni

First Italian edition published by Raffaello Cortina Editore 2023

© 2023, Raffaello Cortina Editore

British Library Cataloguing-in-Publication Data
A catalogue record for this book is available from the British Library

ISBN: 978-1-032-90944-8 (hbk)
ISBN: 978-1-032-90774-1 (pbk)
ISBN: 978-1-003-56064-7 (ebk)

DOI: 10.4324/9781003560647

Typeset in Bembo
by Apex CoVantage, LLC

Contents

Contents

Acknowledgements

This book was born out of a play of glances. It grew in a ferment of affection, and the fact that it has come to fruition is only because of Stefania Nicasi's incisive yet light touch and Alessia Fusilli De Camillis' extraordinary, competent tenacity.

My immense gratitude goes out to them.

The game began a few years ago in Florence, at the end of a conference, *Prendersi in gioco* [*Taking Oneself Playfully*]. In one of those small groups that struggle to break up when good seeds have taken root in the ground, after I had received repeated reminders to prompt me to put in writing the things I was saying, Stefania Nicasi asked me again: "Why don't you write?" My reply: "If you help me, I'll try". An intense exchange of glances and a "yes" was born.

I tried: I collected unpublished works, reconsidered published works, added thoughts suggested by the passing of time, but I would never have reached the end if Alessia's competence and affective support had not intervened with proven effectiveness. Stefania, perhaps a little desperate because of my negligence, decisively offered to be by my side: I accepted, and so began a profuse exchange of emails between Florence, Pescara and Lecco.

In lucky periods, the house in Lecco was a place of work and exchanges, of lakeside walks and moments of trepidation when a beautiful roast prepared for the guests disappeared in a flash into my dog.

It was almost inevitable that in an old house, infused with love and tragedy in equal measure, some fragments of my past would gradually surface, and the connection between personal, analytical and professional history was inevitable.

Since, in the meantime, the years have passed and aches and pains, foreseen and otherwise, have taken their toll, these writings of mine increasingly resemble a testament.

I have loved working in the Italian Society of Psychoanalysis, even though it has not always been easy. I have watched with satisfaction as young colleagues have grown, and I have probed the turbulence of the mind – mine and that of my patients – with passion.

This is my legacy, for those who have the time and wish to draw on it.

About the Contributors

Stefania Nicasi, full member of the Italian Psychoanalytical Society and International Psychoanalytical Association.

Alessia Fusilli De Camillis, associating member of the Italian Psychoanalytical Society and International Psychoanalytical Association.

Preface by Alessandra Masolini-Brown

Taking Oneself Playfully is a fascinating journey into the life and work of Marta Badoni, a highly respected adult and child training analyst in Italy and France. The book is mainly formed of a collection of essays written in different moments of her life, skilfully woven together to recount Badoni's life in parallel with the evolution of her thinking and her clinical work.

Born into a large industrialist family on Lake Como, the last of 12 children, Marta plays with the idea of being "the fifth wheel of the family". Perhaps this predisposed her to work particularly hard as the chair for Europe of the International Psychoanalytical Association (IPA) Committee on Child and Adolescent Psychoanalysis, to ensure that child analysis would no longer be considered the "fifth wheel" in training institutions and be given the space and attention it deserved. But it may also go towards explaining her ability to quietly observe and creatively reposition herself, in her personal life as well as in her thinking and her practice.

Since her first encounter with Daisy de Saugy and Julian de Ajuriaguerra's relaxation psychotherapy in Lausanne, the importance of the body and of the tonic dialogue between analyst and patient has remained central to Badoni's theoretical and clinical development. In Chapter I, she illustrates how she reached her adult patient Maria not only by listening to the description of her symptom – a permanent suffocating pressure on her stomach – or by linking her phobia of mannequins to the distressing experience of wearing an upper body cast as an adolescent: Badoni touches her arms, shares her own perceptions in doing so, and invites the patient to listen proprioceptively to her responses. It is through this attuned work of translation of tensions and sensations into words that Maria begins to discover a body where parts can communicate and come together in her mind.

Resonances with Winnicott's ideas on holding and handling, as well as Bion's concepts of containment and reverie, are very present in Badoni's work, who holds them in mind as she takes the reader on a stimulating *promenade sensorielle*, a sensory walk into her consulting room. We can almost smell and taste the flavour of the sessions in the many clinical vignettes she brings to our attention. In her spirit, they are not presented as neatly baked and finished cakes, but as snapshots of analyst and patient caught with their hands in the dough, to use one of Badoni's favourite metaphors. A process of trial and error in which the analyst's negative capability is a necessary ingredient: "Shut up, you're confusing me", an epileptic girl tells her, overstimulated by her talking. With this young patient, as with an autistic four-year-old boy who throws his ball around and then runs after it, reproducing its random trajectory, Badoni is momentarily lost. However, she is not quite "out of the game", as one possible translation of the Italian *fuori-gioco* suggests. *Fuorigioco* – one word – is also a reference to the football rule of "offside" where a player is too far ahead of the others and the game has to stop. Here we see Badoni realise that she is "offside", too far ahead of the developmental line of her patients, perhaps, to play the game. She stops, looks for the other player, and repositions herself. As she writes in Chapter IV, "The 'listening to listening', to which Haydée Faimberg (1996) drew our attention, is nothing more than making sure that the ball we threw to the patient was caught and thrown back. Throwing back is not, however, a rally, a simple returning – my turn, your turn – throwing back involves some degree of thirdness, a diversion/enjoyment".

One could say that *Taking Oneself Playfully* embraces thirdness and diversions in its very structure. Its chapters are an alternation of biography, autobiography, chronicle, theoretical discourse, and clinical material. It also includes reflections on the role of parents in the analytic process and the transgenerational mandate in the setting, is the focus of Chapter VI, which the Anglophone reader might be familiar with from its publication in the *International Journal of Psychoanalysis*. There we meet Anna, Orlando and Achille, young patients who carry inside, and sometimes embody, their own parents' unmourned ghosts and phantasies.

If one feels a bit lost, at times, among the multitude of characters and the frequent change of scenery, it is, after all, the "play" of a lifetime that we are generously offered here. In Part One, Badoni writes: "In the following reflections, I will try to describe the noticing and realisations that shaped my life and laid the foundations for my professional training". In the same paragraph, she quotes *Winnicott's words in a letter to his wife, Clare: "may I be alive when I die"*.

This book, a true celebration of Marta Badoni's rich, intensely lived personal and professional life, documents the extraordinary liveliness and creativity of her mind through time. I hope the reader will enjoy the journey as much as I did.

Preface by Luis Rodríguez de la Sierra

The Italian title (*Prendersi in gioco*) of this important and exceptional book in the field of child and adolescent psychoanalysis contains an interesting sort of pun, a play on words, as it means both to get caught up in the play and to make fun of oneself. Nothing could define Marta's personality better, as well as what made her into one of the most gifted and interesting child analysts of her time, both in her native country, Italy, and in France, where she had a very important role in the development of child analysis through her work at the European Society for Child and Adolescent Psychoanalysis, the SEPEA. She clearly describes and understands that while child and adolescent psychoanalysis are both serious matters, it is indispensable for the analysts dealing with these patients to possess the ability to immerse themselves in the playing, both with a sense of humour and mostly with the capacity to put ourselves in the place of the child and adolescent to whom play is such an important instrument to communicate and share with the analyst both the obviously conscious and the unconscious aspects of the process. This is what Annie Anzieu referred to as having "l'esprit joueur", a playful disposition, and this is what Marta Badoni shows in her book, and the implication of one of the meanings of the Italian title of the book.

Written with remarkable clarity and concision, the author draws upon a lifetime of enormous clinical experience of working with children and adolescents, and in a series of elegant chapters generously shares her insights into the worlds of her patients, adult and young ones: Maria, Fabiola, Achille, Anna, Orlando, among the many she saw during her life. Making use of her psychoanalytic expertise, Marta Badoni writes about how to help not only our patients, but also their parents and relatives as well as her colleagues in order to distinguish between how much the suffering of our patients is due to the vicissitudes of passing through the different developmental stages of life and how much can be attributed to earlier unresolved conflicts from the beginnings of their existence. The book offers a refreshing and comprehensive psychoanalytic view [mostly] of children and adolescents as they go through different stages of their development, always taking into account its potential and possibilities without ignoring its difficulties and challenges. What is normal and what is not, and what help can be offered to children and adolescents by parents and analysts? These and many other questions are taken on by the authoress with great care and understanding, both of which make this a thoughtful, very well written, imaginative book that merits the attention and admiration of all those interested in staying in touch with all the phases of the adventure in which childhood, adolescence and adulthood are the main protagonists.

Does the connection between child, adolescent and adult analysis, between acting, speaking and playing exist? Marta Badoni replies to this question, showing that there is a shared goal: to help our patients to become familiar with a new language that we are learning together, the language of the unconscious. The patient teaches us the phonetics of this language, and when the analyst understands the sounds he is hearing, he starts to develop a grammar, which will make communication easier. Here we repeat the process that takes place between the baby and his mother, who is listening to him. To take into account the permanence of this process in the inner world of our patients shows the contribution made by child analysis to psychoanalysis, which is one of the many significant messages contained in this book.

Drawing on her knowledge of Anna Freud, Melanie Klein and D. Winnicott, the pioneers of child analysis, Marta Badoni shows her capacity to use their contributions in her work with children without becoming an imitator of her teachers. To illustrate one of the meanings of the Italian title, namely playing the game, Marta Badoni uses the case of Achille, where she does not limit herself only to interpretation but makes use of other analytic tools and, in so doing, tackles what she describes as the perverse game of distinguishing what is analysis from what is not psychoanalysis. She questions her response to Achille and wonders if it was an enactment, but instead she shows her intuitive capacity to incorporate Anna Freud's developmental help into Achille's treatment.

Through clinical examples so vivid that we would think one is in the same room with her, Marta Badoni describes her successes and failures, and tries to gain psychoanalytic insight from the fact that the game has not "taken" at a given moment in the analytic relationship, sometimes because of the patient, sometimes because of the analyst.

Marta Badoni thus describes how with our child patients we start with the game and slowly progress towards talking, without, however, stopping playing. She demonstrates how it is not the words themselves that count but the way the analyst says them and how the child receives them. For this we must have the playful disposition implicit in the Italian title of the book. This expression, in its simplicity, constitutes the essence of how one uses playing and the capacity of an analyst to play with his patient. The analyst must be able to identify with many aspects of his patient, with his ego and his inner world. To play does not mean that one is not being serious, that one is not analysing but to know how to do it is an art, as Marta Badoni teaches us with her book. It is in this context that what she tells us about the diatribe, the "perverse game", can help us to decide on the real nature of child analysis and of adolescent analysis, which is itself an analysis with its own identity.

Marta Badoni's psychoanalytic testament is a rare and precious work for any reader curious to discover how one becomes a psychoanalyst, and how psychoanalysis with the child contains and reveals the psychic movements that are indispensable, in both the analyst and the patient, for the creation of the space for relational and therapeutic play. *Taking Oneself Playfully* is the animated, moving, never devoid of humour, account of the turbulent history and struggles of a psychoanalyst to acquire and have her art recognised and transmitted. It is also a refreshing, extraordinarily accurate and poetic description at the same time of what analytical listening is in the functioning of the clinician.

Marta Badoni goes straight to the point and clearly describes the essence of the psychoanalyst's therapeutic activity: "getting caught up in the game" while making sure that her patient does it too. Without the accomplishment of this double challenge, session after session, there will be no analytic cure, regardless of the patient's age, pathology, and willingness to lend himself to the constraining exercise of psychoanalytic treatment.

This centrality of a dynamic process, which requires a living and moving body-psyche relationship, is of interest to the entire field of the human sciences. Clinicians will find it particularly eloquent and energising to mobilise the observation of their countertransference on a daily basis. Sociologists will discover how the psychoanalytic approach of a child concerns the entire family, educational and school fabric in which he or she is caught. Marta Badoni, one could say, provides us with a deceptively simple, modest but admirable, and profound metaphor of what human life is.

INTRODUCTION

Marta Badoni's path to psychoanalysis

Stefania Nicasi and Alessia Fusilli De Camillis

First steps

Taking Oneself Playfully collects the distilled experience of Marta Badoni, child neuropsychiatrist and full member with training functions of the Italian Society of Psychoanalysis, of which she was National Secretary and Vice president.[1] *A psychoanalyst recounts* the interweaving of her own story, which twists through biographical discourse, clinical discourse and institutional discourse. She passed away peacefully in May 2024.

A good practice followed by the author is the consultation of vocabulary prior to her discourse: taking up an implicit suggestion, we dwell first of all on what is lexically *already known*, in an attempt to trace what is *always new*.

Introduction is what is written or said at the beginning of a book or presentation to give orienting indications; a guide, goodwill in the form of a text containing the essential elements of a discipline; in the field of music, a piece that preludes a composition by presenting its fundamental themes and characters. To *introduce*, from the Latin *condurre dentro* (to lead in), is also to welcome in; to initiate a discourse, a topic of discussion; to accompany, to provide access to a place.[2]

DOI: 10.4324/9781003560647-1

As in René Magritte's pictorial iconography, a half-open window or door reveals an invitation to gaze across a landscape, typically with a glimpse of sky or sea.

The person, the psychoanalyst

Florence, 14 January 2017: Marta Badoni gives a talk at the seminar *Acting – Playing in Child Psychoanalysis*, organised by the Florence Psychoanalytic Centre. The room is packed, students from the various schools of training in analysis or psychotherapy feverishly taking notes, careful not to miss a word, or recording on their phones. At the interval before the discussion, the young colleague sitting next to me[3] asks me where to find Marta Badoni's writings: can I recommend one of her books? In the discussion, Marta is inundated with questions. Not the usual ritual requests, the cloying rhetoric of circumstance, but genuine questions. The audience has realised that they have at their disposal a highly skilled and experienced craftswoman; they want to know *how it's done*. They seem to ask *teach us how to play* with patients, big and small, teach us *how you do it*. I allude to two books, both published by Raffaello Cortina: *L'ascolto rispettoso* [Respectful Listening] by Luciana Nissim and *Le certezze perdute della psicoanalisi clinica* [The Lost Certainties of Clinical Psychoanalysis] by Stefania Manfredi,[4] books coming from the idea of passing on to readers *how and how much* one has understood and learnt in the course of one's professional life, ripe fruits, full of seeds, presented in an open, dynamic and challenging form. Fruitful legacies also because unfinished. At the end of the seminar, I go up to Marta and tell her, "I have a dream". The tone is playful, but the intent is not: she plays along but takes me seriously. Not immediately – we will have to work to convince her to produce her *Artusi*.[5] She is aware of the effort that awaits her: to teach *how to do it*, one has to show *how one thinks*, and, in the case of an analyst, how one thinks is not separate from *who one is*.

Who one is is intimately linked to a cornerstone of psychoanalytic treatment: the progressive shift from the fact to the meaning of the fact. Stefania Manfredi indicated in the tendential search for meaning the quantum of mutative efficacy of psychoanalysis.[6] The transformation of the world of facts into the world of meanings of facts is the product of mental work activated in analysis that depends on the dynamic of *getting involved*, in which the personality of the analyst

2

and that of the patient come *into play*, with their emotions and cognitions, with their particular way of being in the world. Both "walk [like] two wayfarers" on the path of the analytic process, interpreters of transformation. In this sense, the personality of the analyst is considered one of the facilitators of the psychoanalytic method, together with dream work, with its poietic activity, and the work of disassembly, with its deconstructive activity (Riolo, 2018, 82).[7]

Marta Badoni recounts who she is and how she came to be who she is, amidst *misunderstandings and ills understood, agreeable and disagreeable elements,* with just a few brushstrokes, in the course of the book. Born in Lecco, "the fifth wheel of the family", the last of 12 children, all girls apart from only one boy, who lost his life in the war: "Their names?", the analyst Renato Sigurtà asked her, armed with pen and paper, at their first meeting, grasping at the difficulty of finding both her way around and her place. In this complex, numerous, industrialist family, wealthy but dedicated to work, everyone studied and prepared for a profession. Marta graduated in medicine in Milan and, just married in 1966, moved with her husband to Lausanne, where their two children were born. Her background was in internal medicine, and she worked at the Lausanne Cantonal Hospital, but soon became interested in psychiatry and child analysis, moving to the Office Médico Pédagogique (University Service for Children and Adolescents). She became interested in de Ajuriaguerra's Relaxation Psychotherapy and discovered, under the guidance of Daisy de Saugy, that being touched by the therapist "initiates a composite experience in which commonality and separateness converge" (Riolo, 2018, 23). Attention to the child and to the body, which she developed in Lausanne, remained central and intertwined in her clinical practice and theoretical reflection in the years to come. Back in Milan in 1973, she began a new specialisation in Child Neuropsychiatry, which she would finish in 1980 with a thesis on relaxation psychotherapy for mothers of handicapped children. These were intense, difficult years in which she worked with children and adolescents, collaborated with the Child Neuropsychiatry Clinic in Pavia, raised her children, and tried to keep a stormy marriage together. She also started analytical training, but after six months, her analysis with Tommaso Senise was interrupted. In the difficult years that followed this interruption, she quenched her thirst for training in extra-territorial waters. In addition to the valuable seminars with Irma Pick, a lasting trace of this is the emotion she felt in one of the first meetings with Paul–Claude Racamier, when Marta hesitantly asked how fear of interpreting is generated and received in reply a very generous introduction to the psychoanalyst's profession. It would become a profound bond with significant cross-references, such as that between speaking actions and thinking arms. The analysis project came to life again a few years later with Renato Sigurtà: in 1989, having obtained membership, she definitively joined the SPI [Italian Psychoanalytic Society] and the Milanese Psychoanalysis Centre, where she would hold various positions at local and national levels. With the support of Dario De Martis, then President of the Milanese Psychoanalysis Centre, she set up a clinical service for children in the Centre, and in 1993, under the presidency of Giuseppe Di Chiara, the Child Psychoanalysis Observatory was created. In 2004, she took over training, and at the same time, her first grandchild was born, so she became an all-round "grandmother", in both her analytic family and her private one. In 2014, she settled in her family house in Lecco and immersed herself in the archive, reconstructing her parents' history. This led to an exhibition, *Un archivio in-vita. Family and work in the papers of Giuseppe Riccardo Badoni*, conceived and curated with her niece, Francesca Brambilla.[8]

In the shade of the great plane trees that spread over her as a child, her professional and social activities gradually lightened up, leaving room for theoretical reflection, the writing of some important works, and walks with Kelly, the reckless half-breed from the south, taken away from life as a stray, but not from freedom.

Freedom that Marta already announces in the idea of "getting involved", a challenge to dive in.

From the shore of the Introduction, let us delve into a few considerations on the title: *Taking Oneself Playfully*.

A first salience concerns the centrality of the gerund forms: *taking, playing and telling*.

Compared to the use of nouns, the use of gerunds seems to suggest an intention to tame and deal first and foremost with the processual dimension inherent in the dynamics of mental work and processes of transformation and subjectification. In the language of the second metapsychology,[9] the use of gerund verb-forms seems to direct attention beyond the psychic locations of the conscious, preconscious and unconscious, directing it towards early psychic development and the transitional dimensions of the progressive constitution of the process of subjectivation. In this sense, the reference to the gerund form, one of the most recognisable figures of Winnicott's language, has been read in terms of insistence on the processual aspect.[10] Holding, handling and object-presenting are formulae characterised by a syntax structure that, by using the gerund in place of the noun, evokes the semantics of movement and the non-linear temporality of mental development, shedding light on function rather than content. There is a similarly recognisable particularity in the well-known expression *going-on-being*, devoid of both subject and object, rendered in Italian as *continuare a essere, continuità dell'esserci o continuità di esistenza* [continuing to be, continuity of being or continuity of existence].

A second salience, *taking*, concerns being *en-rapport*, the development of the Self in the intersubjective mother-child matrix, and the importance of early relationships, topics on which psychoanalysis and evolutionary sciences converge.[11]

In the background, there is the dialectic between the *classical* psychoanalytic view, which insists on psychopathology in terms of conflict, and the *romantic* view, which insists on psychopathology in terms of deficit – between the *nature* dimension, close to the drive-defence economic model, the intrapsychic, constitutional factors and genetic components, and the *nurture* dimension, close to the ecological model, the intersubjective, interpsychic and relational aspects of experience and psychopathology.

A third salience, *playfully*, concerns the dimension of playing.

In relation to method and technique, playing is part of the observational device of psychoanalysis, as it is considered the equivalent of adults' free associations.[12] In relation to mental development, playing is considered to be an element of great existential value, contributing to the *ontological security* of the person. Already with Husserl and Merleau-Ponty, the semantics of *Spielraum*, room to play, and *spielen*, to play, prefigure the constitution of an Ego-world relationship, of a *space or environment of possibility*: "In all probability the situation is this", Walter Benjamin (1928, 120) observed, "before we transcend ourselves in love and enter into the life and the often alien rhythm of another human being, we experiment early on with basic rhythms that proclaim themselves in their simplest forms in these sorts of games with inanimate objects. Or rather, these are the rhythms in which we first gain possession of ourselves".[13]

By happy coincidence, *Taking Oneself Playfully* recalls the unfolding of the analytical relationship – a way of *being* with the other where moments of taking and encounter alternate with pauses of letting go and solitude – a development in time, the game as a concrete activity, as rhythm and as a mode of mental and relational functioning, analysis of the infant and analysis of the infantile. The reader will note the implicit reference to the pleasure that both patient and analyst derive from the game of getting involved in the analysis. Nor will the reader miss the reference, by amusing assonance, to the expression *prendersi in giro* [making fun of oneself], an attitude that is recommended to the analyst so that there is no abuse of power, narcissism is contained, and humility is developed. We must "know how to make fun of ourselves, of our limited nature" (Benjamin, 1928, 83). An attitude that sees the psychoanalytic paradigm of suspicion (in Paul Ricœur's well-known definition) stripped of dogmatising tendencies and authoritarian overtones in order to be imbued with an attitude devoted to *respectful listening* to the patient. We are in that psychoanalytic literature that warns analysts who *already know* or who *know too much* the *psychoanalysis of response* and of the *administration of knowledge* that risks shipwrecking the game of communication and interpretation.[14]

The book is in five parts – each part labour then delivery. Between the first, *A time for noticing*, and the fifth, *A time for delivering*, there are *Space for training*, *Getting involved in the game* and *The ingredients of care*. Each part comprises a maximum of three works, otherwise two or just one: this is not a voluminous book despite being the book of a complete lifetime. It is, in fact, a distillate, and as such should be sipped – it requires more than one reading. The author works by taking away; she aims at the essential and spends words sparingly, entrusting each one with a mission of meaning.

Searching for freedom

The issue of freedom is close to Marta Badoni's heart, and, although rarely mentioned, it can be traced at the core of her thinking as an inspiring motif, perhaps even *the* inspiring motif. Mother and analyst, analyst of parents and children and trainer of psychoanalyst students, she poses the problem of how to respect the other's freedom to be themselves while accompanying them in the process of growth and change by necessarily exerting an influence. How to nurture, how to treat, how to educate without suffocating or corrupting? For example, what human and educational attitude could mitigate what Kernberg (1996)[15] provocatively called *thirty methods to destroy the creativity of psychoanalytic candidates*? How to put the candidate taking their first steps and training in the psychoanalytic institution in a condition to acquire the words and language of psychoanalysis, while still being able to smile at the dogmatic use of any "well-worn psychoanalytic phraseology"?[16]

The works on understanding and noticing, on the function of the rescuing adult, on betrayal and corruption, on origins and originality should be read with this background in mind. The closer one gets to the origin of life and speech, the more delicate the sprout, the more sensitive the listening must become, and the milder the intervention because the risk of misunderstanding and occlusion is all the higher.

The writing itself, writing on tiptoe, seems to be marked by a concern not to say too much, not to explain, not to impose, but rather to suggest, leaving pauses and spaces for the reader's intuition, in an invitation to play. The author proposes a few moves, but it is up to the reader to make their own.

There is, in this writing, something very feminine. How does a woman write?, Giuliana Saladino asks herself in her *Romanzo civile*. A woman writes "stop and start, stop and start, stop and start, interrupted twenty times, the phone rings, I've lost the thread, begin again, the intercom rings, start all over again . . . the washing machine's finished, I take the plug out, will I hang it up?" (Saladino, 2000, 17–18, my translation).[17] It is not only because women are also overburdened with housework and motherly tasks and are, as they say today, multitasking – with one foot they're rocking the cradle, with their hands they're plucking green beans and with their eyes they're reading a book or watching a screen. It is not just making a virtue out of necessity; it is really a way of functioning by applying oneself to the task in an intermittent manner, interspersing it with life, temporarily forgetting it, picking it up again from another point, always leaving something unfinished, as if half-done, on the edge of the irony by which nothing is sacred or indispensable, apart from the children's health.

And how does a woman investigate? What, for instance, is the internal investigative space embodied by Miss Marple in comparison with Hercule Poirot? Sophie de Mijolla-Mellor asks this question in her essay *Meurtre familiar* [Family Murder] (1995, 150),[18] which takes a psychoanalytic approach to Agatha Christie's detective stories.

The two heroes have different techniques: the former follows a hypothetical–deductive model, progressively saturating the space of known elements down to the last missing piece; the latter works by associative openness. Hercule Poirot "announces his quality as a detective at the first instance and insists that he is universally recognised as the best at it". Miss Marple, on the other hand, "is an observer: from her armchair, where she knits or reads the newspaper, she gleans information that escapes those who fret and live worrying more about themselves than about their neighbours".

Elsewhere, the therapeutic value of an attitude of *Lieutenant Colombo-style curiosity* has been emphasised, a mixture of a *"not-knowing"* stance and curiosity about the phenomena occurring in the encounter and clinical process.[19] Taking a stance with respect to oneself and the patient with the peaceful perplexity of *a cow watching a train go by:*[20] "this type of methodical stupidity is even required of the "supposedly knowing subject", *but on condition that new knowledge of correlations is gained"* (Manfredi, 1998, 74, my translation).[21]

Child psychoanalysis: the fifth wheel?

"There are some things that did not sit well with me: why does the work with children that taught me so much find no place in the institutional organisation? Why is the word "child", when paired with the word "psychoanalyst" considered demeaning? Why do the reports I hear of child analysis often finish prematurely?" (Manfredi, 1998, 44). In the 1990s, these questions became pressing, and Marta Badoni, together with some of her colleagues, worked to ensure that child psychoanalysis emerged from the minority condition to which it was relegated in the institution and in the analysts' attitude, recovering the full dignity it deserved. After all, is it not on the primacy attributed to childhood that the whole of psychoanalysis is based? Do we not always have the child in mind when we treat the adult? Are we not all indebted to the insights of Anna Freud, Melanie Klein and Donald Winnicott arising from work with children? Are not childhood and the infantile the *infinite question* with which psychoanalysis is concerned?

"The appearance in the analysis room of adult patients who can speak but cannot express the attention given to the traumatic events of childhood, and the increasing importance given to the interweaving of the intrapsychic, interpsychic and intersubjective have created a bridge between the world of childhood and the workings of the mind that must be crossed and to whose construction I have devoted a great deal of energy in our organisation" (Manfredi, 1998, 56). We would also add, as serving as a bridge, attention to the body and reflection on action and acting, themes that are now actually fashionable, to which Marta Badoni has devoted pioneering writing, as this book testifies.

If today, in 2022, the national and international panorama has changed and child psychoanalysis has recovered its fortunes, if it is no longer considered the *child of a lesser god*, if it is no longer struck by the anathema that *this is not psychoanalysis*, it is also thanks to the great commitment of those analysts who have toiled in different ways and at different levels in scientific production, in the dissemination of their thought, in teaching and in institutional campaigns, sometimes bitter battles.

In the institution, the game was played out on the training ground: the idea that it is important to train analysts *also* dedicated to working with children and adolescents took a lot of effort and time to gain ground, in the IPA as in the SPI. In the two essays that make up the second part of the book, entitled *Space for training* and *Becoming*, the author broadly traces these events, at both national and international levels, and wonders about the reasoning that made it so difficult, not least the fact that, in a society with a strong male set-up, it was women, and women with an unfortunate fate, who were openly concerned with children.

The opening in the SPI of a Childhood and Adolescence Specialisation Course is relatively recent: an achievement, as long as the introduction of specific training does not end up recreating an enclosure, another sort of satellite nursery, instead of opening minds to scientific debate, to an overall view of analytic and patient care and to the attendance of "an intermediate area shared by children, parents and analysts, each grappling with their own childhood and infantile elements" (Manfredi, 1998, 58). The risk of defining competences instead of promoting them.

At the end of the avenue

Going for a walk with Marta is an experience, as anyone who has been to visit her in her garden knows, among blackbirds and rose bushes, box hedges, borders of daffodils, with Kelly as an impatient escort, turtles popping up, plane leaves and old marbles scattered on the gravel, and a cat lying in the sun. Readers of this book will make discoveries at every turn, in the sort of *sensorial walk* that is her path to psychoanalysis, littered with images and metaphors that stimulate the body along with the mind, children's handprints, masters' footprints, patients' knowledge, flashes of intuition and searing syntheses. While not wishing to spoil the surprise, we must mention the analyst on all fours, the word–noise, the thinking arms of the setting, misunderstandings and ills understood.

As already mentioned, the body and the child, and the work with the body and children, are major and closely intertwined themes, because at the origin of life, the child is a body, a body without words which needs to be understood in order to be assisted. The author's attention and much of her research focus on this crucial and dramatic passage: "Understanding, and above all the function of understanding as formulated by Freud in his *Project* (1895), have accompanied my clinical work throughout my professional life. A function that sees a confrontation as harsh as it is heated between the primitive aspects of mental functioning linked to the impotence of the newborn and the ability of an adult to bring the infant relief as long as he/she is capable of grasping the internal changes created" (footnote 26). Everything here revolves around understanding and understanding oneself, starting with the Freudian intuition contained in his *Project* (1895). The infant flows into the *Hilflosigkeit*, its survival is completely dependent on the environment, and the satisfaction of need is implemented "by *extraneous help*, when the attention of an experienced person is drawn to the child's state by discharge along the path of internal change. In this way this path of discharge acquires a secondary function of the highest importance, that of communication, and the initial helplessness of human beings is the primal source of all moral motives" (Freud, 1895, 222–223).[22] The infant expresses discomfort by crying, for example, the adult *notices*, something in the adult resonates, and, if things go in the right direction, they respond appropriately: they can *understand* insofar as they understand *themselves*. Bion would develop the idea with the concept of *rêverie*.

A body, a story. Functions of the rescuing adult: this essay continues on the same theme and explores *the importance of a comma* that unites and separates. The child is a body, and the adult rescues with their own body and their own story: each sequence takes place in a flash and decides the fate of the infant's possibility of being understood and respected in their singularity, in the construction, brick by brick, of their own story, physiognomy, possibility of expressing themselves, and separation. Originality is rooted in origins. The child who is not understood clams up, falls ill, camouflages themselves or takes refuge in hiding.

As with the child, so with the patient: what happens between adult and child and what happens in sessions between analyst and patient seem to be seamless: understanding is a fundamental and ubiquitous function. Marta Badoni belongs to the rank of analysts who, when they are with the patient, have the mother-child dyad as a model. Serious objections to this approach have been raised from some quarters – for example, that it would risk infantilising the patient – but it is hers, and she supports it convincingly. She has known too many children to be able to forget them. On the other hand, if it is true that the analogy between the parental function and the therapeutic-analysing function is not to be taken literally, it is also true that the analytic situation can reactivate a special form of evolutionary experience whose prototype is the responsivity experienced in the mother-child relationship. In this sense, "developmental orientation frames an approach to psychoanalytic treatment" (Emde, 2005, 117).[23]

Relaxation psychotherapy has made child analysts even more attentive to the participation of the body in analysis, has sharpened their listening and has contributed to the particular sensitivity to speech that, in dialogue, is an embodied word, a voice that touches. Fishing at the same time in the symbolic and the procedural aspects, speech is "a precious object, which can become a tormentor, both because it signals the presence of another who can intrude into the child's world, and because, if it fails to fit into the here and now of the session, it becomes a source of confusion" (Emde, 2005, 96).

The cautious and at the same time effective use of words, the recourse to unsaturated interpretations that invite the patient to add something of their own, the flexibility, the inventiveness and the art of surprising and of playing along are appreciated in the clinical reports, small flashes or extended accounts, such as the stories of Fabiola, Anna, Orlando and Achille, some of which are illustrated with drawings.

"Shut up, you're confusing me": recalling the warning of a very young patient (Emde, 2005, 96), we feel that we can say our introduction is over, silently returning from our walk with Kelly and leaving the reader in Marta's company to wander down her path to psychoanalysis, sensual and brooding, vivid and shadowy.

Notes

1 Executive Committee 1997–2001, President Fausto Petrella, and Executive Committee 2009–2013, President Stefano Bolognini, with Marta Badoni as National Secretary and Vice-President. The past Executive Committees, as well as many other contents concerning the history, training, cultural and research activities of the Italian Society of Psychoanalysis (SPI), can be consulted at spiweb.it.
2 De Mauro, T. (conceived and edited by) (1999), *Grande Dizionario Italiano dell'Uso*. With the collaboration of Giulio C. Lepschy and Edoardo Sanguineti. UTET, Turin.
3 We were both present at the seminar, but here Stefania Nicasi is speaking.
4 "I do, however, want to play and I will do so taking the path backwards, as can happen in boardgames, on the trail of teachers and on that of memories, along the course of my analytical playing, now in my past" (De Mauro, 1999, 83). In *Taking Oneself Playfully*, the author recounts a few moments of her psychoanalyst career: of considerable clinical significance is *playing catch* with Luciana Nissim and Stefania Manfredi, founding personalities for Italian psychoanalysis and her natural interlocutors. " 'So, did the patient take it?', Luciana Nissim asked me during the supervision that started my long journey as an analyst. The question referred to an interpretation of which I was proud, but which was evidently too articulate and too mine for the patient to make it their own, take it and continue the game. It might have been an exciting moment for me, but precisely for this reason I could not share it. Stefania Manfredi told us that when the analyst is too happy with the interpretation he/she has just formulated, something is not working" (De Mauro, 1999, 83–85).
5 Pellegrino Artusi is best known as the author of the 1891 cookbook *La scienza in cucina e l'arte di mangiar bene* [Science in the Kitchen and the Art of Eating Well].
6 Turillazzi Manfredi, S. (1998), *I seminari milanesi di Stefania Turillazzi Manfredi*. Quaderni del Centro Milanese di Psicoanalisi Cesare Musatti. La Tipografia Monzese, Monza.
7 Riolo, F. (2018), "Il metodo psicoanalitico e i suoi funtori". In Bastianini T., Ferruta A. (a cura di), *La cura psicoanalitica contemporanea*, Giovanni Fioriti, Roma, 2018.

8 For an account of the conception and curatorship of the project, see the website of Francesca Brambilla Comunicazione, francescabrambilla.com, and the website of the Politecnico di Milano, archivibadoni.polimi.it. The exhibition is based on the consultation of Giuseppe Riccardo Badoni's personal archive, kept in the family home, and the Badoni family archive, donated to the Civic Museums of Lecco: "Giuseppe Riccardo Badoni, active on the Lecco, national and international scene for over 50 years, between 1910 and 1960, generated two archives during his life: a family one and an industrial one. Marta, a psychoanalyst doctor, has reconstructed not only the story of a father, but of the man and the industrialist he was".

9 Roussillon, R. (1995), "La métapsychologie des processus et la transitionnalité". In *Revue Française de Psychanalyse*, LIX, 5, pp. 1331–1519.

10 Gaddini, R. (1979), *Il processo maturativo. Studi sul pensiero di Winnicott.* A cura di G. Remondi. Cleup, Padova.

11 The chapter *Parents, children and analysts. Resources and challenges for the psychoanalytic institution* comments on some issues of the evolutionary perspective in psychoanalysis: "Freud did not have at his disposal what neuroscience on the one hand, and Infant Research on the other, tell us today. He was, however, curious to understand what bridges linked the adult with the infant world, and on what basis the psychic apparatus was gradually built, starting with the basic biological structure. It would take years, the work of many others and the emergence of non-neurotic pathologies in the analysis room, to understand and develop the breadth of those first intuitions" (Gaddini, 1979, 53).

12 The chapter *Children and the psychoanalytic process* contains a challenging treatment of this point: "The sonority of the sessions is very different, especially in the initial phases, from what we experience with adults: music produced by different instruments, bodily music with its relative dissonances. The analyst's ear has to adapt while the eye is much more involved because children, especially in the initial phases, show more than they express verbally" (Gaddini, 1979., 110).

13 Benjamin, W. (1928), "Toys and Play. Marginal Notes on a Monumental Work". In *Selected Writings Volume 2, Part 1, 1927–1930.* Harvard University Press, 2005.

14 E.g., Winnicott, D.W. (1971), *Playing and reality.* London: Tavistock, 1971. Fachinelli E. (1989), "The Unexpected and Surprise in Analysis". In *On Freud.* MIT Press, Cambridge, MA, 2022.

15 Kernberg, O.F. (1996), "Thirty Methods to Destroy the Creativity of Psychoanalytic Candidates". In *The International Journal of Psychoanalysis*, 77, pp. 1031–1040.

16 Winnicott, D.W. (1965), *The Maturational Processes and the Facilitating Environment.* International Universities Press, Madison, CT, p. 31.

17 Saladino, G. (2000), *Romanzo civile*. Sellerio, Palermo.

18 De Mijolla-Mellor, S. (1995), *Assassinio familiare. Approccio psicoanalitico ad Agatha Christie*. Borla, Roma, 1996.

19 Lemma, A., Target, M., Fonagy, P. (2011), *Brief Dynamic Interpersonal Therapy. A Clinician's Guide*. OUP.

20 Paul Valéry's image.

21 Turillazzi Manfredi, S. (1998), *I seminari milanesi di Stefania Turillazzi Manfredi*. Quaderni del Centro Milanese di Psicoanalisi Cesare Musatti. La Tipografia Monzese, Monza.

22 Freud, S. (1895), *Project for a Scientific Psychology*. SE II, p. 318.

23 Emde, R.N. (2005), "A Developmental Orientation for Contemporary Psychoanalysis". In Person E.S., Cooper, A.M., Gabbard, G.O. (eds.), *The American Psychiatric Publishing Textbook of Psychoanalysis*. American Psychiatric Publishing, Inc., Washington DC, 2005.

PART ONE

A TIME FOR NOTICING

Understanding

Itineraries of an education

This chapter is based on a work presented in 1996 at the International Congress "Translating the Body" (Fondazione Stelline, Milan).

In reconsidering and expanding this work 25 years later, I realise that the title I chose at the time foreshadows a path, accompanying the complex itineraries of an education that marked my life and profoundly transformed it.

Since these passages have profoundly affected not only my life but also my way of understanding the profession and taking part in the life of the Italian Society of Psychoanalysis, it seemed appropriate to me, with a few biographical references, to retrace a very significant time for me in which I matured and brought to fruition the project of becoming a psychoanalyst.

To notice: "To perceive with the mind, to become aware of a fact through clues or through reflection" (definition in the Vocabolario della Lingua Italiana, Istituto della Enciclopedia Italiana). Clues and reflection would therefore be the ingredients of the mental work that accompanies the unfolding of life, guiding its choices; they are also an integral part of professional wisdom, including that of a psychoanalyst.

Noticing urges the sensory apparatus to collect clues, while at the same time reflection calls the ego to a work of elaboration that urges

DOI: 10.4324/9781003560647-2

and sustains it over time, through to the end. Winnicott wished to be alive at the moment of his own death. In the following reflections, I will try to describe the noticing and realisations that shaped my life and laid the foundations for my professional training.

In 1966, 30 years before that Congress, driving up the Simplon Pass at the height of summer, fresh from my wedding and curious about everything new, among the first things I noticed was the lightness of the air compared to the humid summer in Lombardy and a slant of light on the Rhone Valley that still moves me today when, after the last hairpin bend, one looks out over the valley.

There was no shortage of misunderstandings: it should have been obvious that marriage alone would not have solved the weight of resonances that being "the fifth wheel" of the family – as I was told I was – entailed. The last of 12 children, the last and once again a girl from my father's second marriage, 11 women and only 1 man – the engineer from my father's first marriage who died at the age of 27, in 1943, during a naval operation in the Sicilian Channel. My father's first wife died of Spanish flu in 1918, leaving five children between the ages of 2 and 11. A few years later, on marrying my father, my mother would take over, with all the inevitable complications, which were further increased by the birth of seven more children, all girls.

On crossing the border, an encouraging note: in Switzerland, contrary to our local customs, my specialist work was paid with great punctuality. Working at the Lausanne Cantonal Hospital as a researcher in endocrinology, while registered in Milan to specialise in Internal Medicine, was the contract that awaited me. I accepted it with enthusiasm, apart from feeling a bit alienated from a professional choice that, in my intentions, was aimed at relationships with patients, but which, due to the needs of the hospital itself, focused instead on biochemical-endocrinological research.

Two years passed, and things happened: our first child was born, a particularly powerful event, because it was our first and because it was a boy, a very rare event in our extended family.

My husband, specialising in psychiatry, started analysis in the meantime. The stay, which should have been short, obviously went on longer: I tried to keep in touch with the Milan Medical Clinic, but returning to a post in Milan appeared less and less likely, despite the fact that I had managed to specialise in Internal Medicine, no longer in Milan, however, but in Pavia.

In Lausanne, as an evening "diversion", I went to listen to a conference at the Cantonal Psychiatric Hospital: they talked about the analysis of a child, drawings were shown, hypotheses made and, as if by magic, I felt an affinity for this context – I heard words that touched me, that I understood, that resonated.

My subsequent career move into psychiatry, contemplated, requested and obtained, did not appear to create any family turmoil, as opposed to my wish to then start analysis: a misunderstanding!

I regularly attended weekly training seminars for psychiatrists, with a strongly psychoanalytic focus: the year spent at the Psychiatric Hospital was rich in experience, and the following years at the Office Médico Pédagogique (University Service for Children and Adolescents) would prove fundamental. I was intrigued by a proposal for "treatment" for assistants, called Relaxation Psychotherapy, according to de Ajuriaguerra. I requested and obtained permission to follow this course, usually reserved for assistants already in analysis.

In the experience of Relaxation with Daisy de Saugy, a Genevan psychiatrist and psychoanalyst, one fine day I sense that being touched (as happens in relaxation therapy when the therapist cautiously lifts and releases the patient's forearm) initiates a composite experience in which commonality and separateness converge. Being alone in company, Winnicott teaches, is a challenge but also a support for one's own subjectivity; de Ajuriaguerra knew what he was referring to when he spoke of "tonic dialogue".

I remained in Lausanne until the beginning of '73, bidding farewell to the Office Médico Pédagogique with the title of head physician, great gratitude and many question marks.

Our second child, also born in Lausanne, was three months old.

I asked to begin training in the Italian Psychoanalytic Society (SPI): after the three customary interviews (with Pietro Veltri, Giovanni Hautman and Guido Lopez), the reply was positive.

Misunderstanding: a marital crisis, deep and bitter, breaks out, incompatible with analytical work. My first analysis with Dr. Tommaso Senise would be interrupted – a shared decision after six tormented months. I am grateful to Senise for helping me achieve closure without breaking up, thus laying the groundwork for future reopenings.

I tried to resist: the children were too young, my resources too fragile, and leaving a man I had loved too difficult.

17

I resisted and worked – with children and adolescents as I had learned to do in Lausanne. In Milan, I started a new specialisation in Child Neuropsychiatry, completing it in 1980 with a thesis on Relaxation Psychotherapy, aimed at mothers who have had children with handicaps:[1] I realised that the experience of commonality/separateness of body to body with one's own child is crucial and profound for these mothers.

I came to the realisation that I could work, and I met people who are still in my life today as a result of my freelance work: a partial job at Nostra Famiglia in Bosisio (1973–1977) brought me closer to the world of child psychosis, to the dramas of parents and to the importance, already consolidated in Lausanne, of teamwork.

My subsequent relationship with the Clinic of Child Neuropsychiatry at the University of Pavia and with Giovanni Lanzi (1980–1992) allowed me to develop both my work on the body and my work with children and adolescents as a supervisor at the Dosso Verde Institute in Pavia. In particular, as a Contract Professor (1985–1988), I was able to deepen the theme of Relaxation Psychotherapy in the context of training future neuropsychiatrists and, in 1989, contribute to the organisation of a conference on the theme "Un corpo per pensare" ["A body for thinking"], which represented an effective meeting point between French-speaking colleagues and our small working group.[2]

Trained in analytical work, but not an analyst, I was moving curiously through a middle ground, with colleagues who were excellent clinicians and who had made their own personal analytical journeys. I will be forever grateful to Simona Taccani, whom I met again after my university years, for the opportunity to meet Paul-Claude Racamier, with his profound passion for psychoanalysis, at the residential seminars in Monteguidi (1985) and Sestri Levante (1987), and to Carla Marzani for inviting me to the seminars held by Irma Pick on working with children: those occasions gave me great encouragement to continue.

These were important experiences, I learned, I understood: ills understood, but also misunderstandings – what, after all, had become of my analysis project?

Something had remained painfully unresolved: I felt I needed help both to unravel a skein of pain in danger of becoming tangled and to weave together many, even though scattered, realisations matured along the way.

Seven years after my first experience of analysis, I went once more to the SPI to resume the interrupted analytic path.

I was accepted again after a careful interview with Anteo Saraval, and in 1980, I began analysis with Renato Sigurtà.

Misunderstandings: separation from my husband was inevitable and would come about in 1983.

Ills understood: at our first meeting, when I told him that I was the last of 12 children, 11 of them girls, Renato Sigurtà picked up pen and paper and asked: "Their names?". I felt at that moment that I would also find mine.

In 1989, I became an associate member of the SPI.

Intermezzo

The years from 1973, the year I returned to Italy and the failure of my first analytic project, to 1980, when I resumed the analytic path, were years as complex as they were intense and fundamental for both my life and future profession.

I lived in a middle ground still very much linked to the people and the professional skills acquired during my stay in Lausanne. The French language often preceded and pre-empted Italian when I was in a hurry to express myself. On the other hand, it helped me take part in seminars, in particular in the various meetings with the CeRP (Centre for Research in Psychotherapy) group and with Paul-Claude Racamier.

It was a circumstantial way of proceeding, supported by the comments that welcomed my clinical work and first public presentations positively and with interest: I owe a lot to the first patients, difficult patients as often happens to newcomers, from whom I learned a lot. In particular, a fruitful collaboration began with the Carlo Besta Neurological Institute, whose children's sector was led at the time by Dr. Silvana Cumer Bruno. I encountered the drama of autism and the resulting challenges. The habit of taking into account bodily states in the formulation of thoughts was part of my clinical reflection and, at the same time, anchored me to a truth of feeling that allowed me to reach out and tune in to my patients' distant experiences. However, I felt the lack of a container to help me move from clues to reflection and then to an open, systematic exchange with the group of my colleagues (and also how difficult it was for me, coming from a group of siblings, to sustain the impact with colleagues).

This would be taken care of by my analysis and the SPI training course. This was how a way of thinking and working, while not clandestine or secluded, came to be made public, shared and enriched by the response of various working groups and then within the SPI, after I became an associate member in 1989.

Below, I will repropose revised and expanded considerations on the work on the body and on Relaxation Psychotherapy following de Ajuriaguerra. The experience of this treatment, first as a patient and then as a therapist, has accompanied my clinical work, also as an analyst, helping me, I believe, to tolerate states of tension otherwise difficult for me and my patients to handle, to the point of sometimes finding in metaphor a tool capable of giving body and meaning to different histories. I continued with this work even after my association, until my involvement with patients in analysis and subsequent commitments in the Institution led me down other paths, but this experience has always remained in my baggage.

Notes

1 Marta Badoni Benuzzi (1981), "Il metodo di rilassamento di J. de Ajuriaguerra: una psicoterapia nell'ambito della riabilitazione". In *Neuropsichiatria Infantile*, fasc. 243–244, pp. 895–908.
2 The proceedings of the Conference *A Body for Thinking* have been published by Goliardica Pavese, Pavia.

I

MISUNDERSTANDINGS, ILLS UNDERSTOOD

For Paul-Claude Racamier, for his ability to understand.[1]

These days we are just beginning are the final ones in a long journey that has taken the various groups represented here through shared places and thoughts.

Traces of these passages, in which we have dealt in particular with the problem of psychoses, borderline states and psychosomatics, can be found in two volumes edited by Monique Dechaud-Ferbus, Marie-Lise Roux and François Sacco (1994). The last meeting, on the denial of perception (Paris, 1995), is closely related to the theme of this conference. It is the second that our association has organised in Italy; the first – *Il corpo: tra piacere e realtà* [*The body: between pleasure and reality*] – was held in Pavia in 1989 in collaboration with the Department of Child Neuropsychiatry.

Ours has not been a linear path; it has rather resembled a gradual progression, with our patients, testing the ground, but nonetheless interested and curious.

If the terrain has so far been uncertain, the topic we are tackling today has sometimes seemed like a minefield, and the title I have chosen – *Tradurre il corpo: malintesi e mali intesi* [*Translating the body: misunderstandings and ills understood*] – vast in its breadth and intersecting of different theories. To begin with, *Tradurre il corpo* [*Translating the body*] involves engaging in a dialogue with a

DOI: 10.4324/9781003560647-3

code other than that of language, and if for convenience we speak of language through the body (hysterical register), body language (psychosomatic register) and language about the body (hypochondriac register), it is still true that the body has no language. In this absence of language, we still have to distinguish (Amati Mehler, Argentieri, Canestri, 1993, 150) the preverbal from the non-verbal: "Preverbal is defined as meaning an activity of communication, but also psychic activity in general, on the part of the 'infans'; that is, of the subject prior to speech acquisition" (i.e. acquisition ". . . of the mother-tongue language").

In the preverbal, therefore, there is the promise of communication that will eventually become speech, while somatic expression, the non-verbal, is mute to communication: translating it always requires particular caution, and scholars are divided as to its feasibility. Moreover, non-verbal, preverbal and verbal do not occur in linear succession: they are areas that intersect throughout life even when speech has found its way. And again, speech does not in itself guarantee the achievement of a symbolic function. Our patients have, after all, taught us how much and how intensely it can remain anchored to a sensory, concrete stage.

Since we will have the opportunity to encounter this word over the course of these days, I will limit myself here to saying that *it is felt more than listened to, more deeply inscribed in the register of sensations than of symbols*, and is for us a precious clue to ancient misunderstandings between the infant and the care environment. In fact, it signals to us the presence of a hidden subject that thus protects itself from the overwhelming power of speech that, obstructing the body's suggestions, works to decide its fate even before any history is achieved. This subject, a prisoner of their illness, asks to be *first of all understood*, but to do so, we will have to be silent, in the room as in the increasingly crowded world of our theoretical references, and we will also have to know that this silence, both *sought and feared* by patients, requires the therapist to tolerate tensions in the very same moment as proposing relaxation: no guarantee can be given in advance that this silence will not, *a posteriori*, re-actualise ancient invasions and misunderstandings. We are, in fact, in the area of trauma. With the help of the dictionary (Vocabolario della Lingua Italiana, Istituto della Enciclopedia Italiana, founded by Giovanni Treccani, Rome), I will therefore try to familiarise you and myself with the words I have chosen for this text. *Tradurre*, from *trans* and *ducere*: to carry

22

beyond, to transfer. Inherent in this operation of transfer is the idea of a space to be filled, a separation to be faced, an enigma to be solved, a risk to be taken: the misunderstanding.

Corpo, from *corpus*: body, complex, organism. Complex material reality, physical structure, for the philosopher, extended reality, in opposition to thinking reality. To be distinguished from, which has a Greek derivation (*soma*, body), mostly used only as part of a composite word, as we too use it when we speak of *psycho-soma*, and a late Latin derivation (and from the Greek *sagma*, load), which refers to a load, dead body or corpse.

An apparently unitary reality, the body is in fact a complex organism, exposed through the sensory system to an infinity of messages. One of the first passionate devotees of these messages was Julian de Ajuriaguerra.

The tonic dialogue: discrepancies and harmonies

De Ajuriaguerra (1963, 1970) proposes that the infant-mother body-to-body relationship is at the origin of a particular dialogue, the tonic dialogue, and that this dialogue has an essential function in the development of the psycho-soma.

Ajuriaguerra was a curious man and researcher who never took sides. He fled Spain after taking part in the civil war, lived in exile in France, directed the Department of Psychiatry in Geneva for many years, published the first and founding treatise on Child Neuropsychiatry, and, like his teacher Henry Wallon, ended his career at the Collège de France teaching Developmental Neuropsychology, from 1975 to 1981. It was while he was at the Collège de France that, showing himself to be once again ahead of his time, he proposed the establishment of a Chair in Psychoanalysis of Unconscious Processes with the participation of André Green, but the Collège refused (Albarella, 1997).

Psychoanalysed but free of institutional conventions, as a thinker he was passionate about teamwork but also independent, and the works he left us are rich in insights that are still today, so many years later, relevant in many respects (Larrasquet, Claverie, de Ajuriaguerra, 2012). His merit lies above all in having been able to translate the culture of his time, and in particular the thought of Wallon, Merleau-Ponty and Lacan (in particular regarding the mirror stage) into a method of treatment oriented to bring relief to patients difficult to reach by the traditional psychoanalytic method: so-called psychosomatic patients, minor hypochondriacs, and those sick from long-term debilitating illnesses (e.g. TB) and uncertain of resuming their lives once the illness has been eradicated.

The notion of tonic dialogue he introduced allows us to grasp the wealth of communication and information passing between infant and mother through tactile and proprioceptive sensitivity, holding, sustaining and containing: the references to Winnicott's handling and holding are, I believe, inevitable. Furthermore, the tonic dialogue underscores an arcane yet founding relationship in which can be glimpsed the complex itineraries going from Freud's (1895) function of understanding to Bion's (1962a, 1962b) notion of container: it will be the quality of the maternal reception that will be the director capable of producing transformations, of playing with metaphors, or of blocking the dialogue by stiffening body and thought. It should come as no surprise that in such an arcane area, misunderstandings are possible.

Misunderstanding: the result of mistaking or misinterpreting the words or acts of others, often the cause of resentment or quarrels. The resentment arising from misunderstanding is particular in being the result of a betrayed expectation, which, not having a manifest culprit (hence the expression "it was a misunderstanding"), is more exposed than other phenomena of miscomprehension to a grim feeling of uncertainty ("did I misunderstand?"), *doubt as to the rightness of one's own perceptions*, guilt, and persecution. Moreover, it is characteristic of misunderstanding to trigger a chain of consequences, a series of miscomprehensions, resulting in the loss of meaning. We have to remember this well when dealing with the problem of resentments, grudges, aggression – all often hidden – that so many of our patients carry. We have to understand how much the misunderstanding opens up space for a work of verification and an adjustment of communication by re-establishing harmony and harmonisation with one's own body and with the other, as well as how much it opens up abysses of incomprehension, estrangement, distrust, fear or resentment.

Male, from *malus*: bad; *malum*: physical and/or moral evil. Therefore, this word brings us into the realm of offence suffered and of suffering, of physical and mental pain. Offence suffered, physical pain, mental pain, often indistinguishable. At this level, *avere e stare male* [suffering pain and feeling bad] are the same thing. *Understood*, from *intendere*: to turn the senses and the mind to some object . . . to tend to a conclusion, to have intention, to want . . . to perceive and understand, which are in a certain way the effect of tendering attention. Now to return to the title of this work: Misunderstandings and ills understood. We were pleased to introduce this title which, while seeming to be a play on words, in fact circumscribes the territory or context in which we move in our relationship with our patients, and opens up a difficult challenge: whether in the history of the subject the insufficiency of the care environment, the scarcity of the protective function of stimuli, or the malfunctioning of the maternal *rêverie* function have produced misunderstandings. Consequently, whether these misunderstandings, working for a long time and in a subterranean manner, manifest themselves mainly, as is the case with our patients, in discomfort made up of an *indistinguishable amalgam of suffering pain and feeling bad*, of physical malaise and mental pain, we must not be in a hurry to choose and delimit the field of suffering, but rather we must try to understand the ill where it is indicated to us. This implies being able to dwell patiently on the *lament*: the lament is a manifestation of pain that can only express itself through the body, and it is there that it must be encountered, without haste and, above all, without the presumption of being able to enclose it and redefine it as *mental*, because if the patient feels the suffering of the flesh has been rejected, he or she will end up feeling *entirely* rejected, seek shelter and become difficult to reach. It will be important to respect the patient's indications, tolerating this indistinct pain, while at the same time familiarising the patient with his or her own pain. I had written (Badoni, 1994) about allowing oneself to go on a *sensorial walk* with the patient, letting gaze and thought flow over the sensations and then noting them down together. It will be, as we will sometimes see, the metaphor that allows us to extract the lament from the body to then incorporate it in a history that the patient can finally feel is his or her own.

Suffering pain and feeling bad: the tongue ever turns to the aching tooth.

This saying not only brings us back to the desperate insistence with which our patients insist on the symptom, but also to a momentary renunciation of a speech organ as sophisticated as the tongue to put itself at the service of the word, to become an instrument of reconnaissance, of exploration, of communication. The tongue treats the tooth as a foreign territory to be identified and delimited, and the word incessantly returns to the fact in an attempt to give meaning.

Our patients need this *reconnaissance* work in order to return repeatedly to old pains that are never dormant, and to show us, at the same time, the ground to work on: a transformation *from misunderstanding to an ill understood* is sometimes, in these situations, possible. In the therapist-patient dialogue, the body, like an aching tooth, is heard and spoken about.

To speak of translating the body is therefore to attribute a state of foreignness to the body, which may seem quite strange for something we think of as familiar and intimate. But it is precisely this co-presence of the familiar and the unfamiliar, enigmatic and disturbing, that founds the game of identity and identification, which ensures the stability of a person's growth and, at the same time, its continuous renewal.

So how do we translate, without crushing the person, without reducing the text to a dead letter?

If we provisionally consider the body (ours and the other's) as a text to be translated and put ourselves in the role of the translators, *in order to start an attempt at translation, we will have to let this third character grow within the relationship, the fruit of the encounter between us and the patient, a third character who gradually becomes familiar with the context in which the patient moves, as do we with him or her.*

In a meeting between colleagues, I recalled that *ospite* [which in Italian can refer to both *host* and *guest*] is a two-way concept designating both the guest and the host. In this context, it is not only the meeting that counts, but the climate of the encounter, an emotional complex made up of attentions, expressions and tones that can confirm or deny speech, but which above all engage both therapist and patient in a probing work in which the sensory, the imaginary, the thought are exercised.

It is at this level that what de Ajuriaguerra (1963, 1970) called *tonic dialogue* is created: an exchange that, starting from a very elementary level – sensoriality and proprioception – gradually finds a way through to affection and speech. This familiarity with the terrain in which we move, we and our patients, nevertheless entails respect for the patient's otherness and is aimed not at eliminating boundaries, even though this is what patients sometimes ask of us, but at reinforcing them. On the other hand, we would not be talking about translation if boundaries were not close to our hearts.

Alienness and borders: therapeutic choices

But who are these patients who turn to us, and what do they ask of us?

If I had to choose a word, without the fear of restricting the richness of the dialogue that, following different tonic states, is established between therapist and patient, I would choose the word *alien*.

People who are alien first and foremost to themselves, sometimes haunted by an anguish without object or name, desperate without knowing they are, or frightened without knowing of what. Often hammered by a somatic symptom to which they seem to cling like castaways to a raft in a stormy sea.

If these people speak, their speech is often a *word-noise*, aimed at saturating any silence because in the silence the other, the alien, might appear, bringing turmoil and disruption. Such speech, which tends to bewilder the listener by preventing any approach to the actual meaning of the speech, carries within itself, it seems, another message: re-establish stillness, restart from silence.

However, this silence, which, in a single act, opens the door to *feeling*, *resentment* and *grievance*, is both sought and feared. Indeed, it is possible that *a posteriori* (*après-coup*), something that was not forthcoming before may find word and meaning, but so might also the renewal of ancient violence and misunderstanding.

Often, if these people remain silent, chasms open up that evoke sidereal distances. These are patients who, as a last shred of awareness, bring us their pain, made up of an amalgam of fright, fury and somatic suffering, often unnecessarily treated. It can represent a bulwark against psychic disorganisation. Sometimes it is precisely the presence of this troublesome companion – troublesome, but nevertheless still a companion – that guarantees these patients an apparently normal working life. The affective world, on the other hand, is visibly compromised, although it seems a distant concern, almost a luxury that cannot be afforded, things . . . *from another world*. Why do we propose relaxation psychotherapy to these patients and not purely verbal psychotherapy or psychoanalysis? I am speaking here in the first person because the rules, even the most sophisticated rules of indication for psychotherapy, cannot disregard that which is set in motion in the therapist–patient encounter.

When a patient comes to see me, I tend to propose relaxation psychotherapy first if the patient asks for it, because I think that the patient's request should be respected unless there is a contraindication;

secondly, I propose such psychotherapy when I realise that, in the relationship with the patient, my imaginary capability or preconsciousness is scarcely affected by the patient's words, when I feel that words are very little invested as a signifying instrument, and above all, when the body is at the centre of the patient's concerns, whatever they may be.

These are patients who come because they have a pain and because they feel bad, an illness that they can point out precisely but which nevertheless keeps them in check, and with them often their family members, doctors and psychotherapists. Years of experience have taught us that on the body that is suffering pain and feeling bad, and that comes so overwhelmingly to the fore, the body that shows agitation or bewilderment or fear or general discomfort, on such a body we must remain . . . *The tongue ever turns to the aching tooth.*

To these patients who cannot understand what is happening to them, who we are not capable of listening to, who become agitated without understanding what is keeping them in a state of alarm and who agitate us, we propose trying to feel their body. We call this Relaxation Psychotherapy, knowing full well that this relaxation – what we understand as letting oneself go, lying down and entering a dream state to welcome sensations, images and representations – will at best be the final destination rather than the starting point of this work. If anything, it will prepare the ground for analysis. Alongside these patients, in the interplay of gazes, we enter into a shared experience that is precisely the experience of understanding: *to understand* – turn the senses and the mind towards some object . . . tend towards an end, have intentions, want . . . perceive and comprehend – these are in a certain way the effect of offering attention.

We therefore work on the ground of consensus and understanding. If these patients are in difficulty as regards the signifying word, then to avoid further misunderstandings, we must reach them on the ground they show us, the ground of sensation. We make this intention explicit to the patient, and it is an integral part of the therapeutic contract. This is why relaxation therapy begins with the following statement: "Let's try to feel the body and then, later, say what you feel and how you feel it". For example, how does the patient settle onto the couch (and how do we settle into our armchair?)? First and second moments are, of course, often reversed: we often happen to be bombarded at first by a hail of words-sensations that, rather than making themselves heard, provoke an atmosphere of dulling of the sensorium. Or it happens that, if patients speak to us to say what they feel, they tell us they feel nothing (Roux, 1984). By contrast, what happens to us is to be tense: this tension, which our attention is focused on, is an integral part of the effort it takes to *understand*.

In this perspective, first and together with speech, we introduce a *rhythm*: we are the guardians and guarantors of this rhythm. As with any other psychoanalytically-inspired psychotherapy, this rhythm is made up first of all of regular, repeated meetings, usually on a weekly basis. First of all, coming to a meeting repeatedly marks a will not to give up, not to be discouraged at the first misunderstanding – it promotes attention, awakens curiosity, defines a space. But this rhythm is further reinforced by other cadences. I am thinking of the tonic experience of contracting and relaxing, of the alternation of speech and silence that often find a rhythm of their own, of the experience of the rhythms of one's own body, in particular of breathing, the heart, waking and sleeping, day and night, time, ages . . . How difficult it is sometimes to guess our patients' age!

We offer *support*: to begin with, a relatively neutral support, the couch (Dechaud-Ferbus, Roux, Sacco, 1994), but also the support of our presence ("I can't relax alone when she's not there"), our gaze, our thinking. I believe it's good training to be a relaxation therapist to set the *rêverie* function in motion. Little by little, it happens that working on this support allows patients – who literally came with the feeling of being in pieces or of not being able to rest – to recover, with great relief, the shape of their body, the one they feel pressing down on the couch and to which they can little by little give an outline and a measurement.

We give a name to the body and its parts, and in the same moment recognising its unity and complexity. We often find patients who are only able to feel their body in the moment that we call it by name – their arms, legs, back, etc. A kind of accompanied visit within one's own territory, which in another work I called a *sensorial walk* (Badoni, 1994b).

Reconstructing yourself: let the right hand know what the left is doing

Maria, 20 years old, comes to me after a psychotic breakdown: she is being treated pharmacologically and has improved, but is at home with a lack of initiative. For a long time, she always comes to me accompanied. Her psychotic breakdown has left important sequelae – fear of going out alone, fear of the metro, feeling that she is being talked about on television, etc.

She arrives literally bent double and tells me about her symptom and only that; Maria is her symptom. A suffocating pressure at the level of her stomach, which forces her to stand (in fact, sitting down is agonising for her) and to avoid tight clothing – everything squeezes her, she feels suffocated. As I often do when the body is so markedly in the foreground, I ask if there have been other times in her life when her body has given her discomfort. I thus discover (despite the fact that she had come to me after a thorough psychodiagnostic examination) that as a teenager, due to her parents' decision (according to them, she had a crooked back) and with the complicity of an orthopaedic surgeon, Maria found herself squeezed into a plaster cast that enclosed her entire torso, making her breasts stand out, and that, in a state of great anguish, she had managed to make a hole in the plaster at the level of her stomach in order, she tells me, to be able to breathe.

Even now, Maria breathes mainly with her stomach, and it will take some time before she discovers, with pleasure, that her whole chest can be involved in this movement. It is not a stretch to link this experience of plastering, which forcibly moulded her body and posture, with a serious phobia, especially for a girl who would like to work in the fashion world – the phobia of mannequins. But in talking about this with Maria, I am astonished by her overly rapid acceptance of my word, unaccompanied by associations. So I think that the ground must first be laid for the word to settle, without invading and without slipping away.

Without the delimitation of her own territory, Mary would be condemned to speak my language, without being able to translate it into her own idiom, as was probably the case with her mother tongue. Each of us must be able to translate our mother tongue into our own idiom, to make it into something appropriate to the needs of our territory and organisation. Maria, on the other hand, is a bit like the T-shirt she wore on the first day she came to me: on an immaculate background, a small, well-drawn red mouth. Seen like this, she looks like a bizarre object, an excitement with no background to accommodate or define her.

Maria tries to relax, but her arms are very tense, a tension that is confirmed when I touch them. One day I touch her right arm,

30

it is very tense. I touch the left one, I feel it gradually relax, which I notice, and Maria confirms my impression. Comforted by this answer, I propose a possibility to Maria and ask: "Can we think that the right arm sent its ambassadors to the left arm to say that I was about to touch it and that there was no need to be afraid?" Maria accepts this remark of mine with a big smile; she experiences it as a discovery. She now knows that her body is neither passive nor inert, it is not a mannequin. It lives and indicates what is going on around it: these are the first signs of an Ego capable of modulating anguish and using it to protect its boundaries.

The left hand can learn from what the right hand has experienced; it can create a state of waiting, with the tonic dialogue progressively replacing a paralysing tension. Thanks to this tool, Maria is progressively able to move on her own, and she will draw on some working experiences. The relaxation continues.

Finding yourself once more: Fabiola

If the positive evolution of Maria's story seems to be linked to the shared discovery of being able to make use of her body as an indicator of a state on which she can rely, Fabiola's vicissitudes take us into a territory in which extraneousness, trauma and the complexity of family history have produced a risky effect of disorientation whose only sign of constant yet persecutory presence seems to be the body.

The experience with Fabiola, which lasted years, challenged me greatly, leaving me, however, with a knowledgeable legacy of emotions still alive today and of small but significant discoveries about the founding role of metaphor. Presenting herself to me at the age of 48, Fabiola has a bob of short hair and looks like a bewildered little girl. I am amazed at the way she tells her story, with great finesse, but as if in the third person. Her uprooting is clear to her: she feels as if she has no access to her roots, which she nevertheless describes vividly.

The reasons underlying this disorientation are not lacking, but they seem inaccessible, as if unable to go beyond an intellectual, disembodied knowledge. I will summarise them briefly.

Generational disorientation: mother from a strict, cultured, Protestant environment; father raised in a large peasant family, devoted to good wine and good company. Personal disorientation: firstborn, born prematurely in France, at the time of the German

31

invasion; the men escape, and she is left alone with her mother. When her sister is born, her mother *disappears*, apparently as the result of a psychotic breakdown. An especially jealous brother, with whom major conflicts over family decisions will emerge.

At the age of three, she is diagnosed with severe myopia – she cannot see steps, does not perceive passages, feels that from then on, her destiny is sealed: "I was called 'four-eyes', it was understood that I'd study and have a career, but that I wouldn't get married", a destiny instead expected of her sister. At the age of nine, she moves from the village to the city, loses her classmates, and after high school, makes a clean break with her family and moves to the capital. Last disorientation, despite the predictions, marriage: "With an uprooted person like me, a foreigner, who takes me to a foreign land".

In addition to this, she has very small feet, which makes it a struggle for her to find shoes and seems a concrete sign of her difficulty in anchoring herself to reality, putting her feet on the ground. In fact, she struggles to *settle*, a term she herself uses, even in treatment: we will have to wait a long time, without rushing to interpretations, for Fabiola, as an initial acquisition, to manage to keep up with the rhythm of the (weekly) sessions, settling on the couch once a week. She does not want to undergo analysis: she was shocked by her first analyst's weeping when she recounted her father's death. I respect her wish.

Linguistic disorientation as well: she speaks with a strong French accent, but I feel her warning me against expressing myself to her in her own language. It will be a long wait for us to converge one day, not so much on a translation, which could perhaps betray her, but on the discovery together of a metaphor that will finally allow her to flesh out her story.

In the face of such disorientation, the body very painfully takes the lead and seems to represent a sinister anchorage with respect to an experience of impotence, a highly uncomfortable shelter from deep depressive experiences. In her own words, the patient *settles* on illness as a last resort against a mortal void. It will be a good sign for me the day she tells me that she feels *settled* on my couch.

She has not been well for a few years and has worsened after the death, in a short period, of both her parents; she suffers from severe rectal haemorrhagic colitis and, like her sister, has had a bilateral mastectomy for the disease of which her mother died a few years before the consultation and of which her sister will die during our course of therapy. At the end of her life, this sister adopted two Arab children, to whom Fabiola is particularly attached.

To make matters worse, she suffers from glaucoma that makes any movement precarious.

I will therefore be careful *in primis* to familiarise her with the care environment, to avoid obstacles along the way, and to adjust the lighting as best I can. I feel relieved when one day she *sees* flowers (moneywort) in my study and remembers how much her mother loved them.

I could briefly summarise the steps of this long treatment that took place with a weekly session as follows: long silences and feelings of invasion/perception of self in the environment/first metaphors/dreams and dream work.

The first metaphor is proposed by me: we are in a time of mourning, her sister has died, and the two adopted children are being tossed from one uncle to another and are very restless. Fabiola is particularly attached to her nephew, but is frightened by the scenes the child makes about his shoes, which never fit well and are constantly unlaced. At the end of the session, I find myself commenting: "I don't want to lose my shoes at least". A few sessions later, Fabiola tells me how comforted she felt by my words: it was all about accepting, without forcing it, the importance of bonds.

The second metaphor digs even deeper, constructed together as we brought our attention to the body: *the pin/the brooch/the cameo.*

For some time, she has been complaining that her belly is swollen, swollen, she repeats, like a pin [spillo]. For me, a pin does not evoke images of swelling, but rather of stinging pain. I remain thoughtful, and the sessions pass. Shortly afterwards, the swelling of her belly comes up again, and this time the comparison is no longer a pin, but a brooch [spilla].

The brooch, for which Fabiola later uses the French word *broche*, leads us towards something precious, but does not yet provide us with the richness of associations that the third image will instead arouse: her belly is swollen, yes, not like a pin, not like a brooch, but, Fabiola concludes, like a *camée*, a cameo.

While I am struck by the appearance, unveiled by the slightly raised roundness of the cameo, concealing within itself family ties, Fabiola adds, fishing in the intimacy of her original dialect, that *camée*, in this dialect, means a junkie.

The cameo will allow us to work on the searing pain of feeling excluded, given the importance of family conflicts and the abundance of the stakes, as concerns both the inheritance of affection and conspicuous family possessions. Fabiola's sudden, irreparable rages, like *soupe au lait*, milk overflowing from a saucepan, will do the rest, burning her body and leaving her mind disoriented.

The subject will be discussed at length. In the meantime, Fabiola manages to deal better with both her eyesight problems and her work duties, which bring her great satisfaction.

In the last session, years later, she gives a light-hearted, humorous account of a large family wedding and the underlying family rivalries: "They put me at the table of the second-born . . . at a certain point I was amused, and it became clear to me that they were struggling with problems that I had overcome. I thought, I've already understood these things with Dr B.!".

She is happy and tells me enthusiastically about the meeting of her Arab nephews with Linda, the Danish girl who took care of them at the worst times. "I think I can go on alone" – something I agree with.

One afternoon years later, I visit a good physiotherapist. I enter the waiting room, and as I am greeting the physiotherapist, a cheerful voice joins in the greetings: it is Fabiola, who cannot see but has recognised my voice and is very happy to meet me again. "The two of us", she says, "we know how to find the right people".

Ills understood

Note

1 *Understanding,* and above all *the function of understanding* as formulated by Freud in his Project (1895), have accompanied my clinical work throughout my professional life. A function that sees a confrontation as harsh as it is heated between the primitive aspects of mental functioning linked to the impotence of the newborn and the ability of an adult to bring the infant relief as long as he or she is capable of grasping the internal changes created.

Bibliography

Albarella, C. (1997), "Note sulla crisi della psicoanalisi. A proposito di due recenti pubblicazioni". In *Rivista di Psicoanalisi*, 43, 1, pp. 103–118.

Amati Mehler, J., Argentieri, S., Canestri, J. (1993), *The Babel of the Unconscious: Mother Tongue and Foreign Languages in the Psychoanalytic Dimension* (Trans. Whitelaw-Cucco, J.). International Universities Press, Madison, CT, p. 150.

Badoni, M. (1994), "Corps maitrisé et corps soigné: relaxation et facteurs traumatiques externes et internes à la cure". In Dechaud-Ferbus, M., Roux, M.-L., Sacco, F. (eds.), *Les destins du corps*. Érès, Toulouse, pp. 117–127.

Bion, W.R. (1962a), *Learning from Experience*. Karnac, London, 1984.

Bion, W.R. (1962b), "A Theory of Thinking". In *Second Thoughts. Selected Papers on Psychoanalysis*. Routledge, London, 1984.

de Ajuriaguerra, J. (1963), "Le corps comme relation". In *Revue Suisse de Psychologie Pure et Appliquée*, 21, 2, pp. 137–157.

de Ajuriaguerra, J. (1970), *Manuale di psichiatria del bambino*. Masson, Milano, 1979.

de Ajuriaguerra, J. (1994), "Ontogenèse des postures. Moi et l'autre". In Dechaud-Ferbus, M., Roux, M.L., Sacco, F. (eds.), *Les destins du corps*. Érès, Toulouse, pp. 21–35.

Dechaud-Ferbus, M., Roux, M.-L., Sacco, F. (eds.) (1994), *Les destins du corps*. Érès, Toulouse.

Freud, S. (1895), *Project for a Scientific Psychology*, SE, vol. II, 1955.

Freud, S. (1924), *A Note upon the "Mystic Writing-Pad"* SE, vol. X, 1925.

Larrasquet, J.M., Claverie, B., de Ajuriaguerra, J. (2012), "De l'actualité de la pensée de Julián de Ajuriaguerra". In *Osasunaz, Cuadernos de ciencias de la salud*, 12, pp. 23–32.

Roux, M.L. (1984), "Corps affectés et désaffectés". In *Revue Française de Psychanalyse*, 48, 6, pp. 1473–1483.

PART TWO

SPACE FOR TRAINING

Becoming

The 1990s were years of great ferment, both scientific and institutional.

As a new associate, I had to come to terms with an institution that attracted me and urged me on, left me awestruck and questioned and challenged me.

For the first Thursday meetings, it was with great awe that I crossed Via Corridoni, so intimate at the time of my analysis, so mysterious now that I was in institutional, hierarchical and fairly litigious territory. I felt the need to compare my experience as a child and adolescent therapist with experienced colleagues: I would be under a long supervision with Maria Elvira Berrini, with occasional meetings with Giovanna Giaconia and Dina Vallino. I took part in a group led by Pierandrea Lussana at the Milanese Centre, with Nino Ferro presenting a clinical case.

There are some things that did not sit well with me: Why does the work with children that taught me so much find no place in the institutional organisation? Why is the word "child", when paired with the word "psychoanalyst" considered demeaning? Why do the reports I hear of child analysis often finish prematurely?

I took courage: it was Dario De Martis, at that time President of the Milanese Psychoanalysis Centre, who would accept my proposal

DOI: 10.4324/9781003560647-4

to set up a clinical service for children as well, as already existed for adults. I found competent, generous help from Giuliana Barbieri and Simonetta Bonfiglio.

In 1993, the Child Psychoanalysis Observatory was founded in my kitchen in Via Cosimo Del Fante. The proponents of its recognition were: Claudia Artoni, Marta Badoni, Nino Ferro, Magda Viola and Dina Vallino. We received important support in the presidency of Giuseppe Di Chiara.

The institution was eager to help, and I was keen to make up for lost time, as well as feeling ready to transfer my complex family experience of tolerance and organisation to the equally complex analytical family. However, I never thought I would be treasurer and, above all, not fail. With the valuable contribution of Giuseppe Fiorentini, we managed to honourably negotiate the move from the historic headquarters at 1 Via Corridoni to 38 Via Corridoni in 1994. This was an important year for me, as I presented my first work at the Rimini Congress: the theme of being in hiding would accompany me for years. In my life, many people have reminded me of these words addressed by Christ to Martha: "Marta Marta sollicita es et turbaris erga plurima, Maria optimam partem elegit quae non auferetur ab ea [Martha, Martha, you are worried and upset about many things . . . Mary has chosen what is better, and it will not be taken away from her]".

Of course, I also had a sister named Mary, but I think of the institutional Marys who work with the psychoanalytic language. In 1995, I became a full member and found precious companions and friends forever: Anna Ferruta, Paola Molone and Viviana Savoia.

In the meantime, my curious passion for group work took me in different directions: a long, highly significant interaction with the Child Neuropsychiatry Department of Pavia, to which I was introduced by Maria Teresa Aliprandi, whom I had met in Lausanne and who introduced me to Giovanni Lanzi.

These were the first important bridges between the past and the future that would find other links in the years to come.

Encouraged by my analyst, I started a job with the Civil Court of Milan, 9th section. I learned a lot about the drama of couples and families.

Needless to say, my own personal drama served as a model. I raised my children as best I could, obviously with too little time and without adequate earnings. My teenage son, surprised by the lavish welcome I received for a congress in Pavia, ventured: "Mum, remember me when you're rich!". He is still waiting.

Over my head and unbeknownst to me, the Institution had plans: a change of the Executive organisation – Stefania Manfredi Turillazzi and Fausto Petrella challenged each other for the role of president. Stefania asked me if I felt up to being her secretary. Flattered, I accepted and we prepared, but as would happen more and more often, the members' votes reorganised the teams, and so I became secretary with Fausto Petrella, whom I had met as a medical student.

With Adamo Vergine as Secretary of Training, this Executive (1997–2001) would go down in SPI history for the complex, much-discussed passage of our training under the wing of MURST [Ministry of Universities and Scientific-Technological Research] and for the introduction into our training of the advanced course in child and adolescent analysis.

This latest complex passage productively reconnected my previous experience abroad with my current position. In a letter dated 6 June 2000, Terttu Eskelinen de Folch, a former IPA [International Psychoanalytical Association] vice-president and director of COCAP [Committee on Child and Adolescent Psychoanalysis], an IPA organisation dedicated to the training of analysts in the sector of children and adolescents, assured me that she would take care of the request I had sent to Anne Marie Sandler on behalf of the Executive: remembering our training in common at the Office Médico Pédagogique in Lausanne was a good omen. It was to be a friendship that developed over the years, also involving child and adolescent analysis training for Eastern Europe.

Meeting Terttu, who passed away in 2021, was a meeting point as well as a turning point. It seems unreal for me to have been able to bring together such important and such different training experiences by far more experienced colleagues, among whom were Giovanni Hautmann and Arnaldo Novelletto. Relationships around Europe opened up, and at this point, some knowledge of English also became urgent.

The following works are a small testimony to my commitment in this area.

PARENTS, CHILDREN AND ANALYSTS

Resources and challenges for the psychoanalitic institution*

*Revised and modified from the original publication: Badoni, M. (2004), "La psicoanalisi dei Figli: Paradossi". In Neri, N., Latmiral, S. (a cura di), *Uno spazio per i genitori, Quaderni di psicoterapia infantile*, 48, Borla, Roma, pp. 171–186.

If the term "minor" defines the subject-society relationship regarding the aspect of responsibility, that of "child", evoking an emotional bond, introduces not only responsibility but also time, generations, affections and related conflicts.

Psychoanalytic work for early childhood, childhood and adolescence addresses subjects in the process of becoming, children still dependent, albeit with different ties, on their parents.

Daughters and sons, sisters and brothers, to indicate a condition that unfolds not only in a web of relationships between subjects linked by a complex game of identifications but also by a real, daily interdependence, such as that which in our society accompanies us from childhood to adolescence. It is a relationship that differs notably depending on the age of the child and, of course, that of the parents, also subject to time, as teenage children mercilessly remind us. A reality as banal as it is problematic: it is precisely in adolescence that the struggle between generations becomes more intense. This is the age at which children are asked for the courage to keep

DOI: 10.4324/9781003560647-5

going further, without arrogance, and parents for the strength to step aside, without giving up. Here also ends, or should end, the role of parents as the moulders of the generation that will succeed them; the bond does not end, however, with consequences on the psychic and material reality, but the fallout on individual choices and, above all, on the therapeutic process is, of course, particularly varied.

All this has created and still creates problems for the psychoanalytic institution, torn between the fear of betraying its most habitual set-up – the one-to-one relationship between analyst and patient – and the awareness that this different area of work, precisely because of its complexity, can enrich not only practical experience but also psychoanalytic theory.

It is not possible to deal with children without preparation specific to listening to the parents who have generated and raised these children: the request for help that parents pose to the therapist requires attention and tact, before and often during the eventual treatment of the child.

Paying attention to this request does not necessarily mean that the parents themselves should be treated, as is often hastily heard: "It's you two" or "She's the one" – often referring to the mother – "who need(s) treatment". It is necessary to consider that cutting the knot that binds and often suffocates two different sufferings, which might superficially seem to avoid the fatigue of sorting out very tangled balls of yarn, actually deprives the analyst of the emotional experience of finding a common thread between one generation and the next, of making head and tail of, and therefore giving a sense to, apparently senseless stories. Finding a common thread that can also provide valuable indications to the type of answer to be given to the request and the structure to be given to the treatment.

Paying attention to the request means taking some time to understand what parents and children are actually asking for when they come to us, assessing their respective needs, examining the relative compatibility of those needs and then working to ensure that the treatment proposed does not expose any of them to a situation of stalemate or checkmate.

In this perspective, the time between the *first phone call* and the eventual *first session* is neither lost nor dead, but rather a period that, due to the complexity of psychoanalytic knowledge it requires, tests not only the therapist's training but also their flexibility. It is a common and proven experience that it is useful to know how to work *as a team* when the family framework would benefit from a division of tasks between those who will take care of the children and those who will take care of the parents.

The relationship between children, parents and analysts is therefore one of creative mobility. One is never the same parent with one child as with another – children, no less than patients, touch different emotions, different skills and elicit different responses.

Analysts, like parents, will therefore need flexibility, vigilance, willingness to adapt and, at the same time, rigour.

Subjects of treatment: the parents

Parents are such in that they are responsible for and originators of the project of bringing children into the world and raising them. As protagonists, together with their children, of an extremely complex intersubjective relationship, they are also an essential part of therapeutic work. Unless specific attention is devoted to their person and to the suffering (whether admitted or denied) arising from the complexity of this relationship, it is illusory to think of carrying out psychoanalysis on their children. Obviously, their role differs according to the age of their children and the symptoms presented.

In the same way as the setting of the treatment has to take into account the age of the subjects involved and their degree of development, the analyst's mental approach at work must also take into account the shadow that parents cast on their children, *both in the case of it obscuring their personality or illuminating it, functioning as a sundial*, a potentially obscuring shadow according to Freud, capable of signalling the different stages of this relationship and its nuances.

All this requires highly developed, complex training.

Among humans, parents are the beings most exposed to what (following on from Freud's 1915 essay) we call the *work of mourning*. Such work, requiring the ability to deal with the feelings of disappointment that *objects* inevitably inflict on us, is, in the case of parents, directed towards a constant search for balance between the need to invest in their children, to cheer them on while being careful that expectations of them do not create a suffocating cloud, and so tolerating that the inevitable disappointments do not, perhaps silently, undermine trust and hope. Trust also in one's own role as parents, and hope in one's own resources.

42

It is the work of mourning that accompanies birth and forces parents to face the inevitable gap between the imagined and the real child. It is the work of mourning sending the child to the crèche, nursery school or primary school, exacerbated by the first – not always encouraging – comparisons with other ways of being children, of being parents and of being educators. It is the work of mourning that happens when faced with the teenage child, insofar as it is adolescence which, more than the other moments mentioned, together with cheering for the child's successes, brings to the fore the question of generational succession and therefore of time and death.

It is therefore not so strange that in beings already stressed by a more-or-less normal succession, any deviation, discomfort or child's illness can upset balances that are perhaps hard to achieve or can reveal the fragility of constructions that are only solid in appearance.

The vantage point from which to look at parents requesting psychoanalysis for their children will therefore be very varied, not only obviously in relation to the type of request but also very much in relation to the age of the child and, consequently, to the different ages of parenthood.

It is a question of assessing the degree of vulnerability and the emotional impact of a bond, ensuring its functionality.

Precisely because today we know more about parents' vulnerability, we are even more responsible for our actions. The work involved in training cannot be separated from the highly developed, complex experiences concerning the competence to work with children without forgetting the parents who made the initial important effort – requesting a consultation – and who will be guarantors of the continuity of any treatment. With regard more specifically to the structure to be given to the child's treatment, meeting with the parents cannot be reduced to the mere bureaucratic need to define a setting: it is they who are affected by the child's suffering, and it is they who bear the organisational and economic burden of treatment. Much depends on the ability and desire to question and change things, especially when the child's suffering is nothing more than suffering *by proxy*, intended to protect the parents from unresolved conflicts. This is particularly the case when children are unconsciously delegated to solve problems that arose in previous generations, problems that their parents have not been able to process (Badoni, 2002).

A special place must be given to prevention. We know what disasters, for example, maternal depression can be responsible for, even more so if hidden or denied, and we know the devastating impact of unenacted mourning and the narcissistic catastrophes that a child's handicap, even the slightest, can entail. All this can no longer be ignored and should be carefully monitored, in particular through frank, constant collaboration with all the services dedicated to children: from neonatology to nurseries, kindergartens to hospital wards, there are so many areas in which action is possible to prevent problems, with a relatively limited expenditure of energy and money.

Psychoanalytic knowledge can be an excellent tool for filtering such experiences. Of course, the modalities are still very varied and scarcely codified, but, in my opinion, what counts more than the degree of sophistication of the action is being there on the spot, being there genuinely, with the willingness to listen.

The children

We can very roughly divide children into age groups, without ignoring the fact that the extraordinary complexity of human development means that there are many nuances from one moment to the next in relation to biological maturity, the quality of the parent-child relationship and the demands of society.

In Freudian theory, to which we must give great credit for having opened society's eyes to childhood and child sexuality, we find the pre-Oedipal and Oedipal child, the latency-period child, and the pubescent boy or girl.

These ages are directly inscribed in the Freudian theoretical framework relating to the ascertainment of infantile sexuality (Freud, 1905) articulated around the Oedipus complex, its centrality to the formation of the mind (Di Chiara et al., 1985), the latency of infantile sexuality with the prevalence of a defence by removal, the onset of puberty and the signification *a posteriori* of infantile sexuality at the time of adolescence. The body, the investment of its functioning and the changes brought about by puberty play a fundamental role.

It is true that these distinctions mostly interested Freud in formulating the psychoanalytic theory of mental functioning, starting with the emergence of the drive linked to the body and its orifices.

With the formulation of the second principle of the psychic apparatus and the definition of the three elements (Id, Ego and Superego) in constant, though unconscious, dialogue, Freud would modify the theory, without ever disowning his previous work. It is no coincidence that his *Three Essays on Sexuality* (1905) had several prefaces in subsequent editions, the last being in May 1920. There are also numerous notes. In one of these, added in 1924, Freud writes (1905, 168, n. 3 added 1924): "The theory of the instincts is the most important but at the same time the least complete portion of psychoanalytic theory. I have made further contributions to it in my later works *Beyond the Pleasure Principle* (1920) and *The Ego and the Id* (1923)".

Developing it further meant reopening the door to trauma, examining the role of destructiveness and the compulsion to repeat, and thinking of psychoanalytic work as construction as well as discovery. Despite the fact that in the last preface (the 4th Edition), Freud (1905, 133) states: "If mankind had been able to learn from a direct observation of children, these three essays could have remained unwritten", Freud observes that the stakes involved in the child's development from infancy to adolescence are less present than the impact of the growing environment.

However, there is no lack of ingenious insights in Freud's work. In the *Project for a Scientific Psychology* (1895), published posthumously, we find an incredible effort to try to understand how the adult–infant bond works (*adult* as a rescuing object in Freud's lexicon and *infant* as, literally, a child without speech). In just a few, albeit not easy pages, reading the *Project* gives the thrilling idea of witnessing a creation in the very moment it takes place, so numerous are the stimuli that, more than a hundred years later, we recognise to have been grasped and developed by Freud himself, but also a lot by later authors, as explicitly reported by Schore (1994). The infant's emergence from a situation of helplessness relies on the ability of the rescuing adult (how cautious this term is) to understand the signals the infant sends by means other than words, since the child is still without them. Freud did not have at his disposal what neuroscience on the one hand, and Infant Research on the other, tell us today. He was, however, curious to understand what bridges linked the adult with the infant world and on what basis the psychic apparatus was gradually built, starting with the basic biological structure.

It would take years, the work of many others and the emergence of non-neurotic pathologies in the analysis room to understand and develop the breadth of those first intuitions: the situation of powerlessness is in fact a constant threat in the evolution of life, as are the different strategies available from time to time to cope with it.

> I once said: "There is no such thing as an infant", meaning, of course, that wherever one finds an infant, one finds maternal care, and without maternal care, there would be no infant.

With the well-known statement *There is no such thing as an infant,* Winnicott (1960, 39, n.4) inaugurated a new way of looking at childhood and a new way of carrying out psychoanalysis. The immediate consequence: the *talking cure* would have to find new ways to address a being who is not yet endowed with speech or who struggles to use it to communicate. The focus is on the reciprocity of the infant-mother exchange, on the ability to hold (handling), which helps to anchor the child to its own perceptions (holding), creating a sense of continuity of the self.

Regarding the reverberations on the way of being with patients in analysis, also with adult patients, it is a matter of considering that the mind is built, starting from neurobiological bases, on a relationship between subjects, on the feeling of the trustworthiness of care, on the learning together that guarantees a bearable level of frustration, resulting in a progressive recognition of the uniqueness of one's own being that is nourished in and nourishes the relationship with a being other than oneself.

Current psychoanalysis moves along mutually stimulating lines of thought from different points of view: the continuity between before and after its birth (Freud, 1925), which includes legacies and testaments from previous generations (Kaës *et al*,1993); the fruitful bet on the role of the caesura of birth (Bion, 1977), which stimulates mother and infant to find a personal way of understanding each other; and the different modes of symbolisation that include growing attention to a *metapsychology of the act* (Roussillon, 2009), essential in addressing the area of trauma, where events suffered early on, before speech could come to the rescue, initiate specific, different modes of representation. These are areas in which the body and physical expression take the leading roles.

The analysts and the training paradox

The slow, arduous process that the psychoanalytic institution has gone through and is going through in recognising the importance of training psychoanalysts *also* dedicated to working with children and adolescents in their respective growth contexts is cause for reflection.

The founder himself, after the painful break with Fliess and the laboured affirmation "I no longer believe in my neurotica" (Freud, 1897, 264), was particularly concerned about moving psychoanalysis from the seduction-trauma theory to that of unconscious fantasy, the role of the father and the structural significance of the Oedipus complex. In other words, this was Freud turning to the childlike (Guignard, 1995) much more than to childhood, and to the intrapsychic more than the intersubjective.

The fact that in a society with a distinctly male imprint, the first psychoanalysts to deal openly and for an extended period with children were women, and not exactly lucky ones, further weighed on this developing situation. Let us recall (Aliprandi, Pati, 1999) the three pioneers of child psychoanalysis: Hermine von Hug-Hellmuth (1871–1924), Eugenie Sokolnicka (1884–1934) and Sophie Morgenstern (1875–1940), all three of whose lives ended tragically.

As if this were not enough, with Melanie Klein and Anna Freud facing each other on the London scene, the *sibling complex*, now rightly given special consideration by many psychoanalysts also within the family (Kaës, 2003; Macciò, Vallino, 2003), gained attention with particular insistence upon the Freuds' arrival in England, resulting in harsh controversies between Anna Freud, Melanie Klein and their respective pupils. They were divided not only by concrete reasons regarding their respective roles in British psychoanalytic society but also by the notably different weight given to the modes of mental development, organised according to Klein on unconscious fantasy, while according to Anna Freud on the functioning of the Ego and on defence mechanisms.

The *Controversies*, of which we have precious testimony (King, Steiner, 1991), while probably very useful in stimulating the disputants to clarify their respective positions, revealed a minefield in terms of training. Consequently, developing a mentality that takes into account such a complex reality and prepares psychoanalysts to work with couples, parents and families has long been regarded as not relevant, not only for training institutes but for the fabric of society itself.

Pontius Pilate would have recognised the attitude that has led the psychoanalytic institution to wash its hands of the problem of training in this field: only in very recent years has preparation for the psychoanalysis of children and adolescents been delegated to groups or associations operating *outside* the psychoanalytic institution, even if often directed by IPA psychoanalysts.[1]

Thus it was that, alongside a progressive enrichment of psychoanalytic knowledge related to the treatment of children and adolescents, a progressive marginalisation of those working in the field was observed: psychoanalysts who *also* dealt with children and adolescents ended up being considered part of another world, and their training a kind of taboo within organisations and their respective training institutes. Since these patients were until very recently considered *minors*, not to be prosecuted, these analysts were left to their own devices as long as they operated in the margins or in a kind of hidden modality.

The space given to their work in national and international congresses was, until recent years, almost non-existent, as was the attention paid to the method and its foundations in training institutes.

Such was the reaction of *believers* (Kaës, 2003) to the creative ferment of the playroom and the turbulence of working with adolescents.

Works in progress

The appearance in the analysis room of adult patients who can speak but cannot express the attention given to the traumatic events of childhood and the increasing importance given to the interweaving of the intrapsychic, interpsychic and intersubjective have created a bridge between the world of childhood and the workings of the mind that must be crossed and to whose construction I have devoted a great deal of energy in our organisation.

In a supervision group held occasionally in the 1990s at the CMP [Milanese Psychoanalysis Centre] by Pierandrea Lussana, who trained in London, the wish arose to have less restricted and more structured time to meet and talk about our work.

At a meeting hosted in my home in 1993, attended by Antonino Ferro, Magda Viola and Dina Vallino, the idea cropped up of proposing the creation of a working group within the Milanese Centre. We all appreciated Magda Viola's idea of calling it the Child Psychoanalysis Observatory.

Observatory as an observation of the mother-infant couple, but also an observatory aimed at our way of working and the encounter with the complex, often incandescent world I called child psychoanalysis. The idea was accepted by our centre, and the Observatory still functions today in Milan, both as a clinical reference group and as a stimulus for research. From that moment on, the specific aim of the Milanese group was to appeal directly to the institution so that this dual need for clinical discussion and training spaces could be taken on directly within the institution itself. We therefore turned directly to the National Executive of the SPI [Italian Psychoanalytic Society], and its president, Giuseppe Di Chiara.

The request (Artoni Schlesinger et al., 1993)[2] was that a self-certification be promoted by members working in the field while waiting to set up a training course within the society. Particular emphasis was placed on the importance of the preparation acquired in the course of our training, as it was precisely due to this training that we were able to grasp how much of a psychoanalytic element there was in our work, regardless of the age of the patients.

In February 1994, a number of members[3] sent the Executive, which was then reorganising our statute and rules, a highly detailed proposal both on how to census the practitioners and how to launch what would later be called the *Advanced Course*.

This reaffirmed the idea of an advanced specialisation to be integrated into the other training, thus emphasising the uniqueness of the person and the value of training acquired within the Institute.

In May 1994, a questionnaire (prot. 1–742) was sent to all members with the aim of "carrying out a census among SPI members who work or intend to work in this specific field and ascertaining how many of them are interested in participating in a series of seminars aimed at fostering greater reciprocal knowledge among colleagues and providing the opportunity for a theoretical-clinical in-depth study".

The 1999 Roster included the first list of members who were "experts", in that they also worked with children and adolescents. It was drawn up with due regard for previous training and relevant certifications which might concern children and adolescents, or only adolescents. It consisted of 87 members out of a total of 602.

This is important for the interaction that took place in those years between our initiative and a similar one, this time on an international scale.

Things were not easy here either: in a conference (Eskelinen de Folch, 2003), it was recalled how Anna Freud herself had asked for *ad hoc* training in our training institutes as early as 1975. The answer was negative. More than 20 years had to pass before the IPA set up a special committee (COCAP – Committee on Child and Adolescent Psychoanalysis) with the aim of taking stock of the situation, carrying out a census of the expert members in the various organisations and setting minimum standards for the recognition of training. In the years 2001–2005, on the instructions of IPA President Daniel Widlöcher, as COCAP Chair for Europe, I tried to bring together the various organs in Italy dealing with children and adolescents.

Even if today there is broad agreement that the training of professionals should be based on that provided by the training for working with adult patients, the paths to reaching this integration are more complex. However, the evolution of psychopathology and the different ways of symbolisation have opened up a debate to which a section of an issue of the *Rivista di Psicoanalisi* (4, 2019) was recently devoted. This debate has, for example, highlighted the need to acquire, both in theory and in clinical work, the knowledge that allows one to work with children and adolescents in a situation in which the relationship with parents belongs (as well as to phantasms) to the area of family and social reality and intersubjective relationships. It is a question of identifying the tools that, starting from basic training, enable professionals to acquire the necessary knowledge and skills.

As psychoanalysts, we are called upon to deal with the shape the mind is in and how each "mindset" is played out, starting from the conquest of self-awareness and awareness of the other, in an intersubjective relationship shaped by each person's time and age. What counts more than the title of expert is being able to allow the experience of daily work to shape one's mental apparatus without being in too much of a hurry to divide and rigidly designate roles, rather allowing oneself the time necessary to immerse oneself in an area of creative, albeit tiring, play. To avoid creating false experts or false treatments, we should remember this both when working in the field of child psychoanalysis and when thinking about how to prepare psychoanalysts for this task. Indeed, the risk is that the introduction of specific training in institutes ends up creating fenced-off or non-interacting areas, rather than opening minds to scientific debate. It is, in fact, an intermediate area shared by children, parents and analysts, each grappling with their own childhood and infantile elements. It is important for the therapist to be sufficiently immersed in the emotional experiences activated in this area if he or she aims to be sufficiently equipped to answer the complex requirements of this field and be able to help everyone live the experience they are going through with curiosity.

Once the training institute has fulfilled its task of promoting and not defining competencies, it will be up to the organisations to identify, cultivate and keep alive and functioning those forces that show they can operate in the individual areas.

In the SPI, at present, the institution of an advanced course, part of the training that ends after becoming a member, seems to support the opportunity to start from a common basis; the Advanced Course should make the links between theory and different clinical practices more fluid. It should promote the emotional competencies needed to deal with children, adolescents, and parents in particularly complex situations. Clearly, this entails extending an already very long period of training. Those working in the field are aware of this, but only continuous monitoring of the problematic universe in which we find ourselves operating can prevent us from the risk that psychoanalysis perfects itself in defining areas that are more or less protected, thus losing the courage to deal with the demands of a social fabric in turbulent evolution without the fear of losing its specificity. Rather than the distinction between one type of psychoanalysis for adults, one for adolescents and one for children, we should keep alive a psychoanalysis that, being centred on the constitution and modification of the human psyche, has to provide itself with the necessary tools and skills to intervene in the different ages of humankind. The seeds are there, and we can only hope that they will bear good fruit.

Notes

1 IPA, International Psychoanalytical Association, founded in 1910 to coordinate all Freudian organisations.
2 Claudia Artoni Schlesinger, Dina Vallino Macciò, Magda Viola, *Lettera a protocollo (prot. 1–926)*, 14 October 1993.
3 Members of the CMP (Milanese Centre of Psychoanalysis), *protocol 1–539*.

Bibliography

Aliprandi, M., Pati, A.M. (1999), *L'alba della psicoanalisi infantile*. Feltrinelli, Milano.

Aulagnier, P. (1975), *The Violence of Interpretation. From Pictogram to Statement*. Routledge, Hove, 2001.

Badoni, M. (2019), "La psicoanalisi dei bambini oggi: stimolo o scommessa?". In *Rivista di Psicoanalisi*, 65, 4, pp. 943–945.

Badoni, M. (2002), "Parents and Their Child – and The Analyst in the Middle". In *The International Journal of Psychoanalysis*, 83, 5, pp. 1111–1131.

Badoni, M. (2003), "Psychanalystes d'enfants, ou enfants vus par des psychanalystes?". In *Journée des Membres, Société Européenne pour la Psychanalyse de l'Enfant et de l'Adolescent (SEPEA), Société Psychanalytique de Paris (SPP)*, Paris, 17 mai 2003.

Bion, W.R. (1977), *Two Papers: The Grid and Caesura*. Imago Editora, Rio de Janeiro.

Di Chiara, G., Bogani, A., Bravi, G., Robutti, A., Viola, M., Zanette, M. (1985), "Preconcezione edipica e funzione psicoanalitica della mente". In *Rivista di Psicoanalisi*, 31, 3, pp. 327–341.

Eskelinen de Folch, T. (2003), "La formation". In *Journée des Membres, Société Européenne pour la Psychanalyse de l'Enfant et de l'Adolescent (SEPEA), Société Psychanalytique de Paris (SPP)*, Paris, 17 mai 2003.

Freud, S. (1895), *Project for a Scientific Psychology*, SE, vol. II, 1955.

Freud, S. (1897), "Letter to Wilhelm Fliess, 21 September 1897". In *The Complete Letters of Sigmund Freud to Wilhelm Fliess, 1887–1904* (ed., Trans. Masson, J.). Harvard University Press, Cambridge MA, 1985.

Freud, S. (1905), *Three Essays on Sexuality*. SE, vol. VII, 1953.

Freud, S. (1911), *Formulations on the Two Principles of Mental Functioning*. SE, vol. XII, 1958.

Freud, S. (1914), *On Narcissism: An Introduction*. SE, vol. XIV.

Freud, S. (1915), *Mourning And Melancholia*. SE, vol. XIV.

Freud, S. (1926), *Inhibitions, Symptoms and Anxiety*. SE, vol. XX.

Guignard, F. (1995), "The Infantile in the Analytic Relationship". In *The International Journal of Psychoanalysis*, 76, 6, pp. 1083–1093.

Kaës, R. (2003), "Aspetti del complesso fraterno nel gruppo dei primi psicoanalisti". In Algini, M.L. (a cura di), *Fratelli, Quaderni di Psicoterapia Infantile*, 47. Borla, Roma.

Kaës, R., Faimberg, H., Enriquez, M., Baranes, J.-J. (1993), *Trasmissione della vita psichica tra le generazioni*. Borla Roma, 1995.

King, P., Steiner, R. (eds.) (1991), *The Freud-Klein Controversies 1941–45*. Routledge, London and New York.

Macciò, M., Vallino, D. (2003), "Di alcune miserie nella attività intellettuale dei piccoli gruppi alla luce del paradigma fraterno". In Algini, M.L. (a cura di), *Fratelli, Quaderni di Psicoterapia Infantile*, 47, Borla, Roma.

Racamier, P.-C. (1992), *Il genio delle origini. Psicoanalisi e psicosi.* Cortina, Milano, 1993.

Roussillon, R. (2009), "Corps et comportement: langage et messages". In *Revue Belge de Psychanalyse*, 55, 2, pp. 23–40.

Schore, A.N. (1994), *Affect Regulation and the Repair of the Self.* Norton, New York, 2003.

Winnicott, D.W. (1951), "Anxiety Associated with Insecurity". In *Through Pediatrics to Psychoanalysis.* Routledge, New York, 1993.

Winnicott, D.W. (1953), "Transitional Objects and Transitional Phenomena". In *Playing and Reality.* Tavistock, London, 1971.

Winnicott, D.W. (1960), "The Theory of the Parent-Infant Relationship". In *The Maturational Processes and the Facilitating Environment.* International Universities Press, Madison, CT, 1965.

III

PROCESSES OF ANALYTIC WORK
WITH CHILDREN*

*Revised and modified from the original publication: Badoni, M. (2004), "La psicoanalisi dei figli: paradossi". In Neri, N., Latmiral, S. (a cura di), *Uno spazio per i genitori*, *Quaderni di psicoterapia infantile*, 48, Borla, Roma, pp. 171–186.

The nursery: tips and temptations

Thinking about the processes and modes of analytical work with children, I find myself amazed and bewildered. Amazed at the wealth of contributions that have intersected over the course of a century, bewildered because for the psychoanalytic institution, analytical work with children has been and still is both a mine of discoveries and an element of disturbance.

The most immediate comparison that comes to mind is of a building that has housed children who have played there and who, on going away, have left traces. I find here and there, in no apparent pattern, a toy car, a fragment of Lego, a domestic object taken from its usual function to carry out others. One could ask oneself what mysterious purposes these objects were used for, for what ideas, projects, questions. However, if for the landlady this is mere disorder, the temptation to re-establish the known order may prevail.

This is how the psychoanalytic institution has proceeded regarding analytic work with children: great curiosity, but also the temptation

    DOI: 10.4324/9781003560647-6

to re-establish a familiar order: *this* – it has been affirmed – *is not psychoanalysis*.

Like children in a well-ordered house designed for adults, child analysts have often been considered in the psychoanalytic house/ institution as disruptive elements, alternatively as a threat to an established set-up or as objects of curiosity able to draw, from small things, vital cues for psychoanalysis, as long as the rooms were well separated. How many of the fundamental elements of the psycho-analytic construction come from the world of childhood, analysed or observed. On the other hand, can one analyse without observing both oneself and the outside world?

I will limit myself in this work to following the paths of adults who were not afraid to face childhood and their own infantile elements (Guignard, 1996).

Remote investigations: Freud and Ferenczi

Children also think, and with what they have at their disposal (what a small thing Freud's grandchild's reel), they try to represent to themselves and to those who observe them their moods, fears, anxieties, anger and the strength of their affections. Children investigate with their whole body: a body that develops rapidly, that lives and is forged in relationship with the other, and that is, for the child, an object of investigation, curiosity and challenge. This is why children are vulnerable, a vulnerability to which they are exposed because of their extraordinary permeability to the world or the environment, combined with their extreme dependence on the environment, on parental figures, and on their extended family.

This is the child who has been encountered by psychoanalysis and who has also challenged it, in a work of research that is continually open to new developments. Let us start with Freud, to whom we owe the fact that he opened our eyes to infant sexuality, to the strength of the mother-child relationship, the complexity of the Oedipal dilemma, and the dignity of the child's suffering, starting from the initial state of powerlessness, as the motor of all transformation. It is true that Freud was often interested in the child with the adult he was working with in mind, preferring, as in the case of little Hans, contact mediated by the parents to direct contact with the child. There is, however, direct contact, also in the case of Hans, and it is vivid and meaningful, as in the following example:

we know that Hans is struck by the horses' heads, of which he is terrified, and in particular by what the horses have in front of their eyes and by the black around their mouths.

This is the passage (Freud, 1909, 42):

[. . .] as I saw the two of them [Hans and his father] sitting in front of me and at the same time heard Hans's description of his anxiety-horses, a further piece of the solution shot through my mind, and a piece which I could well understand might escape his father. I asked Hans jokingly whether his horses wore eyeglasses, to which he replied that they did not. I then asked him whether his father wore eyeglasses, to which, against all the evidence, he once more said no. Finally I asked him whether by "the black round the mouth" [of the horse] he meant a moustache; and I then disclosed to him that he was afraid of his father, precisely because he was so fond of his mother.

Freud's vision gallops towards the solution of the problem using a *joking tone*: Freud plays with Hans, thinking not only of the frightened child in front of him but also of the infantile elements of the father, already his patient.

I have proposed elsewhere (Badoni, 2004) that this analysis mediated by the father might tend to avoid the often-incandescent contact with the child. Now I also think that in doing so, Freud was accepting a great reality: the child is never alone in consultation. He is a child before being a patient and is still totally dependent on his parents' care. However, as Freud himself notes and as occurs constantly, what might escape the parents can be seen by a trained eye, external to the relationship.

The child analyst will have the difficult task of helping the child to find its own truth and of facilitating the parents in grasping what tends to elude them.

We see in this passage that Freud plays along, giving himself time to observe, allowing himself to be surprised by his intuition, and then *revealing*. This *revealing* shows us the enthusiasm of someone finding confirmation in the field of speculation, as well as indicating a certain ambition of those early analysts: being able to reveal the *truth* of the unconscious rather than suffering the uncertainties of a relationship.

Today, those dealing with children would find the epithet "funny little fellow" that Freud attributes to Hans euphemistic, as well as finding it rare to observe the "irreproachable" behaviour noted by Freud, who describes Hans as "a perfectly reasonable member of human society".

Post-Freud, it is Ferenczi who is rightly credited (Borgogno, 1999) with paving the way for theories and techniques based on object relations and with having investigated beyond removal the offences suffered by the subject due to developmental trauma. Here it is: the emotional fabric that is torn. The person's mind becomes fragile, exposed to dissociative phenomena and to fractures in the mind-body context.

It is also Ferenczi, in pages in which we recognise an attentive observer of infant life, who investigates the development of the child's sense of reality and the underlining of the fundamental contribution of the parents in not hindering the child's will to live and even in convincing the infant to face the adventure of living and forgive the parents for bringing him or her into the world without asking permission (Ferenczi,1929).

In *Child-Analysis in the Analysis of Adults*, Ferenczi (1931) gives us a glimpse of the passion with which he looks at the world of childhood and with which he knows how to capture the nostalgia of childhood and the need for tenderness in adult patients.

Even Ferenczi, however, so fertile in exploring the world of childhood, keeps his distance with respect to direct contact with children – the only exception, in analogy with the case of Hans and this time in a relationship mediated by a female presence, that of the *little chanticleer*, Arpad (Ferenczi, 1913a), a five-year-old boy who, fascinated and terrified by the chicken coop and obsessively attracted by the crudity of the killing of the chickens, ends up becoming a rooster, a rooster in the chicken coop, imitating the rooster's crowing perfectly. Also here in a brief passage, Ferenczi shows his talent when Arpad quickly falls in love with a small bronze rooster in Ferenczi's studio and asks for it as a gift: Ferenczi gives him pen and paper and encourages him to draw.

The child tolerates frustration if encouraged to deal with it, perhaps by transforming it. Otherwise, the child suffers an experience that is too mortifying.

Children seen up close: the pioneers

After these introductions regarding Freud and Ferenczi, of whom it must be remembered that one was the analyst of Anna Freud (1895–1982) and the other of Melanie Klein (1882–1960), it is the turn of women – by fate, by courage? – to take the rugged path of caring for children in the solitude of the analysis room and often facing solitude in relationships with colleagues, when not actually facing the mistrust of the institution.

It happened, most clearly, around the 1920s; 20 years had passed since *The Interpretation of Dreams* (Freud, 1899) and 25 since the writings on hysteria (Freud, 1893–95).

Why so much hesitation, and who were these pioneers? Maria Teresa Aliprandi and Anna Maria Pati (1999) told us about them in a passionate book. Commenting on it (Badoni, 1999), I wrote that the dawn was tragic, tragic for the dramas that marked and accompanied the lives of the three pioneers, the true protagonists of the book: Hermine von Hug-Hellmuth (1871–1924), Eugénie Sokolnicka (1884–1934) and Sophie Morgenstern (1875–1940). Tragic also for that great, silent labour of women who, by immersing themselves – at their own expense – in the contradictions that mark the field of child psychoanalysis, prepared the ground to host its seed and foster its growth. The work and dramas of these three women formed the background to the development of child analysis and influenced its subsequent developments.

Hermine von Hug-Hellmuth worked in Vienna, where Freud entrusted her with a column on childhood in the journal *Imago* from 1909. However, her first important work dates from 1921; at that time, Anna Freud began her own analysis with her father.

Hellmuth's work *On the Technique of Child Analysis*, published in the journal *Imago* in 1920 – based on a lecture given at the 6th International Congress of Psychoanalysis in The Hague – is a *summa* of valuable insights and contradictions. It is a combination of a vigorously educational outlook – the analysis of children is constant character analysis and education – and the ability to recognise how important it is for the analyst to let themselves be helped by the little patient. It proposes resorting to "tricks" to obtain the unravelling of the child's mind while accepting an area of respect, where it is important to be "content" not to do violence, to wait, so as to avoid a situation in which "the soul is disturbed instead of freed"

(Aliprandi, Pati, 1999, 134). Finally, it balances the acceptance given to parental suffering and the idealisation of analysis of the parents as prevention of the child's suffering.

A few years later, in 1924, Hermine Hug-Hellmuth was killed by a nephew she was treating. This tragic incident, followed by a lengthy trial and much press coverage, would wreak havoc on the already difficult practice of working with children and adolescents. It also coincided with Klein's trip from Berlin (where she had resumed analysis with Abraham) to Vienna and undoubtedly had an influence on the failure of this trip. Two years later, after the death of her second analyst, Klein settled in London. Three years later came the first violent attack on a work by Anna Freud, who had meanwhile finished her analysis and published *Introduction to the Technique of Child Analysis* (1927). In the paper, she underlines the importance of establishing a positive relationship with children, helping them to trust the analyst, and – *casus belli* – the fact that children do not really develop transference as they are still too dependent on the reality of their parents.

Klein immediately took a stand against this, and Jones did not make things any easier by publishing Klein's and her group's views in the *International Journal*, leading to a reprimand from Freud for not giving Anna a chance to express her opinion.

We will return to the developments of this controversy later. In the meantime, let us follow the fate of the other two pioneers, also because the migrations of their lives shed light on another important place for child psychoanalysis – France.

Eugénie Sokolnicka (née Kunter, married Sokolnicka) was born and grew up in Warsaw in the rich, cultured Jewish bourgeoisie; she died by suicide in 1934 at the age of 50. Driven by a feverish curiosity, she moved through the Europe of the time: Zurich with Jung, Vienna for a brief didactic analysis with Freud, then in 1913 she attended the *Wednesday Society* sittings. Back to Warsaw and then to Budapest with Ferenczi, who appreciated her as much as he noted her fragility with concern. In Paris, where she was known in the literary milieu that gathered around the *Nouvelle Revue Française*, she was probably overshadowed by the rising star of Marie Bonaparte.

Her work *Analysis of a Case of Infantile Obsessional Neurosis* (1920) was translated into several languages and has come down to us enriched with an interesting commentary by Daniel Widlöcher (1968). This was 1968. It is interesting to note that, by emphasising

Sokolnicka's aptitude for integrating psychoanalytic interpretations with direct interventions on the environment, Widlöcher reminds us that the history of child psychoanalysis can be seen as that of efforts undertaken to manage this essential variant of therapeutic action with the child. To modify the balance of forces, to accelerate readjustments, the psychoanalyst will have to integrate analytical interpretations with direct interventions on the environment.

We are in France, a land where child psychoanalysis has seen a great, valuable development by various therapists, who were also my teachers. And it was in France that the third and last of the three *pioneers* continued her research: Sophie Morgenstern, analysed by Eugénie Sokolinicka, active in Paris in the 1930s and 1940s; she committed suicide when the Germans entered Paris.

Sophie Morgenstern managed to carve out a space for psychoanalytic work in the service led by Heuyer at the Salpêtrière, thus inaugurating that rich exchange between psychoanalysis and institution so particular to France. Her interest in dreams and children's drawings, in the way children construct their thoughts, on the one hand places her reflections at the centre of the theory of technique, while on the other hand they reveal her many uncertainties – uncertainties that the controversy between Anna Freud and Melanie Klein, which had in the meantime become more pronounced, might not have helped. However, it is interesting to note that her work *Quelques aperçus sur l'expression du sentiment de culpabilité dans les rêves des enfants* [*Some insights into the expression of guilt in children's dreams*] (1933) was translated by Servadio and published in the Rivista Italiana di Psicoanalisi [Italian Review of Psychoanalysis] in 1934. It would take another 55 years for child psychoanalysis to find an official place in the SPI [Italian Psychoanalytic Society], and analytical training for child and adolescent analysis was not recognised by the International Psychoanalytical Association (IPA) until 2001.

Discussion and controversies

While London burned under the fire of German bombing, a dispute that had been smouldering under the ashes for some years was ignited between the Kleinian group and the one led by Anna Freud. The coincidence of all this with a serious event such as the Second World War is not by chance: these were years of migration, of disorientation, of great suffering for adults and even more so for children, who were often separated from their parents, safeguarding their lives, but still incurring traumas that would leave lasting traces. Many of Anna Freud's observations, still valuable today, come from the *War Nurseries*.

These were also years in which the functioning of the Society and its Institute (the British Society was presided over by Jones for 24 years) was further complicated by the events of the war, which made contact even more difficult. Many psychoanalysts (including Melanie Klein, Susan Isaacs and Joan Rivière) were forced to leave London. The result was a major loss of contact with the group that had come from Vienna (loss of patients, loss of personal contacts, etc.).

The themes were the relevance or otherwise of transference, the type of setting, the emphasis placed on the vicissitudes of the drive rather than on unconscious fantasy and object relations, the pedagogy-psychoanalysis intertwining, which is also the weight or otherwise of reality in working with children, and the place to be given to parents. Last but not least, who is entitled to training on child analysis, tacitly introduced in different ways and not without controversy by Anna Freud and Melanie Klein.

It is probably a transgenerational legacy of this controversy that training in child analysis took another few decades to be formalised in the IPA, not without the difficulties we still find. It is also an important demonstration, as Steiner also notes (King, Steiner, 1991), that scientific discussions do not take place in a vacuum and cannot be understood without also grasping the extra-clinical variables and interaction with different clinical experiences.

There was, however, an armistice: on the 13th of May 1942, the British Society admitted two distinct training courses: Course A was mixed, while Course B was linked to Anna Freud's theorising. In June 1946, the negotiation was carried out by Sylvia Payne and Anna Freud. There were, in fact, three groups, with the Independents including, among others, Donald Winnicott. We can at this point ask the question: Is a theory of mental development in terms of infantile object relations compatible with a theory in terms of the vicissitudes of drives? More than answering affirmatively or negatively, we should ask ourselves what the psychoanalysis of children (and adults) would be like today without the concept of projective identification, introduced by Klein and developed by Bion in later years, and what the psychoanalytic culture of childhood would be like without the attention devoted by Anna Freud to children and their development in family, school and social reality. Anna Freud, who we know as not only her father's daughter but also the daughter of the institution, seems to have dared more than Klein in opening up psychoanalytic investigation not only to children but also to their world. On the other hand, once it was established that play is the child's real work, Melanie Klein threw herself eagerly into analytical work with children, sometimes ignoring their existential reality but providing us, as we know, with valuable insights into their mental functioning. One only has to think of the theory of internal objects and the formulation of the depressive position, a difficult goal today in a society all geared towards success and adaptation, little inclined to the elaboration of any kind of mourning.

The child and the mother: Winnicott and Bion

To soften and perhaps also to divert attention from the battlefield, it was Donald Winnicott (1896–1971) who, we might say, dared to play with fire where conflict burned, revolutionising the way of understanding not only the analytic relationship but the entire psychoanalytic construct.

There is no such thing as an infant without a mother might seem a self-evident affirmation were it not for the fact that it commits us to widening the area of investigation to the delicate functioning of the dyad, to the mother's capacity to tolerate feelings of hatred towards her child and thus to provide an honourable way to tolerate frustrations, sustaining illusions in due ways and time, respecting private space (no questions asked about the transitional object) and above all knowing how to hold in time (handling and holding), a concept of great poignancy that, as Winnicott wanted, addresses the psychosomatic unity of the infant and the development of a sense of one's own existence in the world.

Winnicott's psychoanalytic revolution was a *silent revolution*, but one that still fuels psychoanalytic thought today. How much does Bion owe to Winnicott?

The upheaval in the British Institute of those years, the work in the Northfield Military Hospital, the first experiences with groups and analysis with Melanie Klein led to further transformations of psychoanalytic thought by Wilfred Bion (1897–1979). What did the concept of *rêverie* bring to child psychoanalysis?

Attributing a communication-carrying function to projective identification and the task of transforming the poignancy of these projections into images to the mother's *rêverie* by giving more digestible representations to the child shifts the focus onto emotions and their development, onto mental functioning and the capacity to think.

Bion rummages through, selects from and rethinks Freud's work, filtering it through Klein's intuitions and his own personal experience of life and work, and thus delivers the necessary tools to psychoanalysts to cope with the social upheavals that took place, especially in Europe, from the end of the 1970s onwards.

Psychoanalysis in France

Across the Channel in Paris, Serge Lebovici (1915–2000) and René Diatkine (1918–1998) built a solid foundation in the post-war period to introduce psychoanalytic thought and practice in the service of childhood.

Who knows whether this extreme attention to the world of childhood in its most distressed reality was not only a response to the social reality of the moment but also the echo of personal transgenerational realities. Both were men fleeing the concrete threat of racial persecution: Lebovici fled Romania, and Diatkine's family moved to Paris after the First World War, from Belarus. Both lived in a Paris torn apart by German occupation and deportations, and Lebovici's father would die in a concentration camp. Diatkine (1994) recalled how, for his generation, being psychoanalysts could not be separated from an indispensable search for truth after the horrors of the war, the Shoah and the Vichy regime.

For a long time, French psychoanalysis remained firmly anchored in Freud's work, orthodox in its theoretical framework, but also very free in its clinical practice. It is sufficient to recall the foundation in 1980 of a Child and Adolescent Psychopathology Service at the Avicenne Hospital in Bobigny, and the experience of the Thirteenth Arrondissement, a mental health service where psychoanalytic thought and practice are placed at the service of people in distress and their families.

Lebovici's work, devoted in recent years to the psychopathology of young children and early interactions between children and their partners, presaged the current interest in early interventions involving the family environment.

Diatkine developed psychoanalytic work with children profoundly, leaving us ample material. I would like to take up just a few points from his last book, from the part concerning the ethics of the child psychoanalyst (Diatkine, 1994).

In particular, he recommends reference to transference as the core of psychoanalytic ethics. He insists that analysts be careful not to enter into situations of omnipotence and not consider themselves a better parent than the child's actual parents. He acknowledges the difficult balance between the need to start from a diagnostic profile and the freedom to be able to contradict it. He insists on the uniqueness of each patient-analyst relationship and therefore on the essential need to safeguard the work from abuses of power, such as the misuse of theoretical concepts *foisted* on the child's or adolescent's head by attributing pre-packaged unconscious fantasies to them, while on the other side, the *sacralisation* of past or current events within the family. He moreover recommends vigilance to keep arousal low and insists on the need to establish a relationship with the family without betraying the child's secrets, as well as on the definition of the object as a mental organisation, whether it is projected onto the representation of external persons or is based on an internal potentiality.

The preparation and tenacity of Florence Guignard (2015) have contributed to the development in more recent years of first Melanie Klein's thinking and later Bion's, with the relative repercussions on the analysis of children, and not only children.

Child and adolescent psychoanalysis in Italy

Having gone over the foundations of child psychoanalysis in other parts of Europe, we can now touch upon the psychoanalytic turmoils in Italy. First of all, it must be said that child psychoanalysis spread thanks to the passion of many members of the two psychoanalytic societies in Italy: the Italian Psychoanalytic Society (SPI) and the more recent Italian Psychoanalytic Association (AIPsi).

A group of Italian psychoanalysts embarked on a journey to France, French Switzerland and Britain. I refer to Algini's text (2007) for an in-depth study of these interesting stories, with a somewhat heavy heart in truth, seeing how much loss of intelligence and affection the psychoanalytic institution's diffidence has fuelled. How many people I met in different ways in my training and who are now no longer with us. We owe it to the efforts of all of them that for some years now training in child and adolescent psychoanalysis has been part of a possible training programme also within the SPI, alongside and complementary to training in adult psychoanalysis.

The circumstances of my life have allowed me, with the support of the Executive chaired by Fausto Petrella (1997–2001), to channel these developments into a training project within the SPI. At a congress in those years, I met Terttu Eskelinen de Folch, then President of the Committee on Child and Adolescent Psychoanalysis (COCAP). It was a fruitful exchange that started a long collaboration, allowing us, with the help of Anne Marie Sandler, to start a first census of analysts dealing with children and adolescents and, later, to set up the Advanced Course.

One might now ask, as Gaddini did (1984), *if and how our patients have changed*: what the children who now turn to us are like, what their families are like. If I think of my own psychoanalytic practice, I believe I can say that I started treating frightened children, while in my more recent practice, I have encountered very excited children. What about childhood neurosis and the age of latency?

We know that since the 1970s, family structure has changed profoundly, especially in large cities. We can think of the rarity of the extended family, of both parents working outside the home, and of the increasing disintegration of traditional family units – elements that introduced children rapidly into the social fabric (crèches, nursery schools), but which on the other hand unfortunately also created the conditions for children to spend a lot of time alone, or at any rate with distracted adults, often themselves excited and in difficulty when it came to setting limits. This is all the more so with the increase in marital separations, with the related phenomena of compensation linked both to feelings of guilt and to a predominantly narcissistic investment in children. Attention to psychic reality, the object of psychoanalysis, is of relatively little interest to today's society, all focussed on adaptation and efficiency. Yet ours is not a society without suffering, and so it is the task of psychoanalysis to take up the challenge and investigate useful methods and models to meet this new society.

For example, are the status and functioning of child sexuality in human psychic development and psychopathology the same today as in 1905?

I began this work with a reference to *little Hans*, a case of infantile phobia, and I wrote earlier that today's children are more excited than frightened. This excitement goes well beyond the Oedipal moment to extend through what used to be called the latency phase, which is today, by almost unanimous consensus, on its way to disappearing. I do not believe that this happens without having to rethink how identity is structured, what consequences this has at the arrival of adolescence, and how the differences of sexes and generations are experienced.

In a conference held in Paris on the relevance of child psychoanalysis in today's Western society, Florence Guignard (2007, 148) specifically highlighted the importance of virtual reality in today's society and emphasised how "virtual reality has a completely different relationship to the pleasure/unpleasure principle and to the reality principle from that of fantasy". While we are alarmed if a child confuses fantasy and reality, we take it for granted that the virtual world proposes an illusory reality, without thinking how much in the long term this movement allows us to dispense with the psychic work that binds and transforms. What about the relationship between the internal psychic world and external reality?

Virtual reality stimulates the sensory faculties at the expense of a more accurate work of perception. One can escape from a reality if it is too painful – rather than working on the transformation of emotions, one engages in avoidance strategies. Ferro (2007) devoted one of his books to the subject. The result is a particular use of language: the word is more and more similar to the act and dwelling on experiences is carefully avoided.

Hence the weakening of neurotic structures and the increase in the pathology of limits, studied in depth by the English and Argentinian schools.

Consequences ensue at different levels (Guignard, 2007). On a phenomenological level, the primary scene fantasy, which moves curiosity towards the parents' world, their sexuality and their history, is no longer the motor factor of epistemophilic drives; the finiteness of life becomes a disturbance, death is hidden and attending funerals is unthinkable. I have happened to intervene in situations where the death of a parent had been kept hidden from the children.

It is difficult to get children out of their virtual game, especially as they often lack the mental tools necessary to deal with reality. This requires psychoanalysts to find a way to access the child's world, to put themselves as players within the game without allowing themselves to become too caught up. I have managed, after other unsuccessful attempts, to draw back to me a child who had withdrawn to the other end of the room, protected by her headphones, by mimicking her attitude, and to convince a reluctant little boy to come into my office by proposing that he lie down on a *magic* carpet and be pulled. In this case, it was a gesture that gave a child, burdened with overwhelming expectations, the chance to be carried, for a moment, on the wings of fantasy.

Difficulties and challenges for today's child psychoanalysts

There are various challenges for child psychoanalysts today. When I started my psychoanalytic practice with children and adolescents, I was very taken up with consultation work, in which one tried to understand *who needed what*. Back in Italy from Switzerland, I was very struck by the lack of attention then (45 years ago) given to parents, and I insisted on this whenever I could: I thought, worked and wrote. Today this is no longer the case. The problem, however, is not so much *who needs what* as *who is who*. The difference between generations has flattened, the transmission of values tends to give way to adaptation strategies, and the reluctance of parents to deal with conflict exposes their children more to what is called intergenerational transmission. The child psychoanalyst today needs to know about adults, children, couples and even groups. Now, if this should make us attentive to the quality of training, it should also create a *habit of humility in the analytical encounter*. One of the traps we are exposed to is, in fact, related to the difficulty of tolerating and exploring our countertransference, tested by the impact with fragmented mental functioning and archaic defence mechanisms.

Discussing the tyrannical qualities of some transferences, I wrote (Badoni, 2006, my translation):

It is therefore up to the analyst to become the interpreter of very painful feelings of impotence and encumbrance at the sensory level. Moreover, it is not enough to sense that this painful, persecutory feeling of impotence has something to do with very primitive communication by the patient, because the analyst knows or learns that the challenge is now, before that between the self and the patient or between the self and the self. The pressure for the analyst to act is very strong in these cases: it is necessary first of all to be able to withstand this pressure, to hold on to one's perceptions in the hope of understanding which regime one is working in, to then cope with it.

Dina Vallino (1984, 181, my translation) writes in her work on participatory consultation:

My impression is that if one gives up wanting to readily explain the situation, one comes to absorb the atmosphere of an everyday family experience. Later, keeping oneself internally in a state of solitude and uncertainty equal to that of the child who has come to us, one manages to find the child.

This is my wish for those about to embark on this exciting work.

Bibliography

Algini, M.L. (a cura di) (2007), *Sulla storia della psicoanalisi infantile in Italia. Quaderni di Psicoterapia Infantile*, 55, Borla, Roma.

Aliprandi, M., Pati, A.M. (1999), *L'alba della psicoanalisi infantile*. Feltrinelli, Milano.

Badoni, M. (1999), "Recensione a Maria Teresa Aliprandi, Anna Maria Pati (1999), "L'alba della psicoanalisi infantile"". In *Rivista di psicoanalisi*, 45, 4, pp. 858–861.

Badoni, M. (2004), "La psicoanalisi dei figli: paradossi". In Neri, N., Latmiral, S. (a cura di), *Uno spazio per i genitori, Quaderni di psicoterapia infantile*, 48, Borla, Roma, pp. 171–186

Badoni, M. (2006), "Tirannia del corpo, tirannia del transfert". Relazione presentata al Congresso Nazionale della Società Psicoanalitica Italiana *Transfert. Cambiamenti nella teoria e nella pratica clinica*, Siena.

Borgogno, F. (1999), *Psychoanalysis as a Journey*. Open Gate Books, London, 2007.

Diatkine, R. (1994), *Il bambino nell'adulto o l'eterna capacità di fantasticare*. Borla, Roma, 1998.

Ferenczi, S. (1913a), "A Little Chanticleer". In *First Contributions to Psychoanalysis*. Karnac, London, 1952.

Ferenczi, S. (1913b), "Stages in the Development of the Sense of Reality". In *First Contributions to Psychoanalysis*. Karnac, London, 1952.

Ferenczi, S. (1929), "The Unwanted Child And His Death Instinct". In *Final Contributions to the Problems and Methods of Psychoanalysis*. Karnac, London, 1980.

Ferenczi, S. (1931), "Child Analysis in the Analysis of Adults". In *Final Contributions to the Problems and Methods of Psychoanalysis*, Routledge, Hove, 1994.

Ferrara Mori, G. (1996), "Recensione di M. Trinci (a cura di) (1993), "Il bambino che gioca"". In *Rivista di Psicoanalisi*, 4, 4, pp. 672–678.

Ferro, A. (2007), *Evitare le emozioni, vivere le emozioni*. Cortina, Milano.

Freud, A. (1927), *Introduction to the Technique of Child Analysis*. Nervous and Mental Disease Monograph Series, Washington, DC, 1928.

Freud, S. (1893–95), *Studies on Hysteria (with Josef Breuer) (1893–95)*. SE, vol. II, 1955.

Freud, S. (1899), *The Interpretation of Dreams (1900)*. SE, vol. IV–V, 1955.

Freud, S. (1909), *Analysis of a Phobia in a Five-year-old Boy*. SE, vol. X, 1955.

Freud, S. (1920), *Beyond the Pleasure Principle*. SE, vol. XVIII.

Gaddini, E. (1984), "Changes in psychoanalytic patients up to the present day". In *A Psychoanalytic Theory of Infantile Experience: Conceptual and Clinical Reflections*. Tavistock, London, 1992.

Grosskurth, P. (1986), *Melanie Klein: Her World and Her Work*. Hodder & Stoughton, London.

Guignard, F. (2007), "Mourning and mental development". In Glocer Fiorini, L., Bokanowski, T., Lewkowicz, S. (eds.), *On Freud's "Mourning and Melancholia"*, Karnac, London, p. 148.

Guignard, F. (1996), *Nel vivo dell'infantile. Riflessioni sulla situazione analitica*. FrancoAngeli, Milano.

Guignard, F. (2007), "Le psychanalyste et l'enfant dans la société occidentale d'aujourd'hui". *Société européenne pour la psychanalyse de l'enfant et de l'adolescent (SEPEA)*, 18 mars 2007.

Guignard, F. (2015), *Quelle psychanalyse pour le XXI siècle? Tome I. Concepts psychanalytiques en mouvement*. Itaque, Paris.

Hug-Hellmuth, H. (1921), "Zur Technik der Kinderanalyse". In *Internationale Zeitschrift für Psychoanalyse*, 7, 2, pp. 179–197

King, P., Steiner, R. (eds.) (1991), *The Freud-Klein Controversies 1941–45*. Routledge, London and New York.

Lebovici, S., Soulé, M. (1970), *La conoscenza del bambino e la psicoanalisi*. Feltrinelli, Milano, 1994.

Morgenstern, S. (1933), "Quelques aperçus sur l'expression du Sentiment de culpabilité dans les Rêves des Enfants". In *Revue Française de Psychanalyse*, 6, 2, pp. 155–174.

Sokolnicka, E. (1920), "Analyse einer infantilen Zwangneurose". In *Internationale Zeitschrift für Psychoanalyse*, 6, 3, pp. 228–241.

Vallino, D. (1984), "L'avvio della consultazione partecipata". In Algini, M.L. (a cura di) (2007), *Sulla storia della psicoanalisi infantile in Italia. Quaderni di Psicoterapia Infantile*, 55, Borla, Roma.

Widlöcher, D. (1968), "Commentaire de "L'analyse d'un cas de névrose obsessionnelle infantile" par E. Sokolnicka". In *Revue de neuropsychiatrie et d'hygiène mentale de l'enfant*, 16, 5–6, pp. 481–486.

PART THREE

GETTING INVOLVED IN THE GAME

Resources and risks

Space dilates: the first decade of the third millennium were years dense with events on intertwined and, as often happens, competing planes: institution, profession and family contended for the hours of the day and night. The tangle heated up and then overheated, finding its melting point in the third weekend of June 2004: in Rome to present my work for training functions, but with an eye and an ear on my phone to finally receive news of the birth of my first grandchild.

Thinking of presenting myself, after being a full member, for training functions seemed a natural thing to me, as it is natural that bringing children into the world is a prerequisite to becoming grandparents.

The work of supervision resembles it a little: the children have been brought up by others, the grandparents now have the task of passing on tradition and knowledge, with the freedom to get involved in the game and, as we shall see, to take themselves playfully while learning to measure the distances between teachers and students, between analyst and patient, and between practice and theory.

The space for both care and treatment in those years included children, adults and couples.

DOI: 10.4324/9781003560647-7

There was a gradual crescendo in my curiosity for the analytical method, in my need to engage with colleagues and to return over the Alps, taking with me, apart from French and English, its culture and practice. I was accompanied by the surprises aroused by exchanges with colleagues, in our centres, at congresses in Italy, Europe and beyond. The year 1999 ended with an exciting congress in Santiago de Chile, but the early 2000s are punctuated by congress meetings that are still vivid in my memory. Between 2000 and 2003, I was in Paris on the fear of thinking, in Annecy, in Bologna for the "Italian-French Colloquium", in Milan for a meeting with Daniel Stern on "Interpretation and Its Limits", in Palazzo Steri in Palermo on "Dream Analysis", in Trieste for the National Congress, in Prague where I presented a paper on the function of accompaniment, and in Sorrento for the European Federation.

You wanted the bike, now get pedalling![1]

Apart from the metaphor, the bicycle is my favourite means of transport in dangerous Milan. It was part of the game, until a treacherous pavement and over-reliance on my abilities stopped the bike rides, but not my commitment: the games carried on.

I lived in Milan for 41 years, from 1973 to 2014, the year I returned to my father's house in Lecco, the only one of 11 daughters to do so. An emotion that had been suspended at the time of my analysis demanded that the games resume, even though I knew that "playing at home" is particularly challenging. I dived into the family archives for a year: the archives of affection resurfaced. It was an intense experience that allowed me to rediscover the adventurous aspects of my father's life and my mother's painful perseverance.

As children we used to play "Rialzo", a game of chase and catch, but if a child jumped on a "rialzo" [a raised surface], he or she had a moment's rest and was allowed to leave the game without betraying the group.

In the game of social life, an occasional "rialzo" has succeeded for me, accompanied, however, by more or less explicit reproaches for having abandoned not so much the game, but the players: "Too bad you deal with children", I was told. Dealing with children has nevertheless been a lesson in irony and humility, indispensable ingredients for survival and, in particular, for working in the fabric of society.

I would once again get back in the game to participate as vice-president in the National Executive chaired by Stefano Bolognini

(2009–2013). It would prove to be a complex job in a world that is becoming, in addition to being poorer, more hasty, more "narcissistic", and more distrustful of psychoanalysis.

It was the beginning of a still unfinished period in which many colleagues are now engaged, and not only in our Society. Many have left us, finding other and more definitive "rialzos" from which they nevertheless manage to spread their passion for psychoanalysis.

To all of them goes my profound gratitude.

Getting involved in the game, Taking Oneself Playfully: sometimes Taking Oneself Playfully happens, sometimes it does not, but it is above all the lost moves that leave traces.

Note

1 [Translator's note] Since in the next paragraph, the author continues the theme of the bicycle, this is the literal translation of the Italian saying "L'hai voluta la bicicletta? Pedala!", the equivalent of which in English would be "You made your bed, now lie in it!"

IV

TAKING ONESELF PLAYFULLY*

*Revised and modified from the original work: Badoni, M. (2017), "Prendersi in gioco". Paper presented at the scientific seminar *Agire-giocare nella psicoanalisi infantile*, Florence Psychoanalytic Centre, Tuscan section of the SPI, Florence, 14 January 2017, Auditorium dell'Ente Cassa di Risparmio di Firenze.

When I was involved in today's work by the Executive Committee of the Florence Psychoanalytic Centre, an unexpected short-circuit gave shape to the title of my talk: *Prendersi in gioco/Taking yourself playfully*. Now all that is left for me to do is play: play at catching each other, play at understanding each other, work by playing, and also know how to make fun of ourselves, of our limited nature.

In the dictionary, the word *play* means an activity that brings pleasure: amusement and *diversion*, hence also disorientation and displacement – in fact, playing includes joking.

The product of play is something, then, that players do not expect, a third product, and it is precisely this that makes the game go on, displacing players in unexpected ways.

To start the game here today, I am therefore going to propose a displacement: I will subvert the order of the questions we were asked and start with the last one. We were asked: *Do the phenomena we are discussing – playing/acting – have counterparts in adult analysis?*

I could immediately answer yes and end the game, say that child psychoanalysis is the same as adult analysis, reassure everyone that we are not playing, like child psychoanalysts, in a minefield.

DOI: 10.4324/9781003560647-8

I do, however, want to play, and I will do so taking the path backwards, as can happen in board games, on the trail of teachers and on that of memories, along the course of my analytical playing, now in my past.

Playing at being taken in: a session under supervision

"So, did the patient take it?", Luciana Nissim[1] asked me during the supervision that started my long journey as an analyst. The question referred to an interpretation of which I was proud but which was evidently too articulate and too mine for the patient to make it their own, take it and continue the game.

It might have been an exciting moment for me, but precisely for this reason I could not share it. Stefania Manfredi[2] told us that when the analyst is too happy with the interpretation he or she has just formulated, something is not working.

Should interpretations be taken? I believe so, and I believe that doing so is equivalent to the patient making it their own, feeling it as their own experience, letting it play in their inner world, searching for other playmates: the events of the day, the encounters of life, the legacy of people who have contributed to our becoming subjects. Associations, when free, are part of the game (Benjamin, 2016). The "listening to listening", to which Haydée Faimberg (1996) drew our attention, is nothing more than making sure that the ball we threw to the patient was caught and thrown back. Throwing back is not, however, a rally, a simple returning – my turn, your turn – throwing back involves some degree of thirdness, a diversion/enjoyment. Freud already warned that it is not so much the patient's ready consent to our interaction that signals the correctness of the interpretation, but the appearance of something new, apparently disorienting, but rich in creative insights. In a recent article (Benjamin, 2016), Jessica Benjamin proposes thirdness as "one configuration in the field, understood intersubjectively as how we are aligned or positioned in relation to the other".

Compared to Ogden's definition (1994), which considers the analytic third as a creation produced by two subjective experiences, unprecedented for both analyst and analysand, this definition seems to me to greatly widen the conception of the third and thus of the game, extending it, if I am not mistaken, to everything needed for the game to take place: getting one's hands messy in the dough, rather than just enjoying the baked cake. This involves repeating, trying and trying again, dosing the ingredients, calculating the timing and putting up with the failures.

But what happens if the players cannot play because they have irreconcilable positions with respect to the game?

Out of the game: a session

I am in a session with a child of about four years old. Among the toys is a ball, part of the setting as an invitation to play. What happens, however, takes us to an unknown and perturbing place: the child takes the ball and throws it with all his strength. The ball bounces off into the room and, after zigzagging through various obstacles, comes back and stops at our feet. To my great surprise, the child, to get back the ball where it is lying, very close to both of us, rather than taking the short, intuitively immediate route, that of proximity, like a puppy following its sense of smell might do, follows the entire bumpy path that the ball has taken. He follows the trail, fascinated, intent on not getting lost, tracing the same path as the ball, as if on precise instructions. Here the ball is an object of fascination, rather than an instrument of play. Bewitched by the movement of the ball, the child becomes caught up in its movement. We are not taken in: amazed and lost, I realise that I am out of the game.

I question myself: we are dealing here with an autistic child, and his playful activity seems to me to be guided by his senses rather than by any desire to play. I see no pleasure in this gesture, no amusement, but a suffused excitement, sustained by the noise that the ball makes banging here and there and by its movement. It is a sensory pathway that excludes contact and could resemble the loss of self in daydreaming of many adult patients (Colombi, 2010). Yet we were apparently playing, but not every ball thrown ends up in play – we were not taken in; at most we were in position, but as distant as stars.

The toys, physically present in the room during the children's analysis, are therefore not automatically transformed into play. They are available to the children as part of the tools they habitually use to express, control or expand their emotional space when words are not yet ready to do so. Adults, even though they may have an accomplished language to express, control or expand their emotional space, may take years to play with the analytical, dreamy, disorienting and unpredictable speech.

Playing at home

At the end of a series of consultation sessions, I asked a child what we could say to her parents in the next meeting, the last one of the consultation phase. This was the immediate answer: "Tell them to invite you to play at my house". An added complication in child analysis is that it is precisely *at home* that one plays, whatever the parents' mode of presence in the analytic setting. Yet this is what the children expect, knowing full well that in the game, the parents, whether materially present or absent, take part as watchful and anything but neutral accompaniers of the analytical experience. Adults expect to talk, and children expect to handle the toys, but, in both cases, before words and play enable us to discover the games, time is needed to meet the players. Playing at home has to take into account the habitat in which one plays but also serves to familiarise oneself with the many characters of childhood, with the roles played changing every time in the theatre of the mind.

It is therefore not the toy that makes the game, but the disposition, often painstakingly acquired by the analytical couple, to put themselves in the game, something that seems very similar to exercising an alpha function and, above all, to its indispensable corollary, a good disposition to negative capability. Usually, when the fun begins, when one can find oneself again after agreeing to be displaced, the analysis is on the point of finishing, for children as for adults.

Before this happens, adults and children act in the session. For adults, words are often acts of speech, useful to fill terrifying gaps, test the other's resistance, or protect themselves from possible intrusions. Children do this by placing themselves very concretely in the room, exploring, often showing off with dizzying movements and attacking the setting with the means at their disposal, in particular the means of the timing of the session: "We're done for today", does not necessarily mean that the children get up, say goodbye and leave. On the contrary, they often engage the analyst in a challenge that is not always easy to contain.

I will therefore answer this question in the affirmative: *there is a correspondence between the analysis of children and that of adults, between acting/playing*, but the instrumentation is inevitably different, which also positions the analyst differently. The child predominantly uses his or her body and the inescapable freedom to move in the space of the room, and the readiness of the analyst to grasp metaphor and meaning in the child's movements will be decisive; the adult predominantly uses spoken language, and it is up to the analyst to understand how much of the patient's corporeality enters into the speech. This is not without consequences, as we shall see.

I have used these brief examples with the intention of inviting you to play with me without knowing where our game would take us. I will now retrace my steps to lead you along the winding paths of the analysts who have grappled with these issues.

A brief history of games and playing

I did not actually start at the end to get out of the game in a hurry, but to remove some misunderstandings about the meaning of games and playing in analysis with children and adults.

The question of games and playing was, in fact, the great misunderstanding psychoanalysis fell into, starting with the weight attributed by child psychoanalysis to playing and its meaning. The result of the controversy was that child analysis was put in a corner for decades, thus depriving analysts of the freedom, flexibility and wisdom that only a disposition to play can awaken. The diatribe excited souls and obscured the desire for research, lost in the perverse game of distinguishing what is from what is not psychoanalysis, until it was realised that adult psychoanalysts were also playing but did not know it yet.

Freud, who did not treat children, but had enough around him to become a keen observer (1920), had, with his famous description of the reel game,[3] laid the foundations for a wide-ranging, disenchanted view of the function of play: a very serious and founding function aimed at representing, repeating and mastering (the emotions and the body that feels them). The reel game, in its dramatic simplicity, nevertheless assumes a peaceful environment and that the player, as Freud put it, is a well-loved child. Only a child who is sure of being found again can, without being upset, play at throwing the mother/reel away and staging her return. These are generally not the starting conditions in our studies.

In order to give a more developed answer to the question you have posed to me, *whether or not it is useful for the analyst to play with the child*, I need, albeit briefly, to trace the evolution of games and playing in theory and in clinical practice.

1929: storm warnings

In 1929, two articles were published in the *International Journal of Psychoanalysis*, one by Melanie Klein on personification in child play, the other by Anna Freud on the theory of child psychoanalysis.

They were the result of long reflection by both and already hint at what would later be the controversial discussions. Both works attribute great importance to the Superego, understood as an instance organising the way of relating to the other, but the conclusions reached by the two authors are opposing. Klein affirms that there is no difference between child and adult analysis precisely because the Superego, although archaic, is clearly expressed in child's play through the characters in the game. Anna Freud maintains that the task of the child analyst is very different from that of the adult analyst in that the child's Superego is still being formed, given that they still have to deal distinctly with reference figures. The analyst is not a shadow, Anna Freud would say, even in those rare cases when the game does not call him or her directly into play. There is in fact an implicit communication, in the unfolding of the game, as well as of the analytical discourse, which contributes to the meaning of the game as well as of speech. The analyst's participation in the game, always active even if the analyst does not actually play, is in fact a guarantee that the game itself can take place. The adult's gaze is an essential component of child play and, for the adult in analysis, is a guarantor for the constitution of the analytic process.

Both Anna Freud and Melanie Klein, through their different theoretical concepts, supported *in primis* their respective clinical practices: Klein's great insights into primitive anxieties expressed through play and Anna Freud's subtle and competent experience in observing and accommodating the family unit in its complexity.

The game described by Klein (1929, 225) as a personification of the Superego describes a path of transformation thanks to the analyst's intervention:

as the analyst assumes the hostile rôles required by the play-situation and thus subjects them to analysis, there is a constant progress in the development of the anxiety-inspiring imagos towards the kindlier identifications with their closer approximations to reality. In other words: One of the principal aims of analysis – the gradual modification of the excessive severity of the super-ego – is attained by the analyst's assumption of the rôles which the analytic situation causes to be assigned to him. This statement merely expresses what we know to be a requirement in the analysis of adults, namely, that the analyst must simply be a medium in relation to whom the different imagos can be activated and the phantasies lived through, in order to be analysed.

The child, by making the analyst play the part of the monster, asks them to do something unbearable for them, something they cannot come into contact with directly. Klein herself points out that, when children ask her to impersonate roles that are too grisly, she only does it for show.

Anna Freud, despite having no doubt whatsoever that she considers the work she does with children to be analysis, conveniently suggests that the child analyst must know who they are playing with, thus having some idea of the mental set-up and skills of the player. Today this seems true on the one hand, but limiting on the other. The equipment of the children's room, like that of the analyst's mind at work, must certainly take into account the relative degree of development, but is it really possible to know *whom one is playing with*? There are two opposing concepts here that are difficult to reconcile concerning the centrality or otherwise of transference – irrelevant, especially in the initial formulations, for Anna Freud and foundational instead for Klein. How to resolve the dispute?

Between the two disputants stood Winnicott (1971), who resolved the dispute by effectively calling himself out of the game but at the same time giving us a comprehensive and quite particular theorisation of what he means by playing. Winnicott in turn had another competent experience to deploy, that of being a paediatrician, a privileged place to observe, from the amusement and misunderstandings between mother and child, doctor and patient, the lengthy work that prepares one for play and its transformations. After Winnicott, the mother comes into play, but the game changes radically.

Meeting while playing

Beginning with the assumption *there is no such thing as an infant without a mother*, Winnicott gradually elaborated a theory of play that envisages "a sequence of relationships related to the developmental process" in which play is prepared, and at some point introduced, in different ways.

In *Playing and Reality* (1971, 108), Winnicott in fact distinguishes different moments of *being-at-one-with*, which I will summarise here:

- The subjective object: the mother is capable of making actual what the child is ready to discover.
- The *to-and-fro* period in which the mother is alternately that which the baby has a capacity to find or being herself waiting to be found. It is a turbulent period and requires the mother to be prepared to participate and give back what is handed out in the game. Disorientation takes place.
- Being alone in the presence of someone. The ability to be alone in presence: playing one's own game even in the presence of another, being able to sustain one's own project. Only when this capacity is sufficient can one participate in the game of otherness without losing oneself.
- Playing together will then be able to intrigue and contemplate knowing how to accept the variants proposed by the other: not only tolerating, but welcoming the overlapping of two areas of play, and enjoying them. Here is the game as it is usually defined – the discard, the enjoyment. At this point, Winnicott adds that interpretation is not necessary; the important thing is that the child surprises himself or herself.

From this theory, we should infer that play presupposes a long, turbulent preparatory sequence, in which the bodies of both the child and the mother are deeply involved, by manipulation, association and metaphor (Modell, 2005). The aim of the game is to contain experience to thus be able to make it one's own and learn from it (Bion, 1962), work that is precarious and always exposed to breakdown and thus to excitement.

Playing also involves that which, in both the analyst and the patient, belongs to their implicit relational knowledge (Stern, 1998), of which playing – and in particular the way one plays (and speaks) –

is a great detector. It is as if to say that alongside and together with the symbolic game, when it appears, there is the constant presence of a way of joining the game which comes from very early experiences, deposited in the bodily memory of the players.

How have our patients, whether children or adults, been prepared for play? This we can only know by getting involved in the game, ready, however, for a to-and-fro between these different moments, never stable and ready to be subverted by regressive movements.

Since Winnicott, play and playing have become a model of the functioning of the mind and, consequently, of the analytical process. Under certain conditions, however, which are partly intuitable from the questions you have posed.

Indeed, Roussillon (2004, 94) emphasises how the fact of proposing play as a model for thinking about analytic work and the work of the session entails the need to specify whether play means a ludic activity or a psychic functioning that involves certain parameters:

> Advocating that particular model has nothing to do with fetishizing play or making an *a priori* model of it, a model "in itself". It is more a case of seeing it as a medium, a means, a "royal road" – an alternative to that of dream interpretation, but in a dialectical relationship with it, nonetheless – that will enable a subjective experience to be grasped and transformed, leading to its interpretation.

Given these premises, I will reply that it is not only *useful*, but I would say *inevitable for the analyst to play with the child*. Why?

Not only because children expect to play, since that is the privileged way adopted to express themselves, but because, from Winnicott onwards, playing, in all its variations, is part of living, of positioning oneself in relation to the other, of losing and finding oneself again. It is necessary, however, to be able to get involved in the game. By getting involved in the game, I mean accepting being surprised by the movements of the game, not so much playing with the child in front of us, as if it were an occupational game, perhaps with the idea of keeping them calm and grateful, ending the session unscathed. Getting involved in the game involves letting one's mind play out the many unforeseen, uncomfortable passages, the doing and undoing, the acting, proposing and arranging in the most unforeseen ways the material involved in the game, including the analyst. All with a rapidity that is often disconcerting and usually makes those who, from dealing with children, then move on to the adult world say: how nice to be relaxed. In fact, to quote Bion, playing in analysis is a great exercise of negative capability.

The rules of the game and their exceptions

Getting involved in the game, first of all, requires a limit, rules. You can say anything, but not do anything – it is customary to tell children that they will not be allowed to hurt or harm themselves. As with adults, a setting is established. You must guarantee continuity and the maintenance of a rhythm. This is also what the toy box is for, one for each child. The box tends to become a representation of the user's state of mind, but also of the progress of the analytical work, something similar to the use that adults make of the rules of the setting, with continuous games of displacement.

The toy box, with its few elements carefully prepared according to the child's age and presumed functioning, can and often does become a bloody battleground, in which one will find fragments of Play-Doh, broken dolls, pencils sharpened to stumps, pieces of paper and even drawings, when they appear. But the box also tells the children that there is a place to put themselves and where they can find themselves in spite of everything.

At the beginning of the analysis, Achille, whom I followed for several years (Badoni, 2005), wrote, and then violently carved, his own name on the cardboard box containing the material at his disposal. His name thus manifested itself as a void, a series of holes, an absence, while the pieces of paper cut out (the tangible entirety of his name) ended up mixed inside the box. They were considered by Achille with wonder, but also with disquiet, because of the impossibility of putting them back together in the right order: a tangible representation of dismantling, in the sense that Meltzer (1975) gives this word.

In the last session of work that lasted five years, Achille picked up his box and, next to the *punched-out* name, quickly and three-dimensionally drew on what remained of the lid his name, not his full name, but the diminutive by which he is known and recognised. This seemed to me to be a good sign of a subjectivity he could rely on. He had found himself and could now leave me. To reach this, however, one has to go through a series of events that you have pointed out to me – enactment, acting out of countertransference, and the analyst's freely fluctuating responsivity are sometimes difficult to distinguish.

How are phenomena such as enactment, acting out of countertransference, and the analyst's freely fluctuating responsivity intertwined?

This is a complex question, and I will try to answer it starting with an example (Badoni, 2005). Achille tyrannised me for a long time, forcing me to make paper aeroplanes that he immediately destroyed, as they never met his expectations. The counter-transferential movements signalled my state of inadequacy, a total lack of confidence in my performance and in being able to understand what Achille was looking for. This was all the more complicated by the fact that the impossibility of making aeroplanes as Achille asked was followed by destructive behaviour – knocking over chairs, trying to unscrew their legs, etc.

Things took a different turn one day when I said (or found myself saying), "If you don't teach me how you want me to make aeroplanes, I can't help you". The atmosphere suddenly became calm and marked a real turning point in our work, which became much more stable from then on and remained so until the end of a long analysis.

This is what happened. Achille set about very seriously teaching me how to fold the paper to make the aeroplane, doing it very meticulously, fold after fold, concerned that I not lose any movement but follow him closely. I felt I had to literally hang on his every word. It was not so much the end result that counted as this intimate, quiet moment of learning. Needless to say, before resorting to this request, I had tried other routes, following my feeling of helplessness and the frustration associated with it. The success of this intervention lies, I believe, in its being located, unbeknownst to me, at the origin of the relationship between Achille and his mother.

At birth, Achille had probably not found a mother able to help him metabolise his feelings and had soon become a violent child, so much so that he was expelled from kindergarten. Distressed by the impossibility of reaching her child emotionally, the mother had tried to compensate by speaking in his place, often literally stealing the words right out of his mouth; the *rêverie* function had been replaced by echoing, effectively leaving the child in the grip of chaos. Achille was imprisoned in a paralysing double bind ("Be spontaneous!") or, following other theories, caught in the violence of the mother's words (Aulagnier, 1975). I thus understood, as the only way out of this *impasse*, a question the child had asked me after the first consultation, when perhaps the hope of being listened to had opened up for him. Before going out the door to find his mother in the waiting room, he had looked straight at me and, foreseeing his mother's attempt to intrude on his world by asking what he had said and done in the session, asked: "Can I say I don't remember?" The question had really struck me, but it took me many years to fully understand its tragic meaning and to help Achille first find and later stand by his own words. I believe that being told, "If you don't teach me, I can't help you" turned the perspective upside down and opened up for Achille the only possible way out of the chaos – having someone close by who could take *his teachings* into account: a malleable object, allowing itself to be moulded rather than imposing itself.

I will leave it up to the discussion to decide whether my intervention was an enactment (taking the place of a dissociated aspect of Achille, the unseen child), a counter-transferential act ("That's enough, it's your turn"), or a freely fluctuating behavioural responsibility (let's try and change the game, you never know). I would, however, stress the importance of the malleability of the object (Milner, 1955; Roussillon, 2008) as a prerequisite for the subject to be able to leave its traces and consequently follow them.

What space is there for speech?

I would reply that the space is delicate and fundamental in its use, in prosody and in giving voice to the characters in the game when welcoming and saying goodbye. The children we see are often brought up with too much or too little speech, words that are often strained and scolding, words that are scarce, because their mothers and fathers are too wrapped up in their own thoughts and conflicts to talk to their children. Speech functions in both the symbolic and the procedural spheres and is therefore a precious object, which can become a tormentor, both because it signals the presence of another who can intrude into the child's world, and because, if it fails to fit into the here and now of the session, it becomes a source of confusion.

In precisely this way: "Shut up, you're confusing me", I was told by an epileptic child on whom my talking probably had the effect of over-stimulation. Speech can, however, also be a cradle that contains, as I realised when I saw a grateful smile dawn on the face of an autistic child, his gaze becoming attentive when I had the idea of addressing him by singing softly. The language of children as well, when it is there and when they use it, has different gradations and is in any case valuable. Moreover, speech in the analysis of children has a lot to do with making sense of what one sees, as well as what one possibly feels. It seems to me that this requires further caution: speech's primary task is to support the child's movement in the room, to give expression to its agitation, and is therefore closely linked to the body, to the use the child makes of it, to the reverberation it has in the analyst's mind and to the images it is capable of arousing.

The child analyst is engaged, as regards speech as well, in a difficult gymnastic activity – the requirement to accompany the regressive movements without getting caught up in them. This, too, is part of the disorientation I mentioned at the beginning and to which Fonagy and Target (2000) draw our attention when they speak of how the mother, faced with characters that frighten the child, does not operate by eliminating them but by confronting them, playing with fear. Seeing a row of ants coming into the house, a frightened little girl cried out: "Go away, go away, I'm scared!". The atmosphere totally changed and became joyful when the adult who intervened did not deny the annoying presence of the ants but lent a hand, offering to teach the ants how to climb. End of the fear and beginning of the game.

What can I say after all this? I have seen children get much better and for a long time with just a few sessions and relatively little effort. I have seen children to whom I had devoted a lot of time get better and start again, but then find themselves in adolescence having to face the facts of life and the turbulence that happens at that age. I am more and more convinced that games start at once and that it is necessary to start early and know how to involve the parents in the analytical work.

In the cases that went well, the relationship with the parents also went well, in the sense that I managed to make them as curious about their child's mental functioning as about their own. I believe Winnicott was right: the game is prepared from the beginning, and when one knows how to play, the analyst and their interpretations can even step aside. The problem is that the children we see have not been through this – inviting them to play also means challenging them to a task they do not have the tools to tackle. Which then opens the question of how to equip them for the game – easier said than done. There remains one hope, and that is the stubbornness with which children continue to send signals and invite us to play: I think this could give us confidence, provided we accept that we must bring to the game ourselves, everything we know, everything that reassures us, to allow ourselves to be surprised. To sustain such an attitude, we need to be able to share it: working together, sharing experiences and learning from the results. For this, I am grateful to Benedetta and those who prepared this meeting, because they have understood that we were here to play, as in any game, very seriously.

Notes

1 Luciana Nissim Momigliano, Turin 1919–Milan 1998. One of the founders of Italian psychoanalysis and the Milanese Psychoanalytic Centre. A strong presence both for her activities in the field of training and for the liveliness and bold strength of her intuitions. Her thought, developed from a Kleinian matrix, was enriched with personal and innovative contributions, with deep investigation into the nature and limits of the analytical relationship. I carried out my first training supervision with her, a direct, profound encounter that resulted in a frank friendship, interrupted too soon. I particularly remember working in a small group that met in the evenings at the Milanese Psychoanalysis Centre, where everyone brought their own contribution. A deep friendship bound her to Stefania Manfredi, with whom she shared thoughts and projects. In 1984, they published *Il supervisore al lavoro* in *Rivista di Psicoanalisi*, 30(4):587–607.

Among her works: *Continuity and Change in Psychoanalysis. Letters from Milan* (Routledge, London, 1992); *L'esperienza condivisa. Saggi sulla relazione psicoanalitica* (raccolta di saggi curata con Andreina Robutti; Raffaello Cortina Editore, Milano, 1992; *Shared Experience. The Psychoanalytic Dialogue*, Routledge, London, 1999); *L'ascolto rispettoso. Scritti psicoanalitici* (a cura di Andreina Robutti; Raffaello Cortina Editore, Milano, 2001).

Her articles include: *A Spell in Vienna – but was Freud a Freudian? – An Investigation Into Freud's Technique Between 1920 and 1938, Based on the Published Testimony of Former Analysands*, in *The International Review of Psycho-Analysis*, 14:373–389, 1987; *The Psychoanalyst in the Mirror: Doubts Galore but Few Certainties*, in *The International Journal of Psycho-Analysis*, 72:287–296, 1991.

Among the essays dedicated to her: *Luciana Nissim Momigliano. Ricordi dalla casa dei morti e altri scritti*, a cura di Alessandra Chiappano

(La Giuntina, Firenze, 2008); *Luciana Nissim Momigliano: una vita*, di Alessandra Chiappano (La Giuntina, Firenze, 2010).

2 Stefania Turillazzi Manfredi, Grosseto 1929–Florence 2015. Founder in 1974 with Giovanni Hautmann, Arrigo Bigi, Giordano Fossi and Franco Mori of the Florence Psychoanalysis Centre. Over the years she was closely linked to the Milanese Psychoanalysis Centre (CMP). For the CMP members, she carried out important training activity, traces of which remain in the clinical seminars published under the title *I seminari milanesi di Stefania Turillazzi Manfredi* in the series *Quaderni del Centro Milanese di Psicoanalisi Cesare Musatti* (Quaderno n. 3).

In her book *Le certezze perdute della psicoanalisi clinica* (Raffaello Cortina, Milan, 1994), we find evidence of a lucid thought open to new challenges, which found a natural interlocutor in Luciana Nissim. I got to know her through Luciana. The most exciting moment for me was when she asked me to stand in for her for a training lesson that she could not give: a lesson on dreams.

3 "One day I made an observation which confirmed my view. The child had a wooden reel with a piece of string tied round it. . . . What he did was to hold the reel by the string and very skillfully throw it over the edge of his curtained cot, so that it disappeared into it, at the same time uttering his expressive 'o-o-o-o'. He then pulled the reel out of the cot again by the string and hailed its reappearance with a joyful 'da' ['there']" (Freud, 1920, p. 9).

Bibliography

Aulagnier, P. (1975), *The Violence of Interpretation. From Pictogram to Statement*. Routledge, Hove, 2001.

Badoni, M., Bolognini, S. (1999), "Gli affetti nella teoria e nella pratica clinica". 41° Congresso Internazionale IPA, Santiago del Cile, 25–30 luglio 1999. In *Rivista di Psicoanalisi*, 45, pp. 641–649.

Badoni, M. (2002), "Parents and Their Child – and The Analyst in the Middle". In *The International Journal of Psychoanalysis*, 83, pp. 1111–1131.

Badoni, M. (2005), "Déficit de la función de "rêverie" y transfert tiránico". In *Revista de Psicoanálisis*, Asociaciòn Psicoanalítica de Madrid, 45, pp. 203–226.

Benjamin, J. (2016), "From Enactment to Play: Metacommunicative, Acknowledgment and the Third of Paradox". In *Rivista di Psicoanalisi*, 62, 3, pp. 565–593.

Bion, W.R. (1962), *Learning from Experience*. Karnac, London, 1984.

Colombi, L. (2010), "The Dual Aspect of Fantasy: Flight from Reality or Imaginative Realm? Considerations and Hypotheses from Clinical

Psychoanalysis". In *The International Journal of Psychoanalysis*, 91, 5, pp. 1073–1091.

Faimberg, H. (1996), "Listening to Listening". In *The Telescoping of Generations. Listening to the Narcissistic Links Between Generations*. London, Routledge, 2005.

Fonagy, P., Target, M. (2000), "Playing With Reality: III. The Persistence of Dual Psychic Reality in Borderline Patients". In *The International Journal of Psychoanalysis*, 81, 5, pp. 853–873.

Freud, A. (1929), "On the Theory of Analysis of Children". In *The International Journal of Psychoanalysis*, 10, pp. 29–38.

Freud, S. (1920), *Beyond the Pleasure Principle*. New York, Norton, 1961.

Klein, M. (1929), "Personification in the Play of Children". In *Contributions to Psycho-Analysis, 1921–1945*. Hogarth, London, 1948.

Meltzer, D. (1975), *Explorations in Autism: A Psychoanalytical Study*. Kornac, London, 2018.

Milner, M. (1955), "Le rôle de l'illusion dans la formation du symbole". In *Revue française de psychanalyse*, n. 5–6, 1979.

Modell, A.H. (2005), "Emotional Memory, Metaphor, and Meaning". In *Psychoanalytic Inquiry*, 25, pp. 555–568.

Ogden, T.H. (1994), "The Analytic Third: Working with Intersubjective Clinical Facts". In *The International Journal of Psycho-Analysis*, 75, pp. 3–19.

Roussillon, R. (2004), "Play and Potential". In *Primitive agony and symbolization*. Karnac, London, 2011.

Roussillon, R. (2008), *Le jeu et l'entre-je(u)*. Paris, PUF.

Stern, D.N. (1998), "The Process of Therapeutic Change Involving Implicit Knowledge: Some Implications of Development Observations for Adult Psychotherapy". In *Infant Mental Health Journal*, 19, pp. 300–308.

Winnicott, D.W. (1958), "The Capacity To Be Alone". In *The Maturational Processes and the Facilitating Environment*. International Universities Press, Madison, CT, 1965.

Winnicott, D.W. (1971), "Creativity and Its Origins". In *Playing And Reality*. Routledge, Abingdon, 2005.

V

CHILDREN AND THE PSYCHOANALYTIC PROCESS*

*Revised and modified from the original work: Badoni, M. (2004), "Bambini e processo psicoanalitico". Paper presented at the Bern Psychoanalytic Centre, Swiss Psychoanalytic Society, Bern, 31 January 2004.

What is a process? These are the possible definitions (from the dictionary *Vocabolario della lingua italiana*. Istituto della Enciclopedia Italiana, Fondazione Giovanni Treccani, Rome): from the Latin *processus-procedere*, first of all, something that takes place over a period of time, comprising a unity of phenomena that make it a homogeneous, regular whole.

Then, a method is adopted with the aim of obtaining a result, an activity of judgement and, especially in computer science, but not only, the way of *dealing with* data (or a matter, as in chemistry) in view of a possible transformation.

Consequently, *proceeding* would imply a change, we might say, of state, a change that could occur for the subject in question over a period of time.

The psychoanalytic process

Freud spoke a great deal about psychic processes but rarely used the word *process* to describe the analytic path. When he did, he

DOI: 10.4324/9781003560647-9

immediately warned his readers against attributing a linear development to it: "He [the psychoanalyst] sets in motion a process, that of
the resolving of existing repressions. He can supervise this process,
further it, remove obstacles in its way, and he can undoubtedly viti-
ate much of it. But on the whole, once begun, it goes its own way
and does not allow either the direction it takes or the order in which
it picks up its points to be prescribed for it" (Freud, 1913, 130). It
seems to be Freud's understanding that the way of treating/process-
ing the subject and the way of proceeding are intertwined, without
a linear correlation being established between the instruments with
which we exercise the analysing function and the course of analysis.

The person of the analyst (EPF, 2003) seems, on the one hand,
central to setting the process in motion, to sustaining the analytical
work and also to unravelling it, but on the other hand, irrelevant to
an unfolding that follows its own course.

After all, the very term *person*, due to its etymology, oscillates
between mask and identity, between a plurality of functions and a
defined, recognisable identity.

Freud must have had it in mind from the beginning and perhaps
considered it so threatening to the seriousness of the science he was
founding that he did not want to make his understanding public.
His *Project* was, in fact, published posthumously. Coping with a situation of helplessness requires an *adult, mature person*, he wrote (Freud,
1895), so with a well-defined identity, but in order to help, one
would not need advice, facts or examples, but recourse to a function,
a function carried out through modifications of unforeseeable and
ungovernable psychic states – processable, yes, but with prudence.
There is no predictability possible in a model whose fruitfulness is
entrusted to the functioning of a couple in a joint work of different
minds: on the one hand, the analyst, their identity and training, and
on the other, the patient's request for help. In analogy with modern
physics, one can, as Riolo (1986) argues, hypothesise a model based
on complexity and its related transformations.

The term *function* would then be developed by Bion (1967):
Freud's rescuing adult, the *adult, mature person*, would, in Bion's
model, become the mother, with the alpha function signalling the
capacity of the mother's mind to *process* the data that her child provides her with, accompanying it in a work of transformation that
gradually transforms from raw sensory data into thinking activity.

Corollary to this work of transformation is the ability to wait for the impact with the raw data to run its course in the mother's mind.

So for the analyst, processing is dealing with and allowing sensory data to settle in the mind. Such data may remain suspended for a long time, arouse emotions or thoughts, and sometimes evoke a figure (Botella, Botella, 2001) whose lines may shape the analytical discourse.

The process and time

As far as the analytical process is concerned, the factor of time seems mysterious and unpredictable: if it does not proceed in a linear fashion, but rather is a path that, once started, goes its own way, what will be the stopping points, the desirable and possible destinations and the goals for the analyst and patient?

In particular, the factors indicating the proximity of the goal remained one of the major questions for me, especially working with children. So I thought I would put the question to a highly experienced analyst. My question was: "How do you know when to end analysis with a child?" The answer was lapidary, scathing and challenging at the same time: "Child analysis ends when the parents decide so".

A frequent reality in child analysis that, in denouncing a problem, foreshadows other possibilities: the parents are not to be forgotten (Badoni, 2002a, 2002b) nor left alone. They will be good companions in the analytical work if one succeeds in making them curious about their children's ways of functioning, with the relative repercussions on their own way of dealing with the dilemmas that bringing up a child poses. This is work that can be articulated in various ways but that cannot be omitted when the subjects under analysis are *first and foremost* children.

Child analysis can also proceed, go its own way and arrive at the finish line of the final session, even if the timing of that finish line is unforeseeable at the beginning. It is, however, possible to sense its proximity in both adult and child analysis if the analyst is able to pick up cues from time to time indicating that the analytical work is leading the patient to a burgeoning awareness of his or her mental states, to cope with them, to tolerate the unexpected, to become curious about other goals and finally to the disquieting, trepidatious feeling of being able to continue alone. These are tentative thoughts, which may become cautious certainties if the analyst gives the patient the opportunity to become aware of these movements and finds the courage to develop them, together with the patient. All this takes shape, particularly for children, from states of excitement that are not always easy to govern, from thought clusters that develop gradually, from presentations that become representations, and from actions that can turn into play, until they find the drive to be able to continue on their own.

Near the finish line: clues, terrors, resources

Marcello is ten years old, and we are nearing the end of a three-session-per-week analysis begun a few years earlier.

He arrives with his brother and paternal grandfather, who leave immediately. He looks happy. Marcello: "At school, there was the spring festival (it's a beautiful day), they were selling primroses". He is holding a personal stereo he has never brought before and earphones to listen to music. Some time passes.

"What music is it?", I ask. In reply, Marcello hands me one earphone, keeping the other and says: "We have to be close together, otherwise we can't hear".

He tells me it is a cassette of his favourite band, 883. We listen together: love songs, farewell songs, songs about sometimes turbulent relationships between boys and girls. The scene changes. Marcello searches in the toy box for toy soldiers and very slowly and unconvincingly arranges them as if for a shoot-out.

I watch and comment that the music speaks of love, while his game speaks of war. He puts the toy soldiers away and continues to listen, rather thoughtfully, then takes a sheet of paper and draws: first, the outline of a cube with the figure of a little man slightly suspended, barely sketched. He scribbles over it and continues with the drawing: a long pole, a character about to dive, the sea. I say that this diver really is diving from very high up . . .! Marcello adds seahorses. I notice that the sea is very rough and that the seahorses look like question marks.

Marcello chooses a felt-tip pen and, in the absence of the colour red, says: "Let's say the fuchsia's red, and draw the first flag red". I comment: "The red flag's a danger signal". Marcello adds: "Of course, you can't swim at all". Then I add: "Yes, but the diver's already taken off, what can be done now . . . Maybe you feel a bit like him, now that we've decided to stop, as if you had to dive into a dangerous sea. You're getting bigger, you've brought me songs about complicated stories between men and women . . . how many uncertainties and question marks about your future . . . what Marcello will be like when he grows up".

Marcello then draws another flag on the dry land, on which he writes: *Forza 8* [Force 8]. I comment: "*Force 8* is rough sea, but it's also part of the name of your favourite band . . . Can someone give the diver a hand?"

Marcello then draws the character of a lifeguard. He draws him with particularly long, bendy arms. He adds that thanks to those arms, he will be able to rescue swimmers without any danger. "Of course", I confirm, "he'll be able to stretch his arms out towards the diver". The session is over: I remind Marcello that we are going to have a small *tuffo* [meaning a break, but literally a dive] for the Easter holidays . . . Marcello smiles and asks me for the dates of the last session and the resumption.

Processing the session: *pacing, timing, resources*

It is the last session of the week: we are faced with separation for the weekend, the Easter holidays and the prospect of the final session, the date of which has been set for June.

Time immediately breaks into the session ("At school there was the spring festival, they were selling primroses"): it is spring, there is a festive trade in primroses. It is a new season for us too. It has recently been the case that in the immediacy of *doing things*, a story with its sequences appears in the session, as happens today. This seems to me to be an indication of Marcello's greater permeability to what surrounds him, along with the pleasure of storytelling.

A new and sparkling season begins and prepares another: it is a *Saturday in the village* that announces a transition, the last year of primary school, the last term of sessions.

Also new is the appearance of music, accompanied by Marcello's sudden request: "We have to be close together, otherwise we can't hear".

Complicity, being in tune, on the same wavelength? Or the depiction of being together, immersed in a sound environment connected by a cord?

I wait. The band *883* is his favourite group; this too is a sign of the times and the approach of adolescence. Perhaps it is too much not to arouse fear – I sense a micro-break, a different way of thinking,

Figure 5.1 Marcello, *Lifeguard with a Force 8 sea*

a discomfort, a digression or regression in the game: the toy soldiers appear, used in the past, and a slow, controlled, thoughtful setting them up. Struck by this discrepancy, I underline it: "The music speaks of love, the toy soldiers ready to shoot speak of war".

Marcello leaves the toy soldiers and takes a sheet of paper. I watch and wait.

The first sketch, a small cube, perhaps a sketchy thought asking for other means to be developed, is scrubbed over, but left in view. I think to myself that Marcello can now proceed by trial and error without tearing up the sheet, as he would have done in the past – there is a work in progress, waiting to be developed . . . I wait.

A very long pole appears, at the top a swimmer taking the plunge; his feet have already left the diving board. Below him awaits a rough sea with large, well-drawn waves.

I am struck by the length of the pole, the clear division between land and sea, the question-mark shape of the waves, and the boldness of the dive. I comment on this, noting that "the sea's rough", adding after a moment that "the seahorses look like question marks".

At this point, time becomes pressing, condensed and packed in both the drawing and thoughts: it is like witnessing a dream. Marcello looks for the red pencil to colour the flag in the sea, cannot find it, takes the fuchsia one and says: "Let's say that it's red". This also pleasantly surprises me: in the past, the absence of the *right* pencil would have led to protests of varying levels of vehemence.

Let's say that. . . leaves a leeway of tolerance and trust, it refers to pretending, to shared work: perfection is not necessary, but thoughts bounce back quickly between Marcello and myself.

"The red flag is a danger signal", Marcello confirms, "Of course you can't swim at all". I follow him, noticing, however, that the diver has already taken off. "He's already taken his feet off the board". The height of the pole, the diver in flight and the impending danger lead me to formulate an interpretation in interrogative form, like the sea-horses: "Maybe you feel a bit like him, now that we've decided to stop, as if you had to dive into a dangerous sea. You're getting bigger, you've brought me songs about complicated stories between men and women . . . how many uncertainties and question marks about your future . . . what will Marcello be like when he grows up?"

The answer is immediate: standing on the floor, Marcello draws another flag, on which, with the same pencil, he writes *Force 8*. The word "force" and the number 8 link up in my mind to an incitement that I formulate: "Force 8 is rough sea, but it is also part of the name of your favourite band . . . can someone give the diver a hand?"

At this point, *the lifeguard* appears out of the blue with well-defined characteristics. In drawing him, Marcello points out that he has made his arms long and bendy so that the lifeguard can rescue swimmers without any danger.

Setbacks at the origin and on the analytic path

We are far from a linear proceeding: sessions proceed in bursts and withdrawals – the work of analysis has left important marks in the freedom of expression, in the tolerance for a thought that is sketched out and then gradually takes shape, and in the pleasure of shared research. Still, the material of the session, as often happens at the end of analysis, poses questions rather than answers. On the other hand, being able to ask questions is one of the accomplishments of analytic work.

The turning point of the session, I believe, coincided with making room for a question by seeing, in the seahorses drawn by Marcello, so many question marks and in giving a name to the figure: Is this really the moment to take off, leave behind solid supports, dive into life and end the analysis? This is what the preconscious tells us, but the unconscious is there and works without our knowledge, if we encourage it.

At the end of the analysis, Marcello brings the experience of a setback at the origin. The analysis began with a weeping mother still reproaching herself for not having had arms ready to welcome this second child, born *too early* with respect to her life plans. Maternal pain and the reproaches of a very demanding superego (the height of the pole?) were the objects of treatment before and during the analysis and again in the parental couple's treatment with another colleague.

Sudden breakdowns and careless repairs ended up making Marcello an unhappy child, full of anger, intolerant of any frustration ("If a battery runs out, he throws everything away"). Unable to play and enjoy the games he has, Marcello often exposed himself to dangerous situations and ended up very bruised.

At the end of the analysis, the theme of separation, faced over and over again, reappears forcefully. Have I, too, raised the bar too high by exposing the analysis to a premature end? Who, in the parental couple's game has raised the bar? It comforts me and leads me to think that we can dare to end an analysis with the appearance of the *rescuing object* and its relative characteristics.

Between land and sea: the lifeguard

At the end of the session, the lifeguard appears on the scene: it is he who will come to the rescue of the precipitous diver. What are his characteristics? He exists in a border zone between two different territories, a land lapped by the sea, leaving marks of its secret life, but also displaying a potentially overwhelming strength.

His arms are long and bendy – Marcello emphasises that in this way they are adaptable to different distances, but above all, they allow him to rescue without the danger of being lost at sea (Winnicott, 1969).

Insofar as his *function* is to rescue, he is presumed to be able to intercept signals while remaining in place, preventing the victim's terror from pulling him into a fatal grip, with no escape.

Rest and refuelling stops: proceeding in a setting

My reflections here concern an age when the child is able to participate in the sessions alone, albeit in a situation of close dependence on the parents. I am thinking of children between the ages of four and pre-adolescence.

In fact, we must take into account the importance of the parents in guaranteeing the continuity of the analytical work and, for the children, the inevitable conflict of loyalties aroused by the analyst's presence (Badoni, 2003).

At the same time, we can reflect on a dual temporality of the analytic pathway with children: the time required by the progress of the analysis makes its mark, but another time breaks in, related to the skills and functions attained and the mental tools available. "Nobody told me how people die", said a child in the first session: a profound intuition of a work of mourning that accompanies every life and every analysis, but which is extremely present in child analysis. Mourning for a change in family intimacy, for bodily functioning that changes in the blink of an eye, from lost teeth to the metamorphosis of adolescence. Mourning for the analyst who is often in a situation of doing what he or she can, compared to what the desire to understand would require, starting with the number of sessions.

Yet even when the attendance is not ideal, the analytical work plays its part if we can convey to the children that we are listening to their *frequencies* regardless of the frequency of sessions. It is, however, important for the analyst to be able, sooner or later, whatever the number of sessions, to distinguish between an avoidant complicity that would exempt both from mental work and a necessary work of mourning regarding the analyst's own expectations.

The regularity and rhythm of the sessions are an indispensable prerequisite that must be developed as the analysis takes shape, protected at all times and analysed when needed. In fact, the analytical process and setting interfere silently, but, as Bleger (1967) made clear to us at the time, the most archaic aspects of the personalities are at play in this interference, as we have also seen in the session described above.

Taking care of the setting in child analysis calls for the collective involvement of the analyst's senses in the sessions. Perhaps the consonance of child's play in sessions with the flow of patients' associations in analysis has been overly idealised.

The sonority of the sessions is very different, especially in the initial phases, from what we experience with adults: music produced by different instruments, bodily music with its relative dissonances. The analyst's ear has to adapt while the eye is much more involved because children, especially in the initial phases, show more than they express verbally: moving, touching, playing, and leaving traces, signs and drawings. On the other hand, children are very attentive and sensitive, not only to the analyst's gaze but also to the level of coherence between gaze and attention. I have noticed that children will suddenly stop a game if they notice that, yes, the analyst is looking at them but does not see them. Anzieu (1985) emphasised the sonority of the analyst's voice as a sound *envelope*. The analyst's gaze has a similar function in child analysis: something similar to a squint, with one eye directed at the scene presented and the other at his or her own psychic apparatus and its processes.

The rapidity of passages is often such as to require genuine mental acrobatics from the analyst, and even physical ones in cases where young patients create situations of real danger. It is a common experience for analysts who have mainly worked with children, when they start working with adults, to have the comforting experience of being able to think while staying seated. Anyway, working with children is excellent preparation for devoting care to patients who need to be looked at and seen, before and beyond interpretation.

I have spoken of frequency as a transmitted wave and the frequency of sessions. The two frequencies are not necessarily related – they can be in tune but also dissonant. It would be a welcome development if psychoanalysis training, especially with regard to child analysis, took this into account.

Bibliography

Anzieu, D. (1985), *The Skin-Ego* (Trans. Segal, N.). Karnac, London, 2016.
Badoni, M. (2002a), "Analisi di bambini, dolori di adulti: consultazione psicoanalitica e costellazione famigliare". In Trombini, E. (a cura di), *Il dolore mentale nel percorso evolutivo.* Quattroventi, Urbino.

Badoni, M. (2002b), "Parents and Their Child – and The Analyst in the Middle". In *The International Journal of Psychoanalysis*, 83, 5, pp. 1111–1131.

Badoni, M. (2003), "Reflexionen über die Analyse eines Kindes im Latenzalter". In *Kinderanalyse*, 11, 4, pp. 437–460.

Bion, W.R. (1967), *Second Thoughts (Selected Papers on Psychoanalysis)*. Heinemann, London.

Bleger, J. (1967), "Psicoanalisi del setting psicoanalitico". In Genovese, C. (a cura di), *Setting e processo psicoanalitico*. Cortina, Milano, 1988.

Botella, C., Botella, S. (2001), *The Work of Psychic Figurability: Mental States Without Representation*. Routledge, Hove, 2004.

Etchegoyen, R.H. (1986), *The Fundamentals of Psychoanalitic Technique*. Routledge, London, 1999.

European Psychoanalytical Federation (EPF) (2003), "Psychanalyse en Europe". *Deuxième conference annuelle de la F.E.P. de Style Nouveau, Sorrento, Italie, 24–27 avril 2003*, Bulletin 57, Année.

Freud, S. (1895), *Project for a Scientific Psychology*, SE, vol. II, 1955.

Freud, S. (1911), *Formulations on the Two Principles of Mental Functioning*. SE, vol. XII, 1958.

Freud, S. (1913–14), *Further Recommendations in the Technique of Psycho-Analysis I*. SE, vol. XII.

Gaddini, E. (1981), "Fantasie difensive precoci e processo psicoanalitico". 4ª Conferenza della Federazione europea di psicoanalisi, Roma, 5–8 marzo 1981. In Gaddini, E., *Scritti 1953–1985*. Cortina, Milano, 1989.

Hermann, I. (1943), *L'istinto filiale*. Feltrinelli, Milano, 1974.

Kaës, R., Faimberg, H., Enriquez, M., Baranes, J.-J. (1993), *Trasmissione della vita psichica tra le generazioni*. Borla, Roma, 1995.

Kancyper, L. (1997), *Il confronto generazionale. Uno studio psicoanalitico*. FrancoAngeli, Milano, 2000.

Manzano, J., Palacio Espasa, F., Zilkha, N. (1999), "The Narcissistic Scenarios of Parenthood". In *The International Journal of Psychoanalysis*, 80, 3, pp. 465–476.

Riolo, F. (1986), "Il "processo analitico": una revisione del modello". In *Rivista di Psicoanalisi*, 32, 3, pp. 389–404.

Winnicott, D.W. (1969), "The Use of an Object and Relating through Identifications". In *The International Journal of Psychoanalysis*, 50, pp. 711–716.

VI

PARENTS AND THEIR CHILDREN, AND THE ANALYST IN THE MIDDLE

Working with a transgenerational mandate*

*Revised and modified from the original publication: Badoni, M. (2002), "Parents and Their Child – and The Analyst in the Middle: Working with A Transgenerational Mandate". In *The International Journal of Psychoanalysis*, 83, 5, pp. 1111–1131.

Transgenerational transmission

In this presentation, I will not write about the inevitable inter-twining of parents' suffering and that of their children, to which I have devoted space elsewhere (Badoni, 2004). Instead, I will try to explore the links between parental suffering that is misunder-stood by the parents themselves and its consequences on the child's mind. This kind of suffering occupies the parents' minds but at the same time blocks the way into their inner world, into their approach towards the child and his or her suffering, and, no less importantly, into the analytical work.

A careful study of the transmission of psychic life among genera-tions has been published by several authors (Kaës et al., 1993). In par-ticular, Haydée Faimberg (1988), through the notion of *télescopage*, indicates the formation of unconscious identities in which unelab-orated events referring to previous generations are condensed: the unacknowledged intrusion of histories that have not been worked through deprives the subject of the possibility of establishing his or her own identity.

Analytical work is in turn conditioned by the presence of silent psychic areas. These often concern couples formed on the basis of mourning that was impossible to process in their respective families or a painfully guarded secret (Torok, 1968).

I have noticed how in these cases the couple tends to be formed as if composed of siblings; the meeting of mortified children becomes a pact between offended *siblings* in search of an impossible reparation. The couple's concentration on such a task tends to compromise their capacity to bring up their own children as beings different from themselves, resulting in a narcissistic scenario, as described by Manzano et al. (1999).

A child's thinking impairment is therefore linked, on the one hand, to the fact that the child's parents are not able to see their own child as a being that is different from themselves. On the other hand, it is equally related to the child's worry that having their own thoughts could, through living their own unique experience, possibly betray the parents, deny the child their own mother idiom (Bollas, 1976) or establish a disturbing distance from the parents, a distance all the more dreaded as it is not sustained by an adequate capacity of representation.

In the absence of adequate orchestration to welcome and harmonise one's own experience – above all the experience of one's own body and its needs – the child is easily exposed to a situation of helplessness (*Hilflosigkeit*) or to an attitude of delegating thought, as if this were the task of others (a view not so out of place given the nature of the transgenerational mandate).

The transgenerational mandate and the analyst's position

When the presence of a transgenerational mandate predominates over other themes, the child analyst does indeed have to work in unusual circumstances.

The fact that the parents have unconsciously given their child the burden of solving a conflict that they themselves have been unable to face up to, or that they have unwittingly passed on to him or her a secret of their own, ends up making the child a marginal presence to the point that it is often difficult for the parents to bring him or her to analysis. The request for consultation becomes charged with pressing expectations of solving the symptom and quickly restoring the family homoeostasis. A child who finds himself or herself entangled in these mechanisms can grow up fearing thinking or even in a situation where thinking becomes impossible. The perceptive system also suffers, since the child cannot find confirmation in the perception of his or her own experiences, the capacity to represent is reduced and his or her mental existence is therefore threatened. Not being subjected to transformation, emotions suffer a double destiny: they become somatic facts and turn into excessive excitement. The extreme excitement in such children is a sign of too much and too little: intrusion that keeps the child in a state of constant threat and absence that arouses separation anxieties.

The succession of psychic events could be summarised as follows: the child is left to work through that which was not carried out in previous generations; the child cannot bear the task and expresses this impossibility through symptoms; the parents are unable to contain the child's anxiety as it reactivates the traumatic experience, and through the request for analysis, they put out an unclear warning signal – treating without curing. In so doing, they are giving the child analyst a mandate in order to free themselves from the task of working through that which is impossible, but at the same time they are closing the analyst and the child in a kind of *claustrum*. The risk of the circle closing therefore becomes very real, suffocating even the analysis.

The child analyst, operating between one generation and another, is a privileged witness, albeit in an awkward position with respect to the events stated above. In a certain sense, his or her role is that of placing himself or herself between the parties, thus reducing the impact of what Faimberg referred to as *télescopage* (1988) between one generation and the other. The problem is not only to be aware of the presence of the mandate but also to try to deactivate it, so that the child can form his or her own identity. It is about transforming the *claustrum* into a protected space where the child has the opportunity to learn little by little from the experience of caring, and, in the happiest cases, the parents can recover their parental function.

Even in ideal situations in which the parents are separately in the care of another therapist, the role of the child therapist is crucial, as the parents must be helped to approach the suffering of their child and understand its meaning and the effect it has upon them: "In such cases the appropriate technique is that which leads the patient to creating his own thoughts, given that his problem is creating them, not learning the thoughts of another" (Vallino, 1998, p. 195, translation).

Anna

I will describe how I tried to cope with the presence of the mandate during the meetings with the parents and the sessions with my patient, Anna. Finally, I would like to show to what extent I was able to give Anna's parents back the sense of their suffering and allow Anna to develop a system of representation of herself and her surrounding environment.

The information gathered during the first meetings with a child's parents goes towards drawing up a kind of draft: it is from here that the analyst's first investments in the child and the child's in the analyst begin. It is not merely a case of gathering important facts concerning the child's background but also of preparing the analyst's mind to listen to what the child will present by activating the function of *rêverie*.

This filtering and connecting is a prerequisite that enables the child to represent in his or her own story those characters from the parents' world that he or she passively acquired, thus becoming alienated from his or her own experience.

At this point, the weight of the mandate has been lightened, and the child can feel *ME*: the protagonist of his or her own story.

First half: attempts at getting closer

Anna's parents asked if they could speak to me about her. When the request was made, she was four years old and had been stuttering quite badly for several weeks (I later learned that this coincided with an increase in her mother's work commitments).

The following information comes from the first meetings (seven in total, over a period of three and a half months). When I met her parents, what struck me was that they seemed to be angry but at the same time affectionate accomplices. The manner they had towards me was very characteristic of this couple, and it tended to repeat itself at times on future occasions as well. At our first appointment, they arrived busily chatting to one another about things that had nothing to do with the request for consultation. While they chatted, they ignored my presence, as if they had some urgent business to settle. It seemed as if they were just passing through because of some inconvenient necessity which was disrupting their busy work schedules, schedules that often took them away on business, each in his or her own context.

Nevertheless, I was able to gather that Anna had a "perfect" brother and also that, as a newborn, she had had serious eating problems. Her mother breastfed her for four months. Only after numerous difficulties was an intolerance to the mother's milk discovered; weaning was difficult. At the age of one, Anna was hospitalised with a serious case of gastroenteritis: she was badly dehydrated, and her life was in danger. She was kept in hospital and recovered with the aid of a drip.

While listening to Anna's parents talking about their history, two things struck me with regard to both content and how they spoke to me, with a combination of ease and reticence: Anna's father's sister had died of anorexia, while in the mother's family, there was a "strange" brother (mental retardation, psychosis?) who was still living at home with his mother.

Asking, as I always do, how the children's names had been chosen, I found out that Anna's middle name was that of her dead aunt. As for her retarded uncle, he would be notably present, not so much in Anna's learning difficulty as in the fact that it was impossible for Anna's mother to notice it and therefore act upon it. By contrast, Anna's brother was presented as being perfect.

These consultations, requested by the parents but apparently an annoying interruption in their affairs, ended up giving me the impression that I was a strange, alien presence, the odd one out, involuntarily listening in to a conversation that did not concern me. Had it been like that for Anna as well?

My impression was that, with their marriage, Anna's parents had sealed a pact of mutual consolation and silence: they seemed to have an unconscious secret in common that made it impossible even for them to meet. Anna's father treated his wife with a mixture of veneration and worry, as if she were important and fragile: he seemed intent on drawing attention to her, as he had previously done with his dead sister, trying in vain to draw the parents' attention to her.

Anna's mother, on the other hand, tended to treat her husband like her brother – a "good-for-nothing". Both seemed busy distracting themselves from mutual pain: "let's not think about it" seemed to be their implicit communication; "don't make me think about it", they seemed to warn each other.

In the middle, Anna, an excited child, was in turn exciting for her parents – a rebound effect that re-presented them with an impossible task to perform. It may be said that, via her stuttering, her body was expressing something she was not ready to speak about (Anzieu, 1968), while her parents were not ready to allow Anna to express her profound suffering.

As for my feeling of foreignness, I believe it was indicative of a transgenerational mandate operating in the setting: I was dealing with an *alien* analytic object that caused unease and demanded attention.

Meeting her parents again after a short holiday to decide if and how to proceed with Anna, I found them very uncertain as to what to do. In particular, they were happy about the fact that Anna had stopped stuttering, but it was also clear that neither one could find the right words to explain to Anna about her future meeting with me or their thoughts on the matter.

The symptom had disappeared, but we had been unable to transform the urgent request – to get rid of the symptom – into an authentic request for help.

Shortly before Anna was due to come to her first appointment, her mother rang to say that things were going much better and that they had decided against coming. I did not hear anything more from them for about a year!

Second half: a bursting, burning head – Anna's analysis

Anna's parents then got in touch with me again to ask me to see Anna once more – other problems had arisen that were "different from before". The difference lay above all in the fact that her parents were now more able to describe Anna's suffering, as well as their own. Anna had recently refused to go back to nursery school after the holidays. She was showing signs of regression, her behaviour was very disturbing, and she cried at every little frustration. However, she was excited and sexually disinhibited – for example, while out walking with her father, she would approach all the women they met, asking them to kiss him.

Anna, who at this stage was five years old, would not separate from her parents for the first three sessions, coming alternately with either her mother or her father.

While Anna's mother was quite detached while watching Anna play, yawning every now and again, her father tended to rouse her excitement, interfering continually with her initiatives. Anna would change the sequence of the game frenetically, making it impossible to follow, and would become discouraged by every little task that she couldn't carry out. She referred constantly to her brother, both in search of a direct comparison and to ask whether he could come, too. I have always felt this request was Anna being uncertain about her right to have a place for herself. As she threw herself into her activity, chasing thoughts that were as excited as they were fragmented, she commented: "My head's bursting, my head's burning".

Towards the end of one meeting, when I asked Anna what I could tell her mother and father when I met them (to draw a conclusion about these first meetings), she looked at me carefully and answered: "Say that I want you to come and play at my house".

After these first meetings, Anna's analysis could begin. It consisted of three sessions a week and lasted four years. The conclusion of the analysis would be the result of hard work and a compromise I felt was inevitable.

Many elements detected in these first meetings would be present in the early months of analysis.

First, there was the separation anxiety that would also appear later and which would quickly turn towards an excited, erotised relationship. There was no space for thinking, which seemed to arouse panic more than it did fear and, even before being feared, was intolerable. Thinking requires attention, a period of reflection and a stage setting in which to place representations, but none of this was present in Anna. Intolerance to frustration was extremely high, and it manifested itself physically by Anna going limp and changing colour, which suggested fainting or a psychosomatic breakdown.

Her excitement was pervasive, her thinking fragmented and roles were confused: "In the car, everyone wants to sit in the front". The raw material brought by Anna and the intense paternal seductiveness raised questions and gave me cause for concern. Her mother's sleepiness seemed to testify to her surrendering to this difficult child, as well as to the fatigue she felt in containing the excitement, excitement which her father not only entertained, but also activated.

The intensity of Anna's excitement and the coarseness of her behaviour made me wonder whether she had suffered some kind of violence: a real trauma, a trauma due to the absence of a function of *rêverie*, or a transgenerational trauma, which led to an inability to organise representations around the original fantasies, in particular around the fantasy of the primal scene?

I also wondered whether Anna's request for me to go and play at her house might be a hint to observe other family members, family events or family games.

Once more, I found myself in the middle: I had to provide a space in which family games could be represented.

In particular, what role did Anna's father's sister, whom Anna was named after, and her mother's brother, this mysterious character whom Anna's mother desperately tried to ignore, play in Anna's relationship with her parents? Who did Anna identify with, and why was so much importance attached to Anna's "perfect" brother? What trauma had made Anna's head burst, burning her thoughts?

Indeed, Anna could not exist in such a situation: breaking down in the face of every little frustration was evidence of this.

In spite of all this, Anna showed an intuitive sensitivity and a keen sense of suffering: her bursting, burning head clearly indicated where her pain lay, and by asking to play with me, she seemed to want to get herself a playmate, possibly one who was smart but calm. Anna needed attention: she needed someone who would look at her without their gaze going blank but who would not intrude too much into her mind.

After these sessions together with either her mother or her father, I asked Anna to come into the consulting room alone. The following is a full account of that session.

The first session

Anna came to the session accompanied by her mother. In the waiting room, facing a vase of fresh flowers that she had noticed when she arrived, Anna immediately became anxious and said: "There shouldn't be cut flowers in the house". When I asked why not, she replied: "A friend of mine said that flowers should stay outside, on the terrace". "Maybe that's because flowers cut from their roots die a little", I said. She immediately became calmer and said, "I'm thirsty, have you got any tingly water?" I offered Anna a glass of *non-tingly* water, and she followed me with no more fears, leaving her mother in the waiting room.

Once in the room, Anna started to speak a lot, but it was impossible for me to follow such broken-up speech. I was, however, able to follow something. She told me that at night she talks, talks a lot to all her little animals and her brother tells her to keep quiet. From here, the frenetic flow started again, she took the toy cars, "Daddy's taking a little girl to the doctor, my big Daddy, no, it's Mummy, Daddy's taking little brother and teaching him how to drive".

Many pairings followed, and then the flood – the animals must be saved. Anna gathered them up in her skirt and decided that they had to be saved inside the books. She began to take the animals to my bookcase. A short moment of silence followed, which, once perceived, seemed to upset Anna, who suddenly stopped playing and went out to go to the bathroom.

On her return, she was very excited: "I'm going to draw a really nice picture!" She scribbled something down, which to me looked like a fish but was actually an enormous mouth. Around the mouth was her mother's face, a little boy's face and then a little girl's face. "How many thoughts there are inside Anna's head!", I said. In reply, Anna quickly drew a sketch on her mother's head and said: "She's thinking about her husband". A second sketch on the little girl's head: "She's thinking about her mummy". I asked: "And who's thinking about the little girl?". She became suddenly maniacal: "Mummy is thinking about when the little girl will be grown up and will have a very handsome husband, that's why I'm giving her flower-shaped eyes". She cut out the little girl's head and glued it onto another piece of paper. While in silence, I was concerned about how I would be able to create a space for Anna and for myself. Anna, as if capturing my thought, continued: "My bear says I can't play with you".

The session was nearing the end, and I showed Anna where we could keep her drawings. She wanted to take them home, but I explained that we would keep them somewhere we both knew and where she could find them again next time. Anna was attentive but frightened: "But I forget everything and Mummy's like me". I said: "It can't be very nice feeling like a flower without roots". She calmed down again: "Let's do this: I'll draw something for you and you can draw something for me". She started drawing and the session ended. At the door, Anna suddenly became distressed, as if she had forgotten coming with her mother. Before making sure her mother was there, she said: "I'm not able to go home alone". Then, finding her mother in the waiting room, she asked her: "What did you hear?"

"Nothing", replied her mother. Anna took her bear and, going quickly back into the consulting room, put it on a bench and said to me: "Look, there's a place for him, too".

Afterthoughts: quenching thirst without excitement

Signs of the mandate and its violence are already evident in the waiting room. Determined and distressed in equal measures, Anna states a pressing, apparently senseless need that must be granted to her, on pain of intolerable terror: there mustn't be any cut flowers. However, when I ask her why not, she is unable to nourish these thoughts and relies on the reflections of a school friend.

It is as though Anna knew but at the same time did not know that flowers cut off from the mother plant soon die. The mandate works like a drug: it nourishes, but at the same time, it impedes separation from the mother plant. It is exciting and works against the perception of the subject, against consciousness and against representation. It seemed to me necessary to intercept Anna's request, to humour her without excitement, to contain her anxiety by accepting that she was blinded to the reasons behind it, and to alleviate the anxiety in order to allow the patient to transform it from an intolerable experience into a signal in search of representation.

In the transference, Anna repeats the violence to which she has been, and continues to be, subjected. This transferential violence tends to provoke an intense and, to some extent, blind involvement of the analyst. The mental stimuli are too intense, and association supports too few to stand up to it. In extreme cases – and this happened working with Anna – the analyst has the feeling of incapacity to think.

Remaining with the botanical metaphor, we could say that Anna works by grafting and uprooting: rooted in the earth/mother or floating dangerously in diffuse excitement. Thirsty for words but at the same time unable to hold and make them her own, Anna stays in the relationship for several seconds and then breaks it. The analyst's interventions must take care to confirm the patient's perceptions to help him or her form a mental space.

Anna's future seems to be left *in toto* to the maternal project ("Mummy's thinking about when the little girl will be grown up and will have a handsome husband, that's why I'm giving her flower-shaped eyes", Anna says as she is drawing).

As in the first session, in many to come, the little boy/girl turns rapidly into an excited adolescent. Time and space are flattened out in the traumatic experience. One might think that Anna's flattening out her excitement about adolescent sexuality represented her need to anchor her excitement, which would otherwise be devastating. At the same time, her parents seemed to be dealing with an ageless child with no future, exonerated from the requests of the surrounding reality.

The object and the word were exciting, like the *tingly* water Anna asked me for and which I avoided giving her, in reality but above all in my interventions, in an attempt to quench her thirst without exciting her.

The lability of a mental space capable of receiving and transforming emotions, on the other hand, involved – as shown in the session – a mental flooding. I believe it is significant that the rescue operation from the flood took place in the bookcase, an ark where words and thoughts could be held. One might ask which flood had, in previous generations, swept away the family order. Just like generational succession, the continuity of time and memory is also completely upset, and separation is sensed as oblivion. Anna was worried about forgetting the way home and was certain that this also happened to her mother. Mother and daughter have no memory, united by oblivion: "I forget everything and Mummy's like me".

Anna is apparently unable to reconcile the relationship with her mother or the newly formed one with me. If she is with me, she is uprooted from her mother and cannot find her anymore; if she goes back to her mother, she will lose trace of the analyst.

In this sense, the presence of her mother in the waiting room, and her reassuring Anna that she had heard nothing of what was going on in the consulting room, seemed to give the go-ahead to continuing working with me: her mother had waited, respecting the space of the session without trespassing. Not just the bear, but also Anna, could continue the work with me.

The first separation: related experiences and fantasies

Anna's first acquisition in therapy seems to have been the feeling of having a place at her disposal, as well as having someone who was willing to *look for her.*

The regular time and space of the setting, my waiting for her when the bell rang repeatedly, and my thinking of her were a reassurance for her: the room in which we worked was definitely her place.

Anna was demanding attention for the neglected child whose parents are unable to provide her with reflexive function. The story of *Le Petit Poucet* (Perrault, 1697), abandoned by his parents and determined to find them again, together with his siblings, would be the *leitmotif* of Anna's analysis. I would be asked to read it countless times, so many that Anna mastered it completely and contributed her own enrichments: it would be her story until the very end.

In particular, we had to find a way of passing from concrete functioning expressed via her own body and the traces left to a mental position capable of working through fantasies, especially the fantasy of the primal scene.

In the consulting room, a place of refuge would become very important in the following months: a curtain that hung in front of a door created a hidden space. For several weeks, Anna had been hiding in there, shouting, "I'm not here, I'm not here!".

Shortly before the first Christmas holidays, Anna hid once again, shouting, "I'm not here, I'm not here!". I kept quiet and could hear her speaking in a very soft voice behind the curtain. I said, "You like being looked for: I heard a loud voice saying, "I'm not here, I'm not here!". Rushing out, she started to clean the room, complaining about how dirty it was. Then she closed the blinds, making everything dark. "I'm putting the invisible little men to bed . . . They disturb me at night, they don't want to sleep". I replied, "Perhaps they want to stay up and see

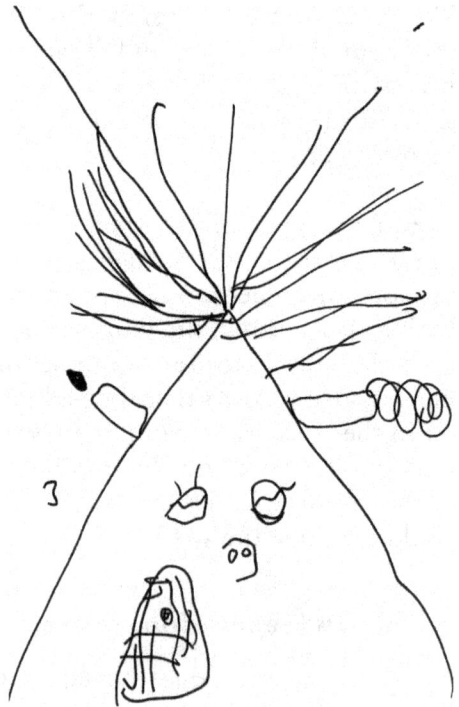

Figure 6.1 Anna, *The first wigwam*

112

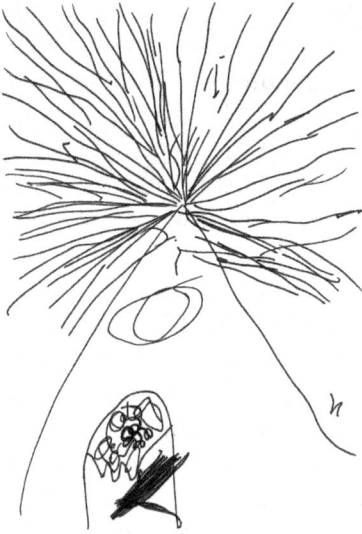

Figure 6.2 Anna, *From fantasies about the body to fantasies in the body*

Figure 6.3 Anna, *A wigwam inhabited by monsters*

Figure 6.4 Anna, *The wigwam gets too full*

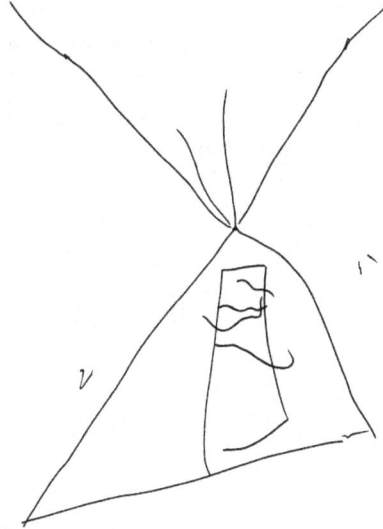

Figure 6.5 Anna, *A session before Christmas*

what happens at night, perhaps they're curious". Anna immediately came to the table and quickly drew an "Indian wigwam". She then started speaking with completely invented "Indian" words. I was very disoriented, and, after a short time, I said, "It must be horrible not to understand words – sometimes that's how it is for children when adults are talking". Anna was very attentive and continued drawing a rapid succession of wigwams, which progressively changed appearance (see drawings).

A threatening face lived inside the wigwam; the door was substituted by a large, toothed mouth. Anna said it was "the house of love". Guns and missiles appeared, and in the end, also teeth (a very recurrent theme). In her last drawing, the door appeared again, but the wigwam was burning. From there, drawing became a very disturbing physical game: as if to make herself vomit, Anna produced saliva and used it to draw on the table. I said: "Now Anna's like a wigwam spitting out smoke and saliva . . . Do you want to leave me with traces of yourself now that the holidays are coming?". "I don't know how to ski . . .", she said. She then wanted to hang her drawings on the wall – "that way you'll remember". She quickly became maniacal and then calmed down to draw the house of two children, commenting: "One who has more, one who has less". She was calm at the end of the session, and, for the first time since the beginning of therapy, she helped me tidy the room.

The effects of transgenerational mandate appear in the child as alienation (Bonaminio et al., 1993). The child is alienated from the mind of his or her parents and consequently alienated from aspects of himself or herself, leading to the extreme declaration: "I'm not here, I'm not here".

The above session seems to highlight considerable changes in Anna's functioning. Although it required great effort, during this session Anna went from a position in which she shouted of her own non-existence ("I'm not here, I'm not here") to a position in which she accepted her own incompetence ("I don't know how to ski"); along with the perception of herself appeared a perception of the relationship with the object, and therefore with time. It was no longer a question of "forgetting everything" (as in the previously mentioned session) but of finding the means to be remembered, kept in mind.

Anna's mental space became more structured, even if, faced with violent fantasies related to the primal scene, her mental functioning regressed, going from fantasising about the body to fantasising within her body (Gaddini, 1981). The fantasy of the primal scene burned in Anna's mind: unable to contain it, she acted it out in her body. All the traumatic potential of this fantasy was exalted: Anna had no choice but violence to her body to avoid violence in her mind. My interpretation attracted Anna's attention regarding not only how she used her body but also how she wished to leave traces of herself. This intervention gave value to Anna's resources rather than insisting on her defences; this approach seemed to help Anna to take on her incompetence, as well as her wish to be remembered.

During the following months, an important but complex game began, enabling us to make some progress.

From violence expressed bodily to fantasy:
a four-legged analyst

We have seen how Anna's mind burned when faced with the fantasy of the primal scene, and how she tried to cope with it by acting through her body. Would it be possible to find a way to pass from concrete functioning to fantasy? How was Anna's suffering to be interpreted to allow her to find words to describe it?

I will now summarise a game that went on for many sessions. Over the following weeks, I would be the one who, playing the part of a neglected, hungry wolf, had the task of being present and giving a voice to the fantasies of the primal scene that had appeared in the wigwam (the task was even more complicated since, once Anna had been entrusted to me – and along with her a conspicuous part of her parents' burden – her parents separated). So, I was the wolf, and as the wolf I had to receive the meaningfulness of Anna's fantasies and the urgency of her needs. The body forced its way into the scene: on all fours and ordered about by Anna, I had to move on command, howl if ordered to do so, or keep quiet. The wolf would have to suffer the pain of exclusion, watch scenes of family life from a distance (a mother looking after her child), and be fed poisoned food, but, gradually, also be nursed.

Little by little, Anna was able to accept that I, as a wolf, would introduce some cautious imagination. During these sessions, if Anna emptied the room of everything that could be carried away and put it all behind the curtain, which swelled up like an enormous tummy, I, as the wolf tied up in the opposite corner of the room, could note the swelling of the curtain, call it a tummy, imagine it full of babies and give voice to the children's fear of coming into the world and of being left alone, hungry and angry, just as I was.

Through the voice of the wolf, Anna was relieved of fantasies that were too fragmented and too difficult to take upon herself and was now more willing to accept my presence during sessions. She began to speak about a little baby boy/girl who had to be born but who, because of some mishap, was not able to be born.

She started trying to write. Her first whole written word would be her name, and then shortly before the summer holidays, her second written word would be "help".

The calendar hanging in my room became an important reference point: through the possibility of gaining experience of her relationship with me and of working with the objects that populated her mental space, her perception of time also changed.

When face to face with a trauma in analysis, the analyst is unconsciously requested to experience the same situation, do something without knowing where it will lead, and so experience a painful absence of thinking. The fear of not being able to think, as well as a profound uncertainty about the distinction between reality and fantasy, becomes the analyst's doubt. It is necessary to go along with this state and be able to come out of it little by little; only afterwards is it possible to understand what has happened and help the patient to do so as well. At this point, the interpreter behaves as if on stage: in order not to betray the author of the text, it is necessary to understand which perceptions have directed his or her mind and given rise to his or her vocabulary – only then can the interpreter/analyst appear on the scene.

By accepting my presence as separate from her own, Anna's mental space widened, and the child that might be born in Anna's game seems to be the result of this work. Once again, however, something happened in her family that hindered further elaboration.

The following autumn, Anna expressed crude, violent sexuality in her game (a dog licks a doll's "vagina-botty"),[1] and over the next few weeks, her behaviour became very difficult. At the next session with her parents, held at their request due to these difficulties, I emphasised once again the need to protect Anna from the excitement I perceived as alienating and annihilating.

116

During that session, I learned from her parents that Anna had been the object of sexual games by older boys her brother had invited home.

A conflict opened up between Anna's parents, as her father had shown the children a cassette on sexual education, and they had found a book about "all the positions" on their father's bedside table. I felt there and then a pain coming from Anna's mother, indescribable in words but acute.

Months later, when analysis risked being interrupted, this expression on Anna's mother's face came to mind – it seemed to me to express mourning, a traumatic event. I wondered whether in that moment Anna's mother had been able to make a link between her own trauma and Anna's story. The fact of declaring out loud a violent episode led Anna into contact with a more ancient violence – alienating identification – and to lighten its burden.

During the weeks that followed that meeting, Anna improved considerably at home and at school, probably relieved by the fact that both she and her parents had been able to tackle with me the problem of her overexcitement: not only to speak openly about a traumatic event but also to acknowledge the parents' uneasiness regarding sexuality, as well as their difficulties in protecting Anna from overexcitement. Anna and her experience could now be accommodated: a *third space* had been created, fundamental in allowing Anna to feel the impact of her alienating identification and consequently distance herself from it. This can be seen in the following session, several weeks later.

The mandate and alien identity:
How much is your own name your own?

The session began with a game in which extremely sadistic fantasies appeared again (characters covered in scars, one particular character called "the nutcase" because his head was full of holes, whom I was asked to treat sadistically with cuts and injections).

A: Look how she's [*the doll*] full of holes, I wonder how she must feel . . .
P: Do you know that when I was little, I didn't want to eat anymore, and they gave me all these injections in my head . . . I'm

    not Anna, I'm Virginia . . . Have I already told you I'm called
    Virginia?

A: You said something about it the last time, but without telling me
    it was you. So, you have another name?

P: When I was born, they called me Anna, and then Virginia, like
    my aunt, my daddy's sister who died.

A: What a difficult name to have! Your aunt didn't want to eat
    either, and that's why she died. Who knows how hungry she
    must have been?

While listening carefully, Anna started to play on her own, which
was quite unusual for her. She made a face out of plasticine and
asked me to work near her. So I began making something with the
plasticine. She was consuming a great amount of the material, and
I commented on how hungry for plasticine she was. In reply, Anna
fashioned a lizard with pointed teeth.

The declaration of a violent act is important for a number of
reasons. It was evident that the seductive game with her brother's
friends (or with her brother?) was a turning point for Anna. But
equally important is the fact that this violence, probably a consequence of Anna being neglected, of not being so important in
the minds of her parents and in the family context, could now be
mentioned.

As a result, not only did Anna's functioning in reality improve
but she was also able to bring to the session the representation of
both the alienating identification and its consequences. While at the
beginning of her analysis, Anna had said that her head was burning
and bursting, now there was the appearance of a mad character, *the
nutcase*, whose head is full of holes. A pierced head, just as had happened to Anna in her first year of life, when she had been hospitalised and risked dying of gastroenteritis; a pierced head because of the
alienating identification, because of the mandate.

Needles of life with which Anna had been saved; needles of death
in that they were bearers of an alien identity. The paradox of the
mandate is this: the sap feeds and at the same time diminishes the
subject's identity. Once again, my interpretation stressed feelings (*I
wonder how she must feel*), and once again, Anna seemed to rely on my
interpretation to construct her discourse.

From here, Anna was able to distance herself from the alienating
identification and get in contact with her mental suffering. This was

the same for her parents, but it was more difficult for them to face up to it. I believe the request soon afterwards to interrupt the analysis must be interpreted from this perspective.

A child is born; an analysis risks being interrupted

The second Christmas holiday now over, Anna announced with satisfaction that the little girl was born, but the atmosphere suddenly became complicated: the little girl and her mother were not well.

Anna confirmed her suffering, as well as her mother's, linked to the awareness of a separation, but Anna's mother wasn't ready to accept the consequences. In a meeting with Anna's parents, together with the substantial recognition of Anna's progress, the mother said, "Anna's breaking away from me", following this with a clear message: "The analysis will have to end in June. Anna won't notice, as there are the holidays". Anna's father was of a different opinion. In the harshness of her mother's intention, as in the assertive paternal defence, I felt it was again mutually impossible for them to think that something concerned them before it did Anna.

Paradoxically, although separated on this occasion by thoughts that were apparently quite different, I felt they were united by an *unspoken* intention: if Anna distances herself from me, I'll die (mother); Anna mustn't die (father) – the paternal fantasy of endless analysis was opposed to analysis being interrupted. Neither of her parents could think of Anna and guarantee her a separate existence

Once again, I was in the middle and felt the need to insert my own thinking between Anna and her parents. With Anna's mother, I would go back to the sense of acute pain that I had noticed on her face months before when she spoke about Anna's relationship with her brother, and to what she had said: "Anna's breaking away from me". It was not difficult for me then, since I too felt acute pain at the thought of ending the analysis, to identify with the mother and feel, in return, a greater trust and alliance. The mother then brought up Anna's middle name, as if surprised that she had never thought of it before: "I just called her that, and never thought about it again". With Anna's father, I would work on his need to intrude on Anna's fantasies, activating and exasperating them. He would thank me after one day when he tried again to enter into her imaginative games, and Anna stopped him, saying, "This is my business".

In this way, I obtained a continuation of analysis for another school year: we had about a year and a half ahead of us. I would have to take on intense mourning work myself to be able to say goodbye to Anna, to her parents, and to the story, and to help Anna and her parents think about what analysis had meant to them. Anna took advantage of this time and enriched the spaces of the mind with new content, and her mental space became enriched with new content, as can be seen in the following session, the last one before the summer holidays (we would have another school year of work ahead of us).

Anna, amidst rapid mood changes, mentioned the holidays: hers, mine, the star of Bethlehem and the children created by God. While expressing her wish to be saved over the summer from mosquitoes (frequent in the summer both in the city and in the countryside), she mentioned a dream in connection with this: "I had a very bad dream that mosquitoes were biting my botty and it was itchy and I was scratching and it was all red . . . Don't tell anyone". I said that botties were a delicate thing for little girls, as they were for grown-up women. "Children come out of there, some from your tummy, some from your botty", she said.

She asked me to read *Le Petit Poucet*, and, in the meantime, she made as if to repair her toy box with an abundant use of adhesive tape. Time was running out, and once again, she got angry and tore up all the paper she could get hold of. A little dismayed by such a stormy ending, looking at the numerous little pieces of white paper Anna had scattered all over the floor, I said: "Look, they're like the pebbles of *Le Petit Poucet*, the ones that helped him find his parents and his home again". Anna calmed down, asked if she could take with her a paper cup to which she had long ago glued a handle, snatched in a moment of anger from a basket, and said, "Today your water was really good!". Stung by curiosity, irritated and sore, during this session Anna fluctuated quickly between the possibility of getting nearer to the fantasy of the primal scene and a definite refusal: children are born of God, and the stable of Bethlehem is a universal manger for children not born of a relationship between the sexes.

However, the crude image of her *botty*, which had already appeared in her playing, was dreamed of, even if it was a *bad dream*, and fits into a context: separation, the prickly fantasies about it, and the tingling, somewhere between pleasure and pain.

Through her quick acceptance of the metaphor offered about *Le Petit Poucet*'s pebbles, Anna reached the possibility of thinking about a connection between herself and her parents, between herself and me, as well as of accepting a distance, a separation.

Moving towards the end of analysis: separation, identity and representation

Once she established some distance between herself, her parents and her alien identity, Anna acquired a greater awareness of maternal and paternal suffering, as well as her own. Now her words came out in a more orderly sequence, rather like the pebbles laid down by *Le Petit Poucet*.

The transference had lost its violent aspects, the countertransference had been enriched with *rêverie*, and the analytical relationship had taken on a more continuative nature compared to the initial *graftings* and *uprootings*. Anna was gradually able to make more sense of her own experiences and, with greater awareness of space and time, face the process of mourning. In everyday life, having repeated the first year of primary school, Anna was now well settled in her class; she read well and could write quite correctly, although she still had some difficulty in the area of logic/mathematics. Her social relationships had greatly improved, as regards both family and school.

Several months later, Anna declared, "Everyone in my family goes to the psychoanalyst, except for my brother, but he should go, too, because he keeps all his secrets to himself". Of course, Anna and I both sensed the fragility of her state and the risk that some new deluge would sweep away the many thoughts we had built together. In particular her brother, "who has never been to the psychoanalyst" and who "keeps all his secrets to himself", could reveal other aspects of Anna's mind and of the mandate that were not touched on during this analysis.

Anna had carefully prepared for the end of the analysis, alternating between moments of gentleness and of anger and disdain towards me, but on the whole, she returned many times to the work done: "Do you remember . . .?", she asked about her drawings and whether she could take some away with her.

She came to the final session with her father and brother. All three of them had an air of being fine. Anna pretended to have her arm in plaster; it was in fact wrapped up in a cushion, which she would tell me about at the end.

Her father told me that school had finished, with Anna getting a good report, and he thanked me. Anna showed her brother her toys and said something like, "You've never been to a psychoanalyst", but in a kind, almost reflective way. Then in the session: "Today's the last time".

For some time, she had asked me every day how many sessions were left. Then began the selection of the drawings. She asked me to read the parts I had written; she was happy when I had written words that she herself could read. She was enjoying herself, and she left me – prudently – the most distressing drawings and the most confused words, saying, "It's better if you keep these", as if I should look after them and protect her from her own madness.

She then decided to draw a picture, and, after not doing any drawing for months, she now produced a very well-drawn picture of her family and wrote her parents' first names clearly (and nearby *mummy and daddy*), as well as her brother's name. "I'm also going to draw my nanny" (who had come to pick her up all those years). Then she decided to make a very small frame out of paper, and, inside it, she drew her family once again: mummy and daddy, herself in the middle "dressed in blue, which is my favourite colour", and near her mother, her brother. She laughed ironically but gently: "I've dressed him in pink".

Above herself she wrote "ME", whereas for all the others she had written their first names. Then she cut out the little picture and took it with her.

She also found a lovely necklace she had made and decided to give it to her nanny. The session ended with an intense hug from Anna and a short speech in which she told me that the cushion she had brought with her that day was always with her: it had protected her once when she fell on the marble floor and hurt her head. My thoughts went back to her first sentence – "My head's bursting, my head's burning" – and to the protective meaning of this cushion. Anna added: "I've had it since I was six".

I will conclude this work with a question from Anna that was fired at me point-blank in one of the last sessions: "Sometimes I call a [children's] helpline . . . who needs it, children or mums?".

I will also take my cue from this consideration to go back to the initial theme of this work: when a child analyst works in a situation in which the transgenerational mandate is active, he or she is caught between the parents' denied suffering and the child's acted suffering. To avoid being suffocated by an impossible request, the analyst's work should be capable of leading the parents to a greater understanding of their suffering and the child to the construction of his or her own mental space. The perennial controversy of whether or not the child analyst has to work with the parents assumes very particular importance here. Whether the analyst likes it or not, he or she is struck by the force of the mandate: this is announced on the one hand by the feeling of extraneity experienced by the analyst from the first meetings, and on the other by the presence of a particularly violent transference, which tends to blind the countertransference and severely tests the analyst's mental functioning.

A successful outcome of analysis will depend on the analyst's ability to go from being witness to an unconscious violence exerted by one generation on the next to having a buffer function, allowing the intergenerational relationship to find a balance.

The notions of Freud's parastimuli, Winnicott's holding and Bion's *rêverie* have different applications here: the parastimuli function (or para-excitatory barrier) is directed to protect the patient from the pressure and violence the mandate has on mental functioning; holding contributes to anchoring the patient to his or her own perceptions, thus reducing the impact of the alienating identification; and the function of *rêverie* is to allow the analyst to move away from the patient's fragmented feelings to gain time and space to *redream* them, following the thread of his or her own associations. The plaster-cushion that Anna proposes to me in the last session recalls the function of a welcoming obstacle (Racamier, 1962): an object that is hard and soft at the same time. Is it possible that the plaster-cushion, as a hard and at the same time dreamy setting, allowed a repair of internal fractures and put Anna in a condition to function again? I feel that all of these aspects together played a part in changing the environment in which Anna, with difficulty, was growing up.

The sessions with Anna's parents preceding therapy probably enabled them to acquire greater awareness of their suffering, which in turn allowed them to carry out their parental function more freely. The analytical work had first acted as a protective barrier for Anna, not only softening the impact of the mandate's traumatic violence but also enabling her mental tissue to repair and take on its own functions again.

As analysts, it is necessary for us to face separation anxiety at many different levels. We must be able to function both in situations in which we have the capacity to think and in others in which we have to bear nonsensical content. Tolerance to being used as an object (Winnicott, 1969) and, as such, to being shaken, is essential.

Work over a long period was necessary to enable Anna to take root in the analytical relationship before being able to represent herself as a separate person within her family. Once nourished by this grounding, Anna, despite her worries, could then separate herself and leave. The end of analysis is not the end of the analytical work, but having tolerated finishing Anna's analysis, plus having worked with Anna's parents to keep it in place, could be a premise for future work.

Note

1 [Translator's note] Anna uses the term "vagina-pisella", with "pisella" being her invented, child's term for "bottom" [rendered here as "botty"], although it is in fact the female form of "pisello", a slang/children's term for penis.

Bibliography

Anzieu, A. (1968), "Sur quelques traits de la personnalité du bègue". In *Bulletin de Psychologie*, 21, pp. 1022–1028.

Badoni, M. (2004), "La psicoanalisi dei figli: paradossi". In Neri, N., Latmiral, S. (a cura di), *Uno spazio per i genitori*, Quaderni di psicoterapia infantile, 48, pp. 171–186.

Bollas, C. (1976), "Le langage secret de la mère et de l'enfant". In *Nouvelle Revue Psychanalyse,* 14, pp. 241–246.

Bonaminio, V., Di Renzo, M., Giannotti, A. (1993), "Le fantasie inconsce dei genitori come fattori ego-alienanti nelle identificazioni del bambino". In *Rivista di Psicoanalisi*, 4, pp. 681–708.

Faimberg, H. (1988), "A l'écoute des télescopage des générations: pertinence psychanalytique du concept". In *Topique*, 42, pp. 223–238.

Fonagy, P., Target, M. (2001), "Attachment and Reflective Function: Their Role in Self-Organization". In *Affect Regulation, Mentalization, and the Development of the Self.* Routledge, London, 2002.

Freud, S. (1915), *Mourning And Melancholia*. SE, vol. XIV.

Gaddini, E. (1981), "Early defensive fantasies and the psychoanalytical process". In *A Psychoanalytic Theory of Infantile Experience: Conceptual and Clinical Reflections*. Tavistock, London, 1992.

Guignard, F. (1997), *Épître à l'Objet*. Paris, PUF.

Kaës, R., Faimberg, H., Enriquez, M., Baranes, J.-J. (1993), *Trasmissione della vita psichica tra le generazioni*. Borla, Roma, 1995.

Kancyper, L. (1997), *Il confronto generazionale. Uno studio psicoanalitico*. Milano, FrancoAngeli, 2000.

Manzano, J., Palacio Espasa, F., Zilkha, N. (1999), "The Narcissistic Scenarios of Parenthood". In *The International Journal of Psychoanalysis*, 80, pp. 465–476.

Perrault, C. (1697), "Le Petit Poucet ". In *Histoires ou Contes du temps passé*.

Racamier, P.-C. (1962), "Propos sur la réalité dans la théorie psychanaly-tique". In *Revue Française Psychanalyse*, 26, 6, pp. 675–710.

Tisseron, S., Hachet, P., Nachin, C., Rand, N., Rouchy, J.-Cl., Torok, M. (1995), *Le psychisme à l'épreuve des générations. Clinique du fantôme*. Paris, Dunod.

Torok, M. (1968), "The Illness of Mourning and the Fantasy of the Exquisite Corpse". In Birksted-Breen, D., Flanders, S., Gibeault, A. (eds.), *Reading French Psychoanalysis*. Routledge, London, 2010.

Vallino, D. (1998), *Raccontami una storia*. Borla, Roma.

Winnicott, D.W. (1969), "The Use of an Object and Relating through Identifications". In *The International Journal of Psychoanalysis*, 50, pp. 711–716.

PART FOUR

THE INGREDIENTS OF CARE

Agreeable and disagreeable elements

A consulting room, but not all of my own: the conquest of a study of my own, in Milan, was long and laborious. I had foreseen it and imagined it, but it took 14 years for the tenant occupying the premises to leave. Once I was in, I myself painted the room intended as the consulting room, while for the ceiling I had patient, precious help. I would like to leave here a grateful thought not only to the skilled workers but also to the colleagues who hosted me from time to time, tolerating the noisy movement of the children I saw. The last precious host was Dino Lanzara, an ironic, affectionate, solid presence in difficult moments.

Finally, my consulting room was ready, but, like every analyst's consulting room, it was not all for me: an analyst's consulting room is always a shared space, populated by ghosts, a space of welcome and of meetings, at times bitter. In his or her mind, the analyst, without always knowing it, hosts the history of his or her life and training. All patients, one by one, bring with them a world that disquiets them and makes their steps uncertain, a turbulent world, to be accommodated and protected before being analysed.

The office must be the guarantor of this intimacy. The door opens to welcome the patient, and the door closes to initiate the session.

DOI: 10.4324/9781003560647-11

As it was for my analysis and then for that of my patients, a soft yet heavy padded curtain sheltered the analytic couple from external noises to allow them to "listen with all their senses"[1] to the sounds of the session.

Yet again, *time* is one of the ingredients. The strict rule defined once and for all between analyst and patient, the 50 minutes of the session, paradoxically opens up a space of freedom: it affects the urges of the unconscious and the work of the preconscious, it can make a scene.

The body in the session: Green said that analytic speech is "speech delivered lying down", "speech" and not "word", therefore spoken, voiced, embodied; "speech delivered lying down" to make room, in a very special situation, for the dream, for rêverie, for affections; a "living discourse", writes Green, only possible if the word is embodied in the feeling of the body.

A body, a story: the idea that the dialoguing presence of the body in the session is at the basis of the exchange, of the relationship, of the analytical investigation, of the game of getting involved or losing oneself, has engaged me since the beginning of my profession, as is also evident from the approach of this book. Today this reflection has broadened to reflect great attention to the analyst-patient set-up in the session. By contrast, I remember the puzzled reaction of my colleagues the first time I spoke publicly about it at the Milanese Psychoanalysis Centre in the 1990s. An expert colleague told me: "As long as you say so . . .", implying that there were other merits that would have earned me credit in the context of the Society: I fell for it!

"Martha, Martha, you are worried". I received many joking – but not too much – compliments from Andreina Robutti, then Secretary of the Society's Executive Board, for having procured a toilet brush for the Milanese Centre's bathrooms. These were the first signs, which introduced me, at first almost unaware, to intense administrative work for the Milanese Psychoanalysis Centre and the Italian Psychoanalytic Society (SPI): days and nights at work in the Executive Committees of the Centre and the SPI to untangle the meandering rules, in the turbulence of the conflicts, while, fortunately, sometimes managing to smile a little.

To return to the **body**: the door opens, the door closes – the journey begins. The idea of an enclosed space was close to Freud's heart, and here is the metaphor of the train (Freud, 1913, 35):[2] imagine the patient at the beginning of the analysis as a traveller describing the landscapes seen from the train windows. Imagine the analyst capable of permeable listening – Bion would say without memory and without desire – but how complex the translating work required to share this journey is (Ricoeur, 2020).[3]

The door opens, the door closes: the body, that of the analyst as well as that of the patient, needs guaranteed times and spaces in which it is important to make room for silence as well as speech. When the session begins, the consulting room expands, the senses are activated. Mina sang: "Quando sei qui con me, questa stanza non ha più pareti [When you are here with me, this room no longer has walls]".[4] This is also true in the session regarding the unexpected irruption of other spaces and times – we need these potentially dilated spaces. And here is another paradox of analytical work: defined spaces/infinite spaces. However, to sustain the paradox and the resulting openings, it is up to the analyst to maintain the boundaries. How many times have I reminded candidates in supervision that the setting, with its spaces, times and rules, is the only instrument the analyst has? The analyst alone is responsible for this special space: maintaining boundaries does not mean rigidity but rather the ability to guarantee maximum freedom for the work of the unconscious and preconscious. The history of the psychoanalytic movement does not fail to point out to us the multiple encroachments, so we must then be equipped: the body lives, feels and suffers. It happens that patients, afraid of sinking, cling to the analyst like people lost at sea: the title of one of my first works, "Aggrapparsi, aggredire, pensare: evoluzione dell'istinto filiale [Clinging, attacking, thinking: evoluzione of the filial instinct]" (Badoni, 1985), published in the journal Gli Argonauti, tackled these problems starting from Hermann's intuitive interpretation, illuminated by Nicolas Abraham. Hermann spoke of the filial instinct, the clinging instinct: on the phylogenetic scale, it is instinct, not love, that promotes the search for the object, and many transformations are needed to help the human infant, overcoming the impetus to appropriate itself, to set out in search of the mother and from there, if the mother appears, to the freedom of being able to think and love.

And the analyst? We know that a clinging survivor at sea risks being lost by clinging to the rescuer, but the rescuer also risks disappearing into the waves of the unconscious in this fatal entanglement. This was suggested to me by, among other things, the drawing of a child whose session I described earlier: in order to face the waves and bring the person lost at sea to safety, he pointed out to me in the drawing, it is necessary for the lifeguard to have his feet on the ground, for the analyst to be firmly anchored in the practice of his or her theories. Then he can throw his rope, and thus the story can take on substance.

Notes

1 Bastianini, T., Ferruta, A., Guerrini Degl'Innocenti, B. (2021), *Ascoltare con tutti i sensi*. Giovanni Fioriti, Roma.
2 Freud, S. (1913–14), *Further Recommendations in the Technique of Psycho-Analysis I*. SE XII, p. 35.
3 Ricoeur P. (2020), *Attorno alla psicoanalisi*. Edizione italiana a cura di Francesco Barale. Jaca Book, Milano. Busacchi, V., Martini, G. (2020), *L'identità in questione: saggio di psicoanalisi ed ermeneutica*. Jaca Book, Milano.
4 From the song "*Il cielo in una stanza*" by Gino Paoli, recorded by Mina in 1960.

VII

A BODY, A STORY: FUNCTIONS OF THE RESCUING ADULT

The importance of a comma

A body, a story. The comma separating those two elements indicates a pause of unknown amplitude: it may be a matter of merely a moment, but it often opens up to abysses which we are irresistibly drawn to look into, perhaps suffering temporarily from that vertigo (Danielle Quinodoz, 1994) which is the awareness of a possible link and the terror of a fall without appeal or future. This abyss, to the edge of which we are brought by those patients – children, adolescents and adults – who ask us to call them and help them exist and enter time, was first looked into by Freud, then by many after him.

The body is a visible and tangible expression of the reality of the person, of the difference between the sexes and of the succession of generations. It is the seat of affections. History is not so much and not only narrative voice but the possibility of access to a living discourse (Green, 1973) in which one's own subjectivity and the impact of the relationship between subjects are present and represented.

The gap exists, like the comma, not to be eliminated, but to be dealt with, along with the emotions it provokes. Its origins lie in an unequal, strongly asymmetrical encounter between an individual who is naked in their corporeity and a subject with their own history. This encounter, suspended at the beginning of a journey, arouses intense emotions and, to be mentally conceived, requires these emotions to be first felt and then sustained. At first, before

DOI: 10.4324/9781003560647-12

speech, newborn babies present themselves with a body, as do patients: on the phone, it is the voice; on the threshold, the body.

But what are the ways of listening and seeing not already imbued with an experience of the beginnings that was already ours and is then reactivated at each original encounter, each time *there is something new*? Above the newborns' cradle, together with emotions, the inevitable and necessary game of similarities begins – in the analysis space, with what eyes do we see and are seen by our patients? How does each new encounter affect our way of existing in the world, of experiencing our personal and professional history and of believing in the possibility of trust? How willing are we to allow ourselves to be affected and possibly changed by the vicissitudes of the encounter? Neither the skills of the newborn nor those of every patient who walks through the door of our offices for the first time, or who in any session, at any time, exposes us to something new, are enough to make the encounter emotionally bearable at first, then thinkable later. This encounter activates and employs structures that we will use not only at the beginning, but every time we are confronted with something original, something new.

Forming a bond between body and history is therefore work that begins at birth and completes its structures in adolescence. It is not that the prospects close at that age, but the adult cannot fail to come back to the game, rules and mental structures established in previous years: he or she will have to revisit them for any possible integration.

"Every act of knowledge is preceded by an act of cathexis and the latter is triggered by the affective experience that accompanies this state of encounter, always present, between the psyche and the milieu – physical, psychic, somatic – that surrounds it" (Aulagnier, 1986. p. 100). At the origins of each new encounter lies an investment and an affective experience, a complex interweaving of intrapsychic work and intersubjective relationship. The structures activated in these circumstances lead, or should lead, the human individual, alone in his or her body from birth onwards, to form an identity, to be able to rely on the awareness of his or her own existence and to feel that he or she is the protagonist of his or her own history, one that is meaningful, narratable, recognised and recognisable.

The comma between "body" and "history" makes explicit a double discontinuity: between subject-body and subject–*other* and between subject and the *physical, psychic, somatic habitat* that surrounds it. The dynamics are between the self and the other and between the

132

self and the self: the intersubjective and intrapsychic work together to help define the origin and originality of each encounter. The comma is not a hyphen, and the transit between body and history, from which the feeling of our existence originates, cannot be other than a complex pathway continually at work, as Freud emphasised and in various ways reinterpreted, understood, commented on, and expanded, leaving us with a body of work that is in motion and courageously open to subsequent developments.

The patients, young and old, to whom we offer psychoanalytic understanding, come to us when the links between body and history are lost, when the competence to deal with emotions, the perceptible manifestation of the *state of encounter,* is not functioning.

In this work, I will attempt to explore the nature and rules at the origins of an encounter and the functions and dysfunctions of the rescuing adult. The competence of the infant alone is not enough to ensure the links between body and history, just as words, in analysis, are not in themselves a guarantee of a living, original discourse. In my text, in addition to my work as an analyst, I will refer to those authors to whom, in the course of this exploration, I have felt closest, without forgetting to be indebted to those many streams of knowledge that, through sharing the psychoanalytic home with colleagues, have over the years flowed into the course of my thoughts.

Strategies and stumbles on the "circuitous paths"

These circuitous paths to death, faithfully kept to by the conservative instincts, would thus present us today with the picture of the phenomena of life.

Freud, *Beyond the Pleasure Principle* (1920) [SE, XVIII, 38]

Although it may appear somewhat funereal, this reflection by Freud, formulated at a moment of great intensity in his life and work, establishes an inescapable link between life and death. By subtracting death from the "sublime Ανάγκη [necessity]", Freud (1920, 230) links it to life and makes it a fundamental part of the experience of living. In the same text in which we sense, along with grief, an extraordinary vital force, Freud throws us a thread to hold on to: the thread of the reel game ["Fort/da", a game with a wooden reel on a thread], a moment of vivid family experience – Freud watching his grandchild playing a game. The evocative force of this game lies in the fact that the child, by throwing the reel under the bed and commenting on its subsequent reappearance, is not interested in dragging the thread and reel around his home and his life, but rather, with an unexpected change of course, plays at making his own the experience of living, made up of disappearances and rediscoveries, absences and encounters. In the absence of his mother, he remembers, repeats, elaborates and represents, gradually acquiring that sense of his own existence in the world which constitutes the common thread of our identity.

Perhaps uniquely among the sciences, psychoanalysis has found itself using terms evocative of death to express the most important phenomena of living: mourning and depressive position, for example. This terminology has often been criticised, but on reflection, it is extremely faithful to the idea that living is only such if one is able to pass through absence, or, at least, not make absence an unbearable, overwhelming threat, but rather an interrogating space.

Freud attributes to the reel game (and to the game of living) a function of *compensation*, which the child obtains in exchange for renouncing a direct expression of the drive and the replacement of the resulting pleasure with *a pleasure of a different kind*, one that leads the child from the passivity of the experience undergone to activity and mastery of the situation.

However, achieving this *pleasure of a different kind* requires a "ferryman", and perhaps, it must be said, a bit of luck: genetic inheritance is not enough. We need to be well received on the world stage (Ferenczi, 1929) in order to be able to take up the challenge and move from immediate pleasure, linked to the body and sensoriality, to pleasure of a different kind, mediated by mental operations. We need a rescuing adult who understands and supports us.

Such is the sense of existence, that *feeling of being understood in what one feels*, to which Marco Macciò and Dina Vallino (2004) have recently returned to reflect upon.

Separation/separateness

For a long time, I have been reflecting on these terms in my daily practice as a psychoanalyst. Separation and separateness are not synonyms, but they express a dialectic that has an effect on analytic work.

Di Chiara (1992) points out how separateness is a vital element in the reciprocal relationship between parents and children and, at the same time, a necessary quality for the psychic world of the analyst. A fundamental element of the Oedipal structure, separateness determines the quality of the relationship between the ego and objects and between the ego and the superego (Di Chiara, 2003). Taking up the theme of post-analytic phases, Gilda De Simone (2002) considers separation as an event for which one prepares oneself through the elaboration and acquisition of separateness.

I am now going to ask my mother tongue for help (Vocabolario della Lingua Italiana, Istituto della Enciclopedia Italiana): *separazione* [*separation*] is defined as "the action of separating, the fact of being separated and the state of what is separated"; *separatezza* [*separateness*] is defined as "a rare form of separation, in a non-dynamic but static sense (i.e. being separated, disjointed, distinct)".

Separateness indicates a state, *separation* an action, and while the definition of *separation* also includes *the state of what is separate*, the definition of *separateness* includes something more in progression: separate, disjointed and distinct. To become pilgrims of the world, subjects among other subjects, it is therefore not enough to be separate; it is necessary to be able to bear being disjointed and, above all, distinct; otherwise, we would have to speak of cloning – a question not of being identical but of identity, a question of freedom.

The advantage of keeping separation and separateness distinct is being able to open the door to a process of great instability, but also of great strength: there is no separation without separateness, and there is no separateness without separation. The state of separateness is the point of arrival and the point of departure for new separations, in a spiral movement that engages corporeity and adult rescuer in its dance.

Separateness and clandestinity

The crucial act of separation, Gaddini (1981, 137) warns, "has less to do with the moment the mother stops breast-feeding the baby, and much more with the overwhelming time when the child has to realize its being separate". Fright is its affect, acting out its response, clandestinity is its habitat, and tyranny is the enemy to be beaten. Acting out, and the resulting clandestinity, Gaddini continues, is an integral part of developmental processes and can be used both against or within the process.

And in analytical work? Gaddini continues: "Participation in psychoanalytic work can only take place in secret, in a sort of clandestinity . . . The messages which the patient's ego sends . . . are coded messages for whoever can decipher them" (Gaddini, 1981, 139).

The analyst will therefore have to understand without intruding so as to prevent the clandestine individual from feeling threatened with being discovered and so changing shelter, hiding again, or, in other cases, seeing their clandestine work made public, thereby triggering a negative therapeutic reaction.

In the perspective of my work, the clandestine people who maintain dialogue with the community uphold their separateness and their rights to exist; otherwise, they will be condemned to a timeless withdrawal. Attention, however, must be paid to the function of the rescuing adult. He or she must first of all perceive the existence of the clandestine individual beyond the overt messages, and understand, support and comprehend what the clandestine person is feeling and the reasons, paying particular attention to the ways and timing with which to approach. If the situation of encounter does not find an adult capable of comprehending, supporting and understanding, body and history lose their connections or establish false connections.

If the rescuing adult does not comprehend but *already knows* what the child is feeling, the subject can only exist by evading the rules of the encounter (space, time and related fantasies) while at the same time alienating the mental structures and competences assigned to it. If the subject is not recognised in what they feel, they will not in turn be able to recognise themselves. They will instead be at the mercy of an imploded body in a sort of autarchic organisation or can invent a story without a body: the comma is a guarantee of a pause and *respectful listening* (Nissim Momigliano, 1989). Clandestinity can therefore be considered a way of reacting to the impact of otherness. It does not in itself jeopardise the existence of the subject or even the relationship between subjects – on the contrary, it can safeguard it. The rescuing adult is not the one who violates the clandestinity, but the one who, in addition to deciphering its messages, knows how to respect times and ways to make them explicit. The fate of such clandestinity and the ways of thinking associated with it are thus largely dependent on the functioning of the rescuing adult. The phenomenon of clandestinity has its privileged moment to reveal itself and be dealt with in adolescence. Adolescence, in fact, resumes *après-coup* the beginnings and mental structures set in motion in childhood. As such, it is not so much, or only, concerned with the specific age of adolescence but is also a resumption of the initial dilemma and the related attempts at resolution throughout life. As a mode of functioning, it can also be reactivated in adults and, naturally, in analytic work.

We might consider adolescence a position as well as a particularly complex period of life.

In terms of age, mental structures and quality of conflicts, we might say that adolescence is the last opportunity to make contact again, *après-coup*, with clandestinity and to act with the aim of integrating subject and *habitat*, subject and collectivity. The success of this operation allows one to regain the inheritance received (Freud, 1912–13) to *exercise* publicly and in freedom.

Separateness and separation can then work together, by progressive oscillations, to create the feeling of one's own identity, in the form of an aphorism: "a tenuous and vital trace, left by the self-perception of the psychic work carried out by the Ego" (Racamier, 1992, 386, my translation).

The result of this work of self-perception seems less important than the ego's awareness of its *own* work in progress, hence of its own separateness, of the continuously ongoing work of separation, of its own existence in the world. Existence leaves traces, the nature of which I will now examine.

The perceptual apparatus

> If we imagine one hand writing upon the surface of the mystic writing pad while another periodically raises its covering sheet from the wax slab, we shall have a concrete representation of the . . . functioning of the perceptual apparatus of our mind.
>
> Freud, 1924 (*SE* 19: 232)

Racamier (1992) reminds us that the trace must be tenuous: permanent, but not immutable (Freud, 1924). As we briefly delve, following the trace into the problem of memory, we must make a further distinction – between memory and recollection. The former refers to the competence to preserve a trace, the latter to the possibility

137

of recalling it to mind. The etymon of remembrance takes us to the heart (considered by the ancients to be the seat of memory), to desire, to investment and to life.

The magic of the mystic writing pad, adaptable in its capacity and available for further notes, does not lie in the miraculous presentation of an *expected fact*, but rather in the renewed wonder (Di Chiara, 1990) at each appearance of a knowledge that is not pre-constituted, but discovered in the authenticity of the experience lived in the encounter. It is the magic of the dream and of the *rêverie* function.

After an interruption, a patient brought to a session a mood between boredom, depression and anger, which seemed destined to cast its dark shadow over the whole session. As I listened to the patient's languor, I immersed myself in atmospheres of my own returning home after school. I thought back to the disappointment of not finding Mum at home and the consequent bad moods. From there, I found myself evoking with the patient an atmosphere of disappointment, of mothers *not preparing a snack* . . . (who disregard a moment for refreshment). After a pregnant silence, the patient tells me: you used a *magic word* – snack – and launches into a long, articulate, lively discourse, bringing up her childhood, missed snacks and collections of snacks.

The trace followed that day lent the patient my persona, an *other* than the patient's, engaged in its own work of integrating psyche and soma, and at the same time in an attempt to make contact with the patient's resentful disappointment. The house was there, as was the session, but we had not really met yet: no snack.

The trace simultaneously marks a presence and an absence; it promotes an investment. Going back to my patient's rancorous mood, I believe that an interpretation limited to dropping on her the well-known refrain about patients' intolerance to the analyst's absence, without allowing her to follow clues, savour pleasures or recognise disappointments, would have been equivalent to one of those snacks that in these hurried times are shoved into children's satchels as instruments of fattening (eat and shut up), but not of nourishment. The image I have managed to come up with is the fruit of a work of integration of the psyche-soma or of a conjunction *of memory and desire*. It is the paradox of the analytical encounter as formulated by Bion (1968), who, aware of the devastating effects of tearing the protective shield (*alpha function – contact-barrier*), recommends that the analyst listening to the patient abstain from memory and desire to welcome and note, to let the patient trace the way, and to protect and support the coming and going of the patient between self and self and between patient and analyst.

Separateness sustains and supports the movements of separation, which continually produce new arrangements of separateness.

On the capacity for understanding: traces or brands

I have touched on the problem of the lightness of the trace – what about its vitality? Due to what phenomena do we come to support the pulsing of life in the infant or the desire to exist in patients? What are the terms of an understanding that, time after time, allows welcoming, understanding, supporting and following the trace without the presumption of finding, thus allowing the ego to base its work on self-perception, to feel its legitimacy and therefore to feel able to rely on it?

In order for the trace to evoke curiosity and thought, we need a fellow traveller, who has passed through before us, to pass on their experience and support us in the search. In the words of Alvarez (1992), we need *live company*, alive in the sense of treasuring their experience, having enough energy to be able to pass it on, and not being afraid of being overtaken.

Imre Hermann (1943) had intuited this when he spoke not of maternal instinct but of filial instinct, as a mother's capacity to retrace her steps to gather and translate the experiences of her infant, and then Bion perfected it with the introduction of the maternal function of *rêverie*.

Work on the trace resembles an initiatory experience, and the initiatory experience is rooted in the culture of origin to also be able to separate from it and produce new experiences to be transmitted.

The function of *rêverie* is not the self-disclosure of the intersubjectivist creed, but rather the offering the mother makes to the child and the analyst to the patient of their own psyche-soma as a method of following the traces, picking up clues and giving the body back to the mind (Ogden, 2001). It is a question of communication, wrote Freud in the *Project*, in a much-quoted passage which inspired the title of this chapter. The quotation refers to the experience of satisfaction (for which the infant's competence is evidently insufficient): "It takes place by *extraneous help*, when the attention of an experienced person is drawn to the child's state by discharge along the path of internal change. In this way this path of discharge acquires a secondary function of the highest importance, that of *communication*, and the initial helplessness of human beings is the *primal source* of all *moral motives*" (Freud, *Project for a Scientific Psychology*, 1895, *318*, my italics).

Freud does not speak here of an object, but of a *mature* individual, capable of sustaining the situation of separateness without imposing his mark, thus promoting the necessary operations for the movements of separation.

It would then be Bion who took up these early intuitions of Freud's; with the notion of *rêverie* and the image of a grid, Bion informs us of a maternal and analytic function, speaking of a body inhabited by a sensoriality that requires transiting through the mother's psyche-soma, in charge of transforming intoxicating elements into elements suitable for knowledge. The capacity for understanding, however, does not always exist and does not belong to everyone.

Helplessness and the capacity to understand

Intendere [understanding] is a polysemic word that calls into question the sensorium on the one hand and the psychic function of attention on the other (Freud, 1911); it presumes an object towards which the understanding turns, it calls into question projects and desires, and it alludes to a cognitive experience.

Work cannot be conducted in solitude; it necessarily bears the matrix of the environment in which it takes place, of its culture. Patient and analyst continually meet and distance themselves in the course of the session.

If the function of understanding is deficient, not only will the mother (or the analyst) not be able to understand, but will end up obstructing and then occluding the exploration work that the child, or patient, is trying to achieve between the self and the self, in the depths of his or her own psyche-soma. At this point, all hope may be lost, and long-term, patient work is often needed to lighten the weight of the mark in which the child remains imprisoned. Taking the side of the mother's word will hinder any further exploration, while betraying it will expose him or her to terrors that are difficult to sustain.

A child of about four turns to his mother and shyly, turning a roll of adhesive tape over in his hands, exclaims: "Mummy, look, it's a snail". His mother looks down at him and absent-mindedly, lets fall the statement: "No, it's a roll of tape".

It went wrong, the game stopped, and with it any further attempt at representation; the child had sought a shell in which to feel protected, separate, distinct – a house-shell in which to play at growing up. He was exploring new forms, seeking encouragement – he did not find it. There was only one truth, lying in the desperate concreteness of the mother's thinking. Separateness cannot be the fruit of an experience of separation – to maintain itself, it must deny otherness and become a fortress (Bettelheim, 1967).

The function of understanding has not been set in motion, help has not come, the rescuer has failed, and the child, marked by the mother's word, retreats into his shell and screams helplessly. They bring him to me because all day long he's been walking around the house mimicking an ambulance. He's looking for help, but no help comes – the child knows the situation of *Hilflosigkeit*, literally, helplessness. Omnipotent, he is putting up with the condition of helplessness: he cannot separate himself from his mother. The function of understanding, which should support in the child a perception that is as distorted as it is essential for creativity, gives way to an unambiguous, unthinking and unappealable judgement.

The exit, at least partial, from this situation and the access to a world of shady representations, but still representations, would then appear in a session in which, opening a gap in the deafening noise that the child makes *being an ambulance*, I commented: "With all this noise, you can't hear if there is a baby crying!" The noise stopped, giving way to a series of memories and representations, finally made public, even if extremely painfully.

Adolescence, a position

The concept of *posteriority* invites us to consider adolescence as a psychological set-up such as we encounter not only in the adolescent but also in the analysis of patients who are now adults, often still grappling with the initial enigma and its myths, among which, alongside the Oedipus myth, I would like to mention the Greek myth of hiding (Vidal-Naquet, 1981; Badoni, 1994), a myth of the double and of a secret elsewhere in which the adolescent, in an initiatory experience, experiences separation and separateness. On the one hand, alone in the woods, they test their own psychosomatic

141

equipment, while on the other, they know they are undergoing a passage and that, at the edge of the forest, the adult generation awaits them, armed, yes, with its rules and culture, but ready to celebrate the adolescent's innovative contribution to the original culture.

We can therefore consider adolescence as a mental position, as well as an age, loaded with the laborious work of integration, of establishing a link between body and history, whose outcome will be not so much a new history as a history *of its own*, in which to recognise themselves and be recognised. Adolescents, in order to be free but not wild adults, have to endure conflicts, often violent ones, process guilt, and savour the insecurity of unknown solitude. As for adults, often lurking anxiously on the edge of the woods and the closed door of the *child's room*, they will have to retrace other anxieties and torments in the opposite direction: the closed door of the child's room recalls the closed door of the parents' room. If the enterprise has succeeded in due time, adults will know how to question and wait; if it has failed, they risk heavy and sometimes tragic misunderstandings and intrusions.

The impact of a new corporeity activates in the adolescent, as in the infant, affects that demand to be sustained. Acting-out is lurking, but, as Gaddini (1981) teaches, the acting-out of a grown person is only a new recourse to the first movements of the infant who is experiencing a situation of helplessness. The task of the adolescent position is, at the same time, to be able to experience separateness without constructing it in a rigid set-up, in a double that does not accept the rules of living and dying, time, gender difference and generational change.

Orlando

"Can it be true, alas!" she cried, "that he
For whom I search, from me attempts to fly?
He whom I hold so dear, despises me?
And he whom I entreat, will not reply?"
L. Ariosto, *Orlando Furioso* (1516) [c. XXXII, vs. XVIII]

Orlando, 33 years old, might appear to be a handsome man were it not for his shabby dress, trousers that look as if he has outgrown them after a sudden increase in stature, an uncertain, slouching gait, somewhere between feminine and unsure of where to put his feet. His speech is well-mannered and bears the traces of a refined education, but his voice conveys complaint, perhaps protest. However, what has stayed with me most from this first meeting is a flash of fury that crosses his gaze as we say goodbye, accompanied by my feeling that he has too many teeth, and that they are too big.

If growing up is a betrayal

His body, already little used in childhood, had definitively betrayed him in adolescence, imposing on him a growth so rapid and sudden as to make him unrecognisable, first of all to himself. The revelation of his growth came to him suddenly when a very tall schoolmate turned to him and said: "We who're the tallest in the class. . .". The revelation intruded suddenly and unexpectedly and upset Orlando; from then on, his life would run on two parallel tracks: lessons and professional growth on the one hand, amorous adventures on the other. The feeling of existing was replaced by an acute feeling of nostalgia: nostalgia for a blessing enjoyed in secret, with no connection to the experience that generated it, which had instead fallen into oblivion. In a dream fragment, described in the second year of analysis: "There was a dragonfly that was responsible for the appearance of two rivulets of blood on the wall, like two tracks. I can't say much about the dragonfly".

As for the tracks, the associations link instead to the derailment of the *pendolino* [commuter train], the train that connects Milan with the capital, Rome. In the imagery of the analysis, the derailment of the *pendolino* speaks of a dysfunction in the connections between capital and periphery, between a Fellini-esque Rome and a professional Milan, between infant and rescuing adult, between separation and separateness, and between a body at the centre of attention and the history that generated it, supporting its growth and subsequent inscription in its own history. Affects and representations run on parallel lines and on unconnected tracks. The dragonfly, a being as perfect as it is ephemeral, bleeds onto Orlando's path with its weight of nostalgia: "The strongest nostalgia does not originate from the yearning need for the pleasure one remembers, but from the pleasure one has forgotten together with the experience that generated it" (Siracusano, 1982, my translation). Orlando's nostalgic affect

143

exudes blood, which is both that of consumed *presumed murders* and of wounds suffered.

The dragonfly questions me and will, I believe, guide the light, inquiring words I use in drawing Orlando back to the meeting places.

The setting, between rule and enigma:
where to find oneself, where to hide

With a body that has grown in spite of the mind, avoiding frustrations and diverting the related fury onto objects of immediate use that fail every time to fulfil their function, Orlando cannot cope with the impact of adolescence and of life. He still has to come to terms with the tyranny of needs and related affects. Frightened and furious, he seeks in analysis a place to hide and, at the same time, find himself, a rescuer who understands his messages and respects his times.

The precision with which the analytical setting defines places, times, and conditions for meeting implies, without making it explicit, the possibility that the rule involves different interpretations, tolerates exceptions and can be broken.

An instrument of initiation, it contains an enigma. It is a testing ground on which, as Bleger (1967) says, the non–differentiated aspects of the self are deposited. It is a meeting place, hosting the experiences of other meetings, with their respective vicissitudes, memories and recollections. It is a place to find oneself, return to oneself, or hide, to be found, and sometimes to disappear.

The setting is experienced by Orlando as a place of testing and will, at the same time, host his *madness*, that mixture of fury and fright accompanying an encounter one is not ready to deal with, and the helplessness that ensues.

Hiding is an ancient game: from the child only a few months old who lights up at the reappearance of his mother's just-hidden face to the older child's game of hiding in order to be looked for in places where it is very unlikely that the adult will not see them and for periods of time dictated by internal laws, which the adult will have to know how to understand.

I recall a short sequence from Ettore Scola's film *The Family*: a child hides, but the adult who is supposed to look for him does not take up the child's request to be found in time; on the contrary, he

144

and the other adults ridicule it, triggering a genuine panic attack in the child.

There is also a type of hiding that is very *animal*, similar to that of a dog enjoying the bone it has just received. It will often bury it in order to find it again and enjoy the experience in private. Approaching the dog at such a time will not lead to any sign of gratitude for the gift received but rather will entail a risk of aggression.

Finally, there is hiding to protect oneself from an intimidating power. Weighing on the timing of this hiding is the degree of complicity between a genuinely tyrannical reality and a tyranny well embedded within the Self. Certain forms of apparent deficit may be part of this, as well as certain inhibitions or bizarre behaviour, which, as in Orlando's case, tend to avoid confrontations or conflicts that are too painful.

Finding oneself in order to say goodbye

Orlando hid the fact that he was in analysis, especially at the beginning, with the introduction of very private times: he got the times of the sessions wrong, he was confused about how many there were, he was uncertain about the times of absences.

In the fifth year of analysis, a kind of oblivion led him to skip session after session, without warning or explanation. The circumstances that convinced me to choose the formula of writing and sending a letter to remind him of me and ask about his intentions were the result of a combination of external facts and mental happenings that I felt I had to treat with velvet gloves.

Like Brandimarte worried about Ruggiero's tardiness, I was in doubt for a long time about what to do, finally choosing – mindful of the intolerable intrusiveness of the mother's phone calls – the formula of a letter, more respectful of separateness and more open to different arrangements.

In fact, it was necessary to take into account the circumstances that had led Orlando away from the analysis for many sessions. These circumstances were complex, ascribable to different levels of functioning in different ways and times.

Orlando had been called to teach in a distant location, too far away to come to the site of his analysis. This new situation was also the result of working together and marked the first affirmations on a professional level, a growing ability to tolerate frustrations and to deal with the group of colleagues. It was an assumption of responsibility, also in view of the fact that, in the meantime, he and his partner had had a child. Alongside an evolutionary aspect and testing himself in initiatory places of knowledge and in the often bitter relationship with his peer group (work colleagues), Orlando, in another place of his own, experienced the nature of our relationship, its *resilience*, my ability to keep him in mind and to tolerate his absence, without daily motherly phone calls. It was certainly also an escape from the analytical rule and, above all, from the emotions this entails. It was an escape from an encounter that was difficult to deal with, tinged with tyrannical power. However, what gave us the most food for thought, and what led me to act with great caution, was not so much the escape itself as the fact that it was an escape accompanied by denial and an unspoken, but very present, veto on talking about it. Violence towards the setting as the right to obtain a space of one's own, but also a den in which to hide one's loot, even at the risk of never being able to use it. Entering the inaccessible places of oblivion entailed paying special attention to transference and countertransference. If the transference bears the traces of Orlando's functioning on parallel tracks (analysis lessons on the one hand, eroticization on the other), the signs of countertransference alternated between a maternal tendency to indulge, allow exceptions, accept unconditionally, and a paternal reprimand. It was necessary to give him a point of reference that would be perceived neither as a lure nor as a call to order.

So I simply wrote to him that I had not seen him for a while and that I wondered what was going on.

Innocent monsters

As a child, he was terrified by the thought of sharks, which he feared to the point of becoming the subject of family ridicule. He was so afraid of their sudden appearance from the depths that he gave up taking pleasure in the sea. I happened to see sharks from very close-up and was struck by the incredible abundance of teeth, together with a total dullness in their gaze.

Seeing Orlando the first time, I had been struck by his teeth. His gaze, however, was furious, vital.

In contrast, dullness had, on many occasions, been the stance adopted by Orlando regarding his absences: session after session swallowed up and dragged into the abyss of wordless oblivion. Things had changed a great deal with the resumption of analytic work, following my letter and its processing.

Orlando brought the need to be sustained in contemplating *wonders*, such as those new and perhaps monstrous apparitions that appear in dreams. This is an achievement, since dreams, for a long time, could not be recounted, being objects subjected to a double discard, which dismayed him: from the image to narrating the dream, from the patient's speech to that of the analyst. "Dreams should be dreamt together", said Orlando – without words and without separateness. To separate, one must instead be able to allow the emotions linked to the origin of the encounter to exist in one's own Self. We must also discriminate guilt, inherited from the Oedipus complex, from innocent violence, linked to an animal instinct: grasping and hiding, biting and carrying into the abyss of the unconscious a prey object, of which no trace would remain.

A few months before the end of the analysis, together with a rediscovered relationship with his mother and sister and much talk of his father, visions of murders, concealment of corpses and . . . sharks began to appear in Orlando's dreams. Now very intent on working on the end of the analysis, he recognised himself in the murderous intentions and sensed his complicity with the shark.

We can now speak of the analytical history, of the separations, of his being swallowed by a shark in the past, sessions and analysts, and then disappearing into the abyss. Many transformations took place in analysis: fury gave way to a manageable, usable aggressiveness, and nostalgia to a veil of sadness. Lost assets were rediscovered, such as his relationship with his sister and his mother, now called upon to be a grandmother. Orlando took on the emotions and guilt associated with them, but to reach this point and remove the emotions of the original encounter from oblivion, it was necessary to recognise the shark's animal innocence and respect its plunging into the abyss. Orlando reappeared in the analysis, the shark in his dreams.

The comma between body and history:
strategies for a gentle pause

Living beings are impressionable, and impressions leave a trace. The nature of this trace is the subject of psychoanalytic research: it occupied Freud from the outset and still occupies psychoanalysts today, who now have at their disposal much more sophisticated scientific supporting material than Freud did, such as the definition of implicit memory, linked to remote emotional and affective experiences and the procedures adopted to cope with them.

If all living beings are impressionable, it seems to be characteristic of humans to potentially feel oppressed by impressions, a frustrating emotion to which the individual can react by attempting to return the impressions to the sender (projective identification) or by alienating, along with the impression, the experience that generated it – alienating the body that gives rise to it.

I have written about the comma between body and history to bring attention to a pause, a moment of suspension and perplexity that surprises those who experience it but does not interrupt the history, nor does it suffer it. It simply participates in it, sometimes with wonder. The pause is the time needed to allow oneself to be impressed by an emotion undergone, thus making it available for possible elaboration, initiating a story. This is also said about love stories.

The first impression in *histories* with our patients activates the sensorium – patients see and hear themselves – before speech. Patients look at us. With which eyes and ears is a matter of enquiry for both participants in the meeting; certainly the impression leaves a trace whose footprints the entire analytical journey follows. Looking at me intensely, almost as if I were a feast for her eyes, Anna, a young patient in analysis, exclaims, "Beautiful eyes", but she does not give me time to be impressed by this comment because she immediately adds, "Lardarse". The transition was so rapid between intake and evacuation as to leave no time to be treated, digested or elaborated. An encounter without time and without history.

If anything, I had to be the one to face it calmly, with an impression of aloofness. In my first meeting with Orlando, I heard complaints and protests in his tone of voice. I saw the shark without knowing why I was seeing it, who it was, or where it was hiding.

It took seven years of analysis for the shark to rise from the abyss, to be dreamt and thought of, freeing Orlando from the terrors of childhood acted out in the analytic setting.

The companionship of feeling is valuable if it provides a tenuous, vital trace, ensuring the work of perception and the feeling of existing. The companionship of feeling can become tyrannical if the rescuing adult does not withstand the impact with emotion while, however, also supporting the other's ability to cope with it. How? By letting patients teach them. I have often noted, also in this work, how the analyst's interventions in the form of questioning help patients, as they can thus identify with a learning function that is the analyst's before being theirs. Dreams without associations (the patients' teachings) are often blank proxies to an analyst's supposed knowledge, obstacles placed in the way of the analytic process, rarely clues to an ongoing process. To a traumatised and frightened patient, it is more useful to ask what they mean than to tell them that what they said is something other than what they said. Emotion announces an otherness; it exposes vulnerability: the situation of separateness must be sustained in order to allow a separation. The function of understanding is valuable in that it supports the subject in what he or she feels, but it does so by relying on its own distinct experience and history, albeit in contact with that of the person to be helped. The function of understanding in Freud heralds the function of *rêverie* which, according to Bion, implies being able to rely on negative capability, on pauses, therefore on commas.

Rêverie is all the more indispensable the less the patient is predisposed to the encounter, tends towards a *mannered* participation, or is there without being there, hiding their state *in primis* from themselves. The comma between body and history disappears, and with it the patient in its truth. If the patient is not supported in this uncertainty, they tend to hide.

Ways of hiding

There are various ways of hiding. A particular case is the hiding that I have called *animal*. It responds to an attempt to hide from oneself the times and places of an encounter and an exchange while nevertheless enjoying the continually renewable flavours of the encounter, with no connection to the experience of the encounter, buried (like the dog's bone in the ground) in oblivion. Returning to the initial theme, we could say that oblivion signals a fault between body and history, a failure of the function of understanding, a paradoxical encounter without loss and without memory. The unveiling of oblivion does not correspond to exposing the subject to a second loss (Siracusano, 1982) so much as to confronting it with the marasmus of the beginnings and the original, unsustainable encounter.

149

While hiding has to do with curiosity or, in the case of *animal* hiding, with the need to secretly savour old and new tastes, absences, whether they be justified or unjustified, call into question responsibility and therefore guilt. The adolescent's first move is to self-justify absences from school: an act of rebellion against *the father or whoever acts for him*, and at the same time an attempt, perhaps crude, to take responsibility, but also to try out temporary adventures in a secret elsewhere, distant from the official places of culture. In these terms, teenagers who go AWOL know they are elsewhere, savour the experiences and question themselves, often with the invaluable help of their peers. However, they have to deal with guilt, not only that of betraying the trust placed in them, but more profoundly that of stealing the father's signature and, along with it, his identity.

In the former case, although it burns, the sense of guilt signals that trust has been there; in the latter case of identity theft, we are dealing with a relationship that brands, from which one can only escape by stealing the signature and tearing off the brand. These two sources of guilt cannot be treated in the same way. The former belongs to the area of neurosis, the latter to very precarious states of the Self that must be approached with caution.

Disappearing is something else again: getting quickly out of sight, vanishing, but also dying. It suggests the sudden materialisation of a danger or an unbearable feeling of shame (I would like the ground to swallow me up) – it is necessary to vanish, possibly without leaving a trace, or go into hiding.

Hiding is an attitude that enlightens us about archaic forms of thought and a pertinent illustration of analytical work. It speaks to us of both intrapsychic work and the relationship between subjects. The concept is adaptable to the need – particularly pressing in the presence of trauma – to keep one's emotional turmoil alive, provided one has access to a secret space. The hidden individual does not cease to live, nor to experience, nor to think – they certainly do that in their own way, in secret. However, the hidden individual cannot call themselves such except as regards their relationship, as particular as it may be, with the reality from which they have fled; they maintain a relationship with subjects who are not living in their clandestine state. They do not break off communication but do not say where they are. They send messages, but it is necessary to be able to decipher them. They disappear not for the sake of disappearing, but because disappearing is necessary to their mental life (and some-times to their life), although hiding would be a failure of living if it did not have a time limit.

The time limit, as I learnt from myth and reconsidered in my analytic experience, is adolescence, the effective age that re-engages body and history. I proposed thinking of it also as a *position*, reached in adolescence, aimed at sustaining a separation without denying the experiences that have promoted and supported it. This is also the case for the concluding phases of analysis, which often reactivate and re-elaborate emotional arrangements linked to the *adolescent position*.

Reading Vidal-Naquet (1981), I was struck by a clandestinity erected as a rule by Greek society in the definition of the status of the adolescent.

The ancient Greeks told us little about the status of children, relegated like women to an elsewhere without history. Myths and poets, however, deliver us torrents of children who are devoured or exposed on mountains in the hope of not having to reckon with the grown child, the adolescent. From myths and psychoanalytic work, we know that an exposed child corresponds to a ferocious adolescent. The theory of *posteriority* tells us that we cannot escape this correspondence. Psychoanalytic work takes charge of making contact with the clandestine patient.

A final consideration regarding guilt. Clandestinity is not sub-ject to censure; it is a statute of exception outside the rules, which claims to become the rule. It makes no sense, therefore, to call the clandestine person to order without first getting the reasons for their clandestinity out of the way. Time is what it is, often the time of an analysis. An untimely call to order may, on the contrary, expose the clandestine patient once again to the tyranny of needs and affects, and the reaction may be violent. And yet, indulgence of the excep-tion with no time limit leaves adolescents and patients in a non-place, lost, timelessly encountered, in analyses that, not being the result of work that is also initiation, cannot be concluded.

On vulnerability

I will now try, with the help of my patients, to show how the ability to sustain one's separateness and the drive towards separation move-ments are combined in the creation of identity and the assumption of temporality.

Achille

Figure 7.1 Achille, his first drawing

It is no coincidence that I call my little patient (five years old at the first consultation) Achille. His first drawing reminds me of the Homeric hero (see drawing), the only son of Peleus and Thetis, possessed by a ferocity equal to the threat of death hanging over his sad fate – *doomed to a short life*, Homer tells us in the Iliad (Book XVIII). Powerful and vulnerable at the same time because of a flaw in his mother's extreme attempt to secure him for eternity. The mother who holds her child by the heel while trying to immerse him in water (the Styx) that would make him immortal is a mother who struggles to leave her son to his fate. With the same act with which she wants him to be hers forever, she consigns him to a destiny of vulnerability. This vulnerability is not so much the fate of death, to which all humans are subject, but it is a mental position constantly on the alert to avert precisely this fate, unacceptable even before unthinkable. The position of vulnerability implies the more or less remote threat that the encounter with the other will result in an assault aimed at overwhelming the subject. The perception of one's own vulnerability, if not rescued, generates an experience of helplessness that becomes a challenge to omnipotence. If the encounter becomes possession, the tyrannical set-up that derives from it is repeated in the transference: the analytical work, accommodating

152

excluded aspects of the self, will try to give these aspects the right to existence first and then to speech.

I will briefly summarise Achille's situation in his family: the son of separated parents, his mother suffers from a hidden but desperate resentment towards her family of origin, her own mother in particular, and her husband. Two lost pregnancies, the first a miscarriage and the second an abortion, the former before Achille's birth and the latter after it. Achille functions simultaneously as a repository of maternal resentment and as her avenging arm for the offence suffered. The father in turn reacts to this scenario by distancing himself not only from his ex-wife but also from Achille, which helps to confirm the child's experience of being a worthless child.

Achille is clumsy in his movements, suffers from nightmares, draws little and in dark colours, and attracts the (hostile) attention of adults (at kindergarten in particular) with excited, aggressive behaviour. His friends are generally the unruliest in the class, and he is often punished, so much so that the teachers have reported his behaviour to his parents several times.

I realise that I am dealing with a very distressed mother who would herself need help, with a child struggling with anxieties which risk impeding harmonious development emotionally, socially, and at school, and with a parental couple incapable of communicating without accusing each other and using the child as proof of the other's dysfunctions.

Rather than a couple asking for help for their child, I feel that I am caught in a tangle of characters who function by echoing. The mother attributes to Achille suffering that is above all hers ("He's still back in the time his parents were together"), the father blames him for an attitude that is now above all maternal ("He always wants to win"), and Achilles feels that he is nothing, threatened and powerless, and reacts violently: a tyrannical bond is gradually established between us too, one that is very difficult to undo.

I am leaving out the work done on the family distress and the attempt to differentiate the areas to focus on Achille, his way of functioning and my response.

However, I must point out that my experience of intrusion and increasing impotence in the face of this family's burden of suffering constitutes a countertransference clue to a tyrannical, all-encompassing transference: meeting is dying.

So I will begin with the first meeting, at the start of our journey.

If meeting means dying

Achille arrives accompanied by his mother. He is a good-looking child, albeit on the verge of obesity, with an inquiring gaze. He leaves his mother without difficulty, but first strongly reproaches her for always repeating the things he says.

Once in the consulting room, he seems heartened when I tell him that his father has (meanwhile) phoned me and that I will see him.

When I tell him who I am and then show him the calendar to indicate when we will see each other again (after the summer holidays), he exclaims: "And when all these months have passed, will we die?" I ask why he worries about that. He adds: "No one tells me, I've never seen anyone die". However, he quickly abandons these reflections to throw himself at the material at his disposal, which he grabs and then immediately drops. For perhaps the first and last time, he uses family characters to put all the children in the toilet, laughing sarcastically. Towards the end of the session, he asks me if his mother will have heard what we said and asks (expecting a questioning from her about the content of the session), "Can I say I don't remember?"

The resentment shown by Achille, who in the waiting room reproached his mother for repeating everything he says, confirms to me an echoing functioning between Achilles and his mother. He and his mother live in a controlled space. They need and simultaneously suffer from the presence of shared speech, which bounces from one to the other, without being able to take charge of their emotions.

Achille complains, not unjustly, that no one has accompanied him in a mourning process: "No one tells me, I've never seen anyone die". The fact that he functions in echo to his mother makes him feel enslaved by his relationship with her, but at the same time, separation makes him too vulnerable a being and constitutes a mortal threat to his psyche.

Achille is unable to sustain the state of separateness, as shown by his eager, unconstructive throwing himself onto the play material. He is relentlessly searching without finding. His body, through obesity and perpetual hunger, signals the presence of an anxiety without containment or answer.

I sense that he is capable of getting excited, although much less of pausing with his emotions, which he seems instead to get rid of together with the children, transforming in real time, we might say, the intrusion suffered because of the emotional movement into an expulsion laden with sadism. Helplessness without succour or understanding is transformed into tyranny. In the places of the mind, this will cause aspects of the Self and the relationship between subjects to go into hiding; in the analytical relationship, it will exert its fierce violence and dull intolerance.

Achille was first probably invested by the long shadow of his mother's depression due to the two miscarriages, one before and one after his birth, and then by the vortex of his parents' separation, without either of them being able to help him elaborate his mourning for so many painful separations. In deeds, before words, he will express what appears in the gesture of putting all the children in the toilet: he feels like a poop-child, evacuated from his parents' minds, and so unable to be guided by the trace of an encounter – a worthless child. Much later, he will say, in a particularly dramatic moment: "I never wanted to be born".

On the other hand, if the only means of defending himself from maternal intrusion is not remembering, we can imagine how difficult it is for this child to learn from experience, intent as he is on erasing the experiences he has, lest they be taken away from him by his mother's word.

To prevent the trace left by his encounter with me from being captured and dissolving into echoes in his mother's word, Achille ends up burying the trace and losing it himself. His advancement will tend not to be a journey but rather a repetition of the same thing.

In the second consultation, almost two months later, Achille simultaneously behaves as if no time has passed and as if years have passed. He quickly recognises and remembers all the material used in the previous session but interrupts himself and, looking at me carefully (despite the fact that I feel in good shape after the holidays), exclaims: "How you've aged". In vain, I try to understand what might be the signs that have led Achilles to this observation. I speak to Achille about time (which seems so long to him that he has had to remove it). He then repeats the same concern he expressed in the first session – that his mother will grow old and die, that I will die and that he too will die.

The activity is feverish, marked, like the first time, by great verbal aggression. However, in the confusion, a sound rises up, barely audible – Achille hums "I'm a little strange" and struggles to leave my studio at the end of the session.

155

The secret paths of communication:
notes from the underground

Figure 7.2 Achille, drawing two years later

I will now recount a session that took place almost two years after the above-mentioned moments.

Achille immediately begins to draw (a rare event). At the edge of the sheet he draws a child, then some very dark musical notes. He tells me that the child is him. I simply comment that the notes are big and dark (to me, they also seem sad and belligerent, but I keep quiet about this). He then adds some lighter notes and draws a coloured line between himself and the notes, a boundary (hardly visible now). He tells me that he likes singing, we talk about sad notes and happy notes, and little by little he fills the whole remaining part of the sheet with brown, covering the traced boundary and concealing himself completely. Struck, I ask, "Where did you end up . . . in a pile of dirt?" Achille looks at me surprised (I will better

156

understand why at the end of the session) and says: "I'm in a dark room, I'm dreaming of singing, the room is all made of wood, that's why it's brown". I comment that he is trying to get me to understand how much music he has at his disposal, but perhaps he is a bit lonely in this all-wooden room (which, at that moment, makes me think of a coffin). He then tells me about the colours of his room at home – white and green.

On leaving the consulting room at the end of the session, he unhesitatingly walks over to some children's books I keep in the waiting room and pulls out one depicting a mole in a pile of brown earth.

Like playing, the drawing a child makes in a session is not just any drawing, but can move from act to representation and vice versa. It still remains a shared operation, with nuances: like certain dream narratives, it can be presented and immediately torn up without any possibility of further shared work. At other times, however, as in the session presented, it unwinds and is modified following associative movements: it is redrawn following an evocative word, just as the detail of a dream can be recalled following a word from the analyst, as can be recalled. The drawing presents analogies and differences with the dream narrative: if it is true that the dream is nocturnal and the drawing is created in daylight, it should be noted that daytime remnants and dark thoughts are interwoven in the drawing as in the dream. Just as the dream narrative can take on different shades depending on the vocabulary used, the temperature of the relationship established in that moment between analysand and analyst, and the resonance that the words uttered in the session evoke, so too does the drawing, in the way it reveals itself in the sequence of themes presented, the quality of the stroke, the spatial arrangement, the choice of colours, as well as the vocal commentary that the child gives, when it happens to be given. The drawing in these cases resembles a dream had in the presence of the analyst. Waking dream thought. Both the telling of the dream and the evolution of a drawing trace in the analyst's mind a scenario in which sharing and discarding alternate.

Dreams and drawings are therefore productions to be handled delicately and with the indispensable help of the analysand.

The drawing by Achille that takes place before my eyes is a rare occurrence and therefore all the more delicate. So I will not say to Achille that his notes look to me like cannonballs, that his notes are dark, an anonymous word, but one that evidently evokes something in Achille, who immediately juxtaposes the dark notes with light ones. Thus, we have different voices here, as in opera – dark voices and light voices. In the shading, solids and voids. Dramatically different tones: the appearance of this duplicity, evoking an encounter, a confrontation and possibly a conflict entails risks, and so Achille literally disappears.

This sense of *losing sight,* of Achille's retreat into a dark, clandestine refuge is the overriding affect I feel in the session, which leads me to comment on it all with a question: *Where did you end up – in a pile of dirt?* The surprise is both mine and Achille's. I was lucky, I guess, because this sudden brown overlay concealing the child-Achille had also made me think of a pile of poop, of being in Achille's shit and also of my own, often, being with him. Better *earth,* an unsaturated word that tastes of life and death and allows further additions to the drawing and its narration. My surprise is intertwined with Achille's and his response, extended, was probably helped by being the answer to a curiosity of mine, to a not-knowing (another would have been to explain to him my hypothesis about his hiding place): "I'm in a dark room, I'm dreaming of singing, the room is all made of wood, that's why it's brown". Here, then, dream and drawing intersect, but it seems as if Achille, looking for his (all-wooden) sounding board, is in danger of ending up in a coffin.

He retreats for now to a clandestine hideout, from where a *mole* can come out to carry messages and observe, but also spy and betray: this is Achille's daily task between one and the other parent. It concerns as much the hidden exchange of messages between one and the other of the spouses as, more distantly, other mournings and aborted ideals that cannot be spoken of. Suspending the memory of the many sessions in which both Achille and I were effectively in the shit, I question and interrogate myself (*where did you end up?*). Uncertainty that allows Achille to give me *his* position and give voice to a dream, thereby opening a dialogue.

Being, experiencing, knowing: Teresa

In solitude or with others always
alone I remain, I myself do not keep
the company of feeling. An uninhabited ship,

I sail the sea of life,
more alone than solitude. I am outside
of that which in me thinks.

Pessoa (1988, 109) [my translation]

Masud Khan (1974) argued for distinguishing three levels of psychoanalytic work, according to the nature of the patient's problems. These levels are being, experiencing and knowing.

These levels appear to us most emphatically in psychotic, borderline and neurotic patients, respectively, but they are intertwined, as Bion also showed us, in everyone's experience and in every analytic treatment.

Being, experiencing and knowing seem to have to come together to allow the body to inscribe itself in its history and to allow the subject to become a person and thus be able to tell their story in the changing multiplicity of characters of their own internal world and in the incessant interaction of identifications.

If the connection between body and history is lost, the body becomes a place of implosion where impotence and omnipotence face each other and fight the last, desperate duel, without commas and without history.

In order for the encounter to leave its trace and for that trace to constitute a *point of reference*, a companion, albeit a secret one (Gaburri, 1986) and a starting point for subsequent encounters, it is necessary to be able to support the subject in the state of encounter, allowing them to be, to feel and to know. The impossibility for the rescuing adult of establishing a belief (Zapparoli, 1987), an integration between *saying* and *feeling*, has as its first consequence the fact of not being able to rely, as Pessoa evokes, on the *company of feeling* in constructing that feeling of continuity in time on which identity is founded. Instead of bearing the traces of an encounter with the rescuing adult, the body becomes alien, turning into a double that becomes a threatening elsewhere, a den of nasty surprises, an otherness to be exorcised. The encounter leaves no trace, and the company of feeling (experiencing, trying) is bypassed by a violent, excited and exciting short-circuit between impotence and omnipotence.

Analytic work tends to take on miraculous expectations, and the analyst risks being trapped as an accomplice in an omnipotent enterprise. It is necessary to be able to come out of this *claustrum* to open up to a feeling of curiosity and hope (belief, trust), in which it is possible to sustain one's own separateness, perceive one's environment, feel curious about new spaces, and prepare new separations.

Teresa was in her third year of analysis (four sessions a week). Married with children, a job that she was unable to move beyond being a hobby to become a worthwhile activity, and, by her own admission, an ageless, sexless body. Starting in her teens and continuing into her 20s, Teresa had used hard drugs, of which her injured body still bore the results and traces.

The panic attacks from which she suffered severely restricted her movements and the possibilities, despite being available to her, of affirmation.

The first crucial step in our journey saw an attempt to transform an all-encompassing request – *deliver me from evil* (Green, 1988) and from the panic attacks – into an encounter in which we could try to understand each other. I had observed, from one session to another, that alongside the moment of being overwhelmed leading to the panic attack, there was a particular attitude of the patient towards what was happening in her body: if *experiencing-feeling* led directly to the panic attack, the other escape route was that of an indifferent detachment (*blissful indifference*), of an alienation from her own body, and of a development of a series of strategies bordering on magical exorcism, in which the patient, closed in her own magical crypt, distant from herself and the world, relied not on *experiencing-feeling*, but on magic aimed at exorcising the perturbing experience, the encounter with otherness. In the background, there was the idea of being able to present herself to the world without paying the price for her dependence on the world – an attempt at self-generation that denied gender and generational differences.

Highly evocative in this sense had been her description at the beginning of the analysis of the impossibility, in spatial terms, of distinguishing the boundary between the "antiquarians' district", her mother's place, a herald of nobility and professional perfection, and the "junkies' district", inhabited by a population, like her, with neither hope nor time, by beings intent on heating themselves up, in the often fatal embrace of heroin. No boundary between zones, no comma between body and history, no mental work. If anything, when needed, false papers were made, dressing up a stealthily stolen identity to be exhibited, at the risk of being continually unmasked.

The failure of the function of understanding had led Teresa to visualise the state of encounter as a tyrannical occupation by the object. In order to remove the sentient body from this tyranny, Teresa had made it into a refuge as hidden as it was explosive, occupied by an evil from which to be freed, without wasting any more time in the complex entanglements of an encounter, with its rules and structures. In the transference, Teresa repeated her search for an object that would release her from feeling panic – not an encounter, not a signalling anguish, not an initiation, but an unpredictable alternation between an object colluding in an omnipotent operation and an object reduced to helplessness, a useless spectator of strategies devoted to failure.

One day when these mental operations appeared clearer to me, speaking partly to myself and partly to the patient, I said: "I don't know if I can do anything for your panic attacks, but maybe together we can do something for you".

She jumped up furiously, got angry with me, then quietened down and her speech became more communicative, more alive.

Fury, together with fright, are the affects of helplessness, an act purely in response to a nameless terror, to the perception of an encounter with an other than the Self, with whom one is not ready to deal.

However, the trace, albeit slight, of the previous encounters allowed the patient a rapid transformation of fury into angry aggression. She sought and found, as Racamier (1962) would say, a welcoming obstacle on which to mould herself: the work carried on, but, at least for a while, it was work for two.

Paradoxical communication on my part, which nevertheless, along with the declaration of helplessness regarding the panic attacks, introduced an appreciation of the patient's contribution and a hope. We would have to try to learn, and she would have to try to teach me, somewhere between the maternal trust that the infant will show the way and the paternal firmness that says: "You can do it yourself".

Two years later, a dream. If the contact barrier becomes *périphérique*

I will now recount a sequence of dreams and events, some two years later. In the meantime, the panic attacks have diminished, the patient's work position is more defined and stronger, her relationship with her children has improved a lot, while the conjugal relationship remains mysterious, apparently good, but with a strained sexuality and a veiled conflict. The fact remains that the patient returns, periodically, to the refrain: "I'll never get out of this".

The session is on a Wednesday, the third of four weekly sessions (in italics are the comments the patient makes while narrating the dream). After a brief beginning in which she tells me of her difficulty those days taking the children to school (partly real, partly associated with her own difficulties bringing herself to the session), she recounts:

I had a dream. We were in X., me, M. [husband] and the children, and the architect, the one who helped me with the house in X. (she adds: *the relationship with him is becoming a true friendship, so much so that I feel I can be myself with him, and he with me too, I saw him yesterday as well because we went to see a house together that my sister wants to buy in Milan. . .*). We were walking around X. [foreign city]: in my dream I saw the neighbourhood where we lived, which is a very long neighbourhood, between the centre and the suburbs . . . towards the centre, the houses are very beautiful, then half and half, then the suburbs begin, the boundary is the *périphérique* [ring road, but Theresa uses the French term] beyond which, in the dream, there was a green space, left completely free of buildings . . . I said to myself, in the dream: *How good the French are, leaving a little bit of nature and don't immediately rush to build. . .* Then the dream scene changes, this time I am with C. (*do you remember? That friend of mine from London, for years she couldn't have children and recently had one*). We were at the tollbooth of the motorway, the tollbooth keeper (half tollbooth keeper and half policeman) had a dog, the aggressive kind, the dog put his muzzle into the car, I wasn't that worried because the car was closed . . . then all of a sudden the dog jumped in and put his muzzle right next to my face, so with my hand I gave him a little rough scratch behind the ears, I know that dogs like it.

In this session and the following one, Teresa continued to work around the dream, her professional projects and her affects, swinging between a pleasant feeling of reality and, once again, the ambush of anxiety.

As for me, although aware of the skill attributed to the French for leaving ample free space, my mind was very crowded with material from the dream.

The next sequence of sessions took place in the following week.

I remember Monday's session as one of the most difficult of the whole analysis. Teresa is in pain, she fears she won't make it, she is gripped by a fear, not unreasonable, that it is serious and that I can't understand her: "I can't say I'm afraid, my mother wouldn't understand and as for my father, I see him there like a wet rag".

I sense this risk: I oscillate between the impression of understanding the patient's experiences and the sensation of losing her again. I try not to abandon her, even though I feel the difficulty of the undertaking. We return to the landscape free of buildings beyond the *périphérique*, something that now seems to us to be related not so much to the need for uncontaminated spaces but to a very painful sense of emptiness, symmetrical to the excessive organisation of the city that she would like to leave, to the rigidity of its layout and to the noble aspect of the centre.

In Tuesday's session, the patient, who seems to be feeling better, brings to the analysis a double: as a child, she had given herself another name and another surname, an *alter ego* in which to hide. Its first name, Federica, was a name she considered much nobler than her own, while her surname (or family name), Galbusera, she had taken from a completely anonymous factory whose name could be read through the windows of her school.

Here is Wednesday's session, the third of the week:

P: Walking up the stairs the other day, I heard two ladies talking about the people on the fourth floor always leaving the lift door open. One of them sounded like my mother with that air of confidence and superiority that made me feel constantly scolded and scorned . . . Maybe the lady isn't like that, but with my mother, in addition, there's that her confidence came from nothing . . .

A: Rootless?

P: I know almost nothing about my grandparents, half Sardinian half Friulian, my grandfather was the manager of for a nobleman, in fact he didn't work much but he liked antique furniture and everything that the nobleman he worked for liked . . . it was as if he was him . . . my grandmother was more concrete . . . my mother must have been beautiful, a beautiful body, blue eyes, black hair, so beautiful that she was sometimes photographed for fashion magazines . . . I know little about her, although I'm trying to find out more. When she was very young, she went to babysit for a noble family in Y. It was in a castle and every now and then she tells us about this beautiful place . . . she had also babysat in Y and had become a family friend . . . then, when she was 25, she went to Z. (an auction house), I don't know how she got there, then she returned to R. with the director of Z., they moved into a beautiful flat in the square, and opened the first Z. gallery in Italy . . . then my father arrived, and yes, he was well-to-do, but his character was nothing like hers . . . Mama seems to be made of rock, but in fact the impression is that she is made of sand and if you lean on her, she falls apart and sinks. I dreamt last night: in the first one, there were sculptures and chimps, it seemed like a philosophical problem, how to bring chimps closer to art, in fact they were going in and out of . . . something that looked like sculptures . . . Then, towards morning, I had another dream: I was in a boat, in the cabin, under the surface of the water, but through the porthole I could see a beautiful sunset, red on the horizon, I thought happily that even though I was locked in there, I could look out and enjoy the sunset . . . in fact in the boat there was a prisoner who was still me . . . at a certain point the horizon changes and I see that we've reached land . . . happily, I break the porthole and jump into the water, I'm a bit surprised that the hunt for the prisoner isn't starting, that it's me and it's not me . . . they let him go and instead they scurry around the anchor. I can say about this dream that coming out of yesterday's session [further work on the *périphérique*], I was happy because I finally felt more real, even if the image was disturbing. I recognised myself in that terrible feeling of emptiness . . . however I have the impression that I need small measures to get out of the porthole, it wasn't the arrival in New York . . .

A: We've talked about roots, and here there's an anchor, a kind of umbilical cord that keeps you close to the earth . . . and there is still a limit in this dream, the line of the horizon, for example, but it's a warmer limit than the *périphérique*, and there is a sense of time, the end of a day . . .

P: Now I remember something else from the chimp dream: at one point an aunt of my mother-in-law's, a gallery owner, appeared and said, "Have you been to Paderno Dugnano?". As if it were a very famous place for art, like Sabbioneta.

A: Everything's more domestic in this dream: not Sabbioneta, but Paderno Dugnano.

P: I went to Paderno Dugnano some time ago, overcoming a lot of fear, because a friend of F.'s [her son] had invited him to a birthday party . . . it was a beautiful 17th-century villa, but the owner was very easy-going and I was comfortable with her . . . a bit older than me, a bit masculine . . . Strange, this morning for a while I still had that nice feeling of being real, of having a body, then I said to myself, I'll drink some coffee to give me a boost, and suddenly I got anxious [the dosage of coffee is one of the alchemies she practises to ward off attacks].

A: [*Throwing it out there*] No coffee for the chimps?

P: [*With a cheerful giggle*] We were playing a silly game yesterday, in the studio, with my workmates. One said a word and the other an association, my colleague said "coffee" and, by association, I said "tranquiliser", instead coffee was matched with sex . . .

Old gridlocks and new travel companions

For Teresa, the state of encounter does not find connections to allow the body to access and take root in its own history but turns into a state of *impasse*, presented in the symptom of panic attacks and represented in the dream by the impassable limit of the *périphérique*, with its chaotic traffic, difficulties in finding the right exit, and its fortified aspect, a rampart. If the shield protecting against stimuli fails, it creates at the ego's limit a state of perpetual, excited and noisy gridlock, which allows no way out. The rescuing adult (*architect-analyst*), even though seeming to facilitate the patient's movements within the city and within her own psychic space, does not yet seem able to ensure a passage to somewhere else (even a clear place where she can wander about, experimenting with her own psychosomatic equipment, perhaps temporarily under a false name). This passage is instead watched over by the *tollbooth keeper-police officer*, half guarantor, half at risk of exchanging guarantees and power. The *contact barrier*, whose function should be "protecting reality perception from being overwhelmed by emotions and phantasies emanating from within" (Bléandonu, 1990, 153), is in fact configured in the dream as a gridlock of sensory impressions (beta elements) that condemns the subject to a vertiginous spinning in on themselves. This situation makes the exchange between culture and nature impossible, while the idealisation of the Origins and the city centre constitutes an overflow that ends up projecting itself as an emptiness beyond the limit, at the same time making nature a virgin terrain to be conquered, access to which is nevertheless impossible. It is no coincidence that the whole thing takes place in a city half known to the patient, who has lived there for years but is still a stranger to it. There appears, however, to conclude the dream, a character with two faces and two functions, half guarantor of the journey, half policeman, and a movement of integration that is announced with the appearance of the dog, with its entry, perhaps a little abruptly, into the car, and with the patient's perception that she knows how to handle it. An animal on board and an integrating instinctuality.

Perhaps one of those dreams that *turn the page* (Quinodoz, 1999), dreams that appear unexpectedly at times when the patient manifests a better integration of psychic life, revealing, paradoxically, the original matrix of the phantasm and its regressive aspects.

It is difficult to say how much the malaise of Monday's session is related to a dysfunction of the analyst, or if it is an enactment, or a repetition in the transference of absolutely dramatic moments in Teresa's life.

If I listen to the countertransference clues, I find anguish and helplessness, together with a great vital force (*a living, secret companion*): "Come on, we'll make it!".

In fact, the *périphérique*, even if it is too busy, is still a limit and is arranged in a very different way from the deceptive and treacherous continuity between the junkies' district and the antique dealers' district. In order to cross this boundary, to establish links between body and history, between nature and culture, it would be necessary to enter one's own time, to make the unattainable and bogus nobility of the mother and father more usable and familiar. My reminder of time and affects brings to Teresa's memory a fragment of a dream and a memory: in the dream a maternal *alter ego*, who, in the dream recounted a few sessions later, invites her to visit Paderno Dugnano and not Sabbioneta, where Paderno Dugnano, which lies beyond the outskirts of Milan, is not a place of high monumental prestige. In her recollection: "I went to Paderno Dugnano some time ago, overcoming a lot of fear, because a friend of F.'s [son] had invited him to a birthday party . . . it was a beautiful 17th-century villa, but the owner was very easy-going and I was comfortable with her . . . a bit older than me, a bit masculine".

The *périphérique* has been crossed, as Teresa proudly asserts when associating with the dream. Not a noble stone mother, rather one who crumbles into sand at first contact, but a noble villa with an easy-going owner, who (perhaps precisely because she combines paternal and maternal functions in being *a bit masculine*) helps Teresa to feel well, more real.

As for the sequence of the sessions, I think I can say that Monday's session was, in more dramatic terms, similar to the session in which I had told the patient that I was not sure I could get rid of the panic attacks but that I would be by her side to understand.

In Tuesday's session, we had understood, to the great relief of the patient, that the emptiness beyond the *périphérique* was in some way linked to the overflowing of the inside, which had allowed Teresa to take up, together with her own history, the painful history of her parents' uprooting, obliged, before her, to fill an emptiness with heavy, not very usable constructions.

The name of the double chosen by the patient as a child seems very interesting in this context, as, in a somewhat dreamy, alien state, she let her gaze and thoughts wander beyond the window (another limit) of her classroom.

Federica Galbusera is the name and particular figure of a double. Federica is a noble name, in the idea of the patient as a child, but it is not the name that ensures the passage from one generation to the next, transmitting the relative inheritance. The surname, on the other hand, is entirely anonymous, taken from an equally anonymous factory, suggesting fabricated children, with no meeting of the sexes and no thought. An incongruous identity, perhaps what in the dream drew the attention of the *tollbooth keeper-police officer*. Limits are also present in that dream fragment: the motorway tollbooth, at the origin of a journey and the car with the windows barely open. It is a double limit that should be at the origin of a journey: to set off, in addition to an identity document certifying one's origins, one must take on board, with the dog, also animality and affects, an experience that now seems possible if the dog, from a ferocious animal, is transformed into a travelling companion. The friend-travelling companion, who could not have children, seems to allude to an

167

impossibility to generate, linked to an impossible encounter between generations.

   The incongruous double is a character consigned to hiding, from which she only emerges when, looking out of the porthole of the ship, Teresa can first glimpse the warm line of the horizon, enter time and drop anchor. Another fragment of the chimp dream can thus appear: exiled from their habitat and forced to contend with stone sculptures. It is interesting that, as with my asking Achilles, *where did you end up?*, here too, in the dream, there is the interrogative formula: *Have you ever been to Paderno Dugnano?* It really seems that the questioning helps these patients to feel like protagonists and not that they are just carrying out a programme set by some travel agency.

Bibliography

Alvarez, A. (1992), *Live Company*. Routledge, Hove.

Ariosto, L. (1516), *Orlando Furioso*. (Trans. Harington, J., 1591).

Aulagnier, P. (1985), "Birth of a body, origin of a history" (Trans. Weller, A., 2015), in *"Naissance d'un corps, origine d'une histoire"* in *Corps et histoire*, Les Belles Lettres, 1986. pp. 100.

Badoni, M. (1985), Aggrapparsi, aggredire, pensare: evoluzione dell'istinto filiale. Argonauti, 27, 301–316.

Badoni, M. (1994), "La clandestinità nella organizzazione sociale e nella relazione analitica". Atti del X Congresso Nazionale della Società Psicoanalitica Italiana *La risposta dell'analista e le trasformazioni del campo analitico*. Rimini.

Bettelheim, B. (1967), The empty fortress: infantile autism and the birth of the self. Free Press, New York.

Bion, W.R. (1968), "Opacity of Memory and Desire", in *Attention and Interpretation*. Tavistock, London, 1970.

Bléandonu, G. (1990), *Wilfred Bion – His Life And Works, 1897–1979* (Trans. Pajaczkowska, C.). Free Association Books, New York, 1994.

Bleger, J. (1967), "Psicoanalisi del setting psicoanalitico". In Genovese, C. (a cura di), *Setting e processo psicoanalitico*. Cortina, Milano, 1988.

De Simone, G. (2002), "La memoria e l'oblio". In *Rivista di Psicoanalisi*, 48, 3, pp. 551–565.

Di Chiara, G. (1990), "La stupita meraviglia, l'autismo e la competenza difensiva". In *Rivista di Psicoanalisi*, 36, 2, pp. 441–457.

Di Chiara, G. (1992), "L'incontro, il racconto, il commiato. Tre fattori fondamentali dell'esperienza psicoanalitica". In Nissim Momigliano, L.,

Robutti, A. (a cura di), *L'esperienza condivisa. Saggi sulla relazione psicoanalitica*. Cortina, Milano.

Di Chiara, G. (2003), *Curare con la psicoanalisi*. Cortina, Milano.

Ferenczi, S. (1929), "The Unwanted Child And His Death Instinct". In *Final Contributions to the Problems and Methods of Psychoanalysis*. Karnac, London, 1980.

Freud, S. (1895), *Project for a Scientific Psychology*, SE, vol. II, 1955.

Freud, S. (1911), *Formulations on the Two Principles of Mental Functioning*. SE, vol. XII, 1958.

Freud, S. (1912–1913), *Totem and Taboo*. SE, vol. XIII.

Freud, S. (1920), *Beyond the Pleasure Principle*. SE, vol. XVIII.

Freud, S. (1924), A Note upon the "Mystic Writing-Pad" (1925). SE, vol. X.

Gaburri, E. (1986), "Dal gemello immaginario al compagno segreto". In *Rivista di Psicoanalisi*, 32, 4, pp. 509–520.

Gaddini, E. (1981), "Acting out in the psychoanalytic session". In *A Psychoanalytic Theory of Infantile Experience: Conceptual and Clinical Reflections*. Tavistock, London, 1992.

Green, A. (1973), *Fabric of Affect in the Psychoanalytic Discourse*. Routledge, Hove, 1999.

Green, A. (1988), "Pourquoi le mal?". In *Nouvelle Revue de Psychanalyse*, 38, pp. 239–261.

Hermann, I. (1943), *L'istinto filiale*. Feltrinelli, Milano, 1974.

Hillman, J. (1983), *Healing Fiction*. Station Hill Press.

Homer, (1990), *The Iliad* (Trans. Fagles), Penguin Classics, Book XVIII.

Kerényi, K. (1951), *The Gods of the Greeks*. Thames & Hudson, London.

Khan, M.M.R. (1974), *The Privacy of the Self*. Routledge, Hove, 1996.

Macciò, M., Vallino, D. (2004), "Il senso di esistere del neonato e l'attrazione fatale dell'identificazione". In Borgogno, F. (a cura di), *Ferenczi oggi*. Boringhieri, Torino.

Nissim Momigliano, L. (1989–1990), "Psicoanalista allo specchio". In *L'ascolto rispettoso. Scritti psicoanalitici*. Cortina, Milano, 2001.

Ogden, T.H. (2001), *Conversations at the Frontier of Dreaming*. Routledge, Hove, 2002.

Pessoa, F. (1988), *Faust*. Einaudi, Torino.

Quinodoz, D. (1994), *Emotional Vertigo: Between Anxiety and Pleasure*. Routledge, Hove, 2002.

Quinodoz, J.-M. (1999), "Dreams that Turn Over a Page: Integration Dreams with Paradoxical Regressive Content". In *The International Journal of Psychoanalysis*, 80, pp. 225–238.

Racamier, P.-C. (1962), "Propos sur la réalité dans la théorie psychanalytique". In *Revue Française de Psychanalyse*, 26, 6.

Racamier, P.-C. (1992), *Le génie des origines. Psychanalyse et psychose*. Payot, Paris.

Siracusano, F. (1982), "Il messaggio nascosto nell'oblio". In *Rivista di Psicoanalisi,* 38, pp. 320–328.

Vidal-Naquet, P. (1981), *The Black Hunter: Forms of Thought and Forms of Society in the Greek World.* Johns Hopkins University Press, 1998.

Zapparoli, G.C. (1987), *La psicosi e il segreto.* Boringhieri, Torino.

PART FIVE

A TIME FOR DELIVERING

Generating

When the black landline still used to ring in the waiting room, it was my pride and curiosity to get to it first: disappointment was lurking . . . "Who's speaking?" "Badoni". "Which Badoni?" "Marta Badoni". The last of 12, 11 of whom were girls, the conclusion was soon drawn: they were not looking for me. The first consequence was that I became very fond of the name my parents, having exhausted the resources of relatives whose memory they could pass on, found for me: it was original.

So original that in my first years as a member of the Milanese Psychoanalysis Centre, I was much more Marta than Badoni for all my colleagues.

But it did not end there. Before me, a packed line-up of females had already worked hard to find their position: ancient literature, architecture, engineering for the first and only male; engineering, however, also for the first daughter of the second marriage, more by imposition than by choice, given the premature death in the war of the only male child. The workings of the family industry gave precise indications on the subject to be passed on.

At that time, I was five years old. Perhaps the war, perhaps a more hidden need to escape from undue constraints had made me choose, at home and in the garden, two safe hiding places: no one

DOI: 10.4324/9781003560647-13

would find me there. I liked being in the world; I was fascinated by the play of light that the leaves of the plane trees created with the help of the wind, I liked playing with dogs and cats and listening to the adults' discussions, even though I understood little. There were many topics swirling around the family dinner table, a moment of great vulnerability for me if the adult discussions challenged my ability to understand. As a reaction, I tried to find my own way of intercepting the "grown-ups'" statements and joining in with my own considerations or tangential jokes, sometimes amusing, sometimes outlandish. That was how I came to be called the Queen of Fools: that was the price to pay to be able to think in my own way. Over time, I lost my realm, but not the pleasure of originality.

So it was that, through the power of repetition, I arrived last at the Italian Psychoanalytic Society (SPI) as well, and as the last, I allowed myself a few antics, of which this text bears some testimony.

VIII

BETRAYAL AND CORRUPTION

On the corruptive power of maternal love and the *good use* of betrayal★

★Republication of the original work: Badoni, M. (2016), "Tradimento e corruzione". In Ambrosiano, L., Sarno, M. (a cura di) (2016), *Corruttori e corrotti. Ipotesi psicoanalitiche.* Mimesis, Milano.

My reflection regards the events that the process of subjectivation requires in order for the subject to be guaranteed the feeling of their own existence and the possibility of occupying their own free position in the world. This is a process that originally involves the child and his or her care environment but which is repeated with continuity and ruptures throughout life.

In particular, I would like to look into the indispensable role of the mother and the care environment and a release that is necessary, but fraught with pitfalls: the mother is her child's *spokesperson*. She must know to some extent what is happening to them in order to be able to help them, and yet the risk that the mother's word is not directed at promoting the constitution of the subject but becomes a law to be followed is constantly present. Since the mother's word is imbued with her own sensations, emotions and affects, the child will end up disinvesting their own perceptive system and will consequently experience increasing difficulties in their choices, and in particular in their affective choices.

DOI: 10.4324/9781003560647-14

Introduction: vicissitudes of a bond

Hatred stirs up strife,
but love covers all sins.

Proverbs, 10, 12

I begin with this passage from the book of *Proverbs*, which seems to warn us against all feelings of hatred and proposes a powerful, saving love: a sort of great amnesty that extinguishes all judgement and suspends thought. In fact, in the course of life, events appear much more complex: love certainly binds, but it also envelops, while hate provokes quarrels, but it is also a precise indicator of position and, as such, foundational in the constitution of the individual. Sometimes children, when they feel crushed by their parents' power, may say "I hate you" as a last bulwark in defence of their own subjectivity. Love is more complex, especially when the adjective "maternal" is added to it, which seems to shut out any possibility of questioning. In this absolute, women first of all risk being caged, to the detriment of the great, thoughtful work that is childcare.

Yet every man (and perhaps even more so every woman) will have to work hard to free themselves from a bond so inevitable that it can be paralysing. On the inevitability of the bond, there is not much to add, given the great *prematurity* of the infant, who, although endowed with the skills required to establish contact, is in absolute need of such contact to live. If anything, it will be a question of understanding on what procedures the bond is based and, above all, to what extent it is capable of guaranteeing future freedom.

I would therefore like to devote my attention to the misunderstandings of maternal love and, in particular, to its corruptive power. Here I give the term *corruption* its primary meaning: to spoil, to alter, to contaminate (according to the Istituto della Enciclopedia Italiana, founded by Giovanni Treccani, Rome). Corrupted matter loses its identity until it is no longer recognisable. Corruption speaks of death. When being corrupted refers to the Ego or the Self, we are faced with alterations that make it not only unusable but also unalive. It is above all the perceptive system that is affected and threatened in its proper functioning as guarantor of the harmony of the Self. In the absence of a smooth functioning of this system, in the absence of the ability to pick up clues and produce transformations, the individual will end up oscillating between states of excitement and inertia. Perhaps the very word love should warn us – a potentially contaminating love that does not do justice to the complexity of mental states required of the mother to take care of her child and does not allow the infant to be able to trust their own perceptions. The love that "covers all sins" becomes corruptive when the sin is that of existing, guilt that needs to be transformed, not covered.

My background for reflection will be the process of subjectivation as currently described and developed in psychoanalysis. Although this process has been observed and considered in different ways in the various theoretical models that study it, I believe that they can all be considered to have a common goal: the development and acquisition of the meaning humans seek regarding their own existence in the world, and thus the strength to sustain and defend their own free subjectivity.

Not an easy task because in the word *subject*, two opposing realities are brought together which are in open contradiction and yet are at the base of our uniqueness. In fact, *subject* is both the *subjectum*, the subjugated being, and the ego, thinking and acting, that which I am (Cahn, 1991), the ego, which Freud already said had to manoeuvre between the demands of the id (the unconscious), external reality and the superego, precipitated by inherited experiences and the introjection of parental dictates.

The process of subjectivation has its basis in very early childhood, but continues throughout life. It moves from extreme states of the mind, such as the feeling of helplessness (the *Hilflosigkeit* described by Freud), promotes dark, powerful feelings that also coagulate in feelings of guilt, guilt for one's own existence. When I write about the corruptive power of maternal love, I think both of a love that, raising children in the shadow of a faultless security, obscures the meaning of their existence, and of those patients who, according to Green (1993), oscillate between the obligation to survive and the impossibility of coping with the aspiration to live.

The human psyche is shaped in the relationship with the other from the original situation of helplessness. After Freud, who had already intuited in the *Project* the essential contribution to the infant of a rescuing adult, it was Bion, among the post-Freudians, who probed the ways in which this rescue happens and constructed a theory that has allowed us to follow the oscillations between intra-psychic, interpsychic, and intersubjective.

Around the exchange of messages between subjects, especially as they are rooted in bodily experience (from Bion's alpha function to Roussillon's messenger function of the drive), it is therefore of vital importance to be able to *notice*, in the relationship with the other, what is coming from the other, from the degree of resonance to the degree of compatibility that these messages bring with respect to the identity structure (what I myself am) and the sense of cohesion of the Self. *Noticing* means "becoming aware with the mind, becoming aware of a fact through clues or through reflection" (according to the Istituto della Enciclopedia Italiana, founded by Giovanni Treccani, Rome). Noticing also contains *correcting* – it is therefore by nature oscillating, doubtful, and sometimes in a state of alarm, like Dante's "helmsman in a great storm". It is not a matter here of rejecting that which is other than oneself but of setting in motion a discriminating function (that is why I speak of *noticing*) capable of sifting through the world of the senses, of establishing differences and gradients of compatibility with one's own structure. In this wandering between internal and external, noticing, precisely because it is mobile and oscillating, will have its own natural ambiguity, as a participant of two different natures, with the role of coordinating them. In emotional storms, it is important that the mind can work in ambiguity. Ambiguity is at the origin of creative instability; it interrogates but draws its richness from a suspended questioning. It is vital precisely because it does not close in on a given answer or certainty. In the world of the emotions, ambiguity does not have a positive or negative value – it warns, it creates connections, but it does not envelop. What is at stake here is the work that the ego carries out as a corporeal reality; it has its foundation in the work of perception and in the function of attention (Freud, 1911), whose task is to approach sensory impressions, instead of waiting for them to appear, its instrument. It is an activity of exploration and storage: exploration of reality, storage in the memory, activation of an activity of judgement, of thought, therefore, as an action of testing, as noticing. Since memory carries within it the traces of lived experiences, the problem that arises is the subject's ability to preserve the sense of its own identity in translating the traces. I have mentioned elsewhere (Badoni, 2014) how the operation of translating, in making the trace usable to one's own subjectivity, one's own idiom, entails running the risk of betrayal. This is the theme I would now like to explore.

Corruption and betrayal in the process of subjectivation

When the discriminating function fails to be sustained, the subject's sense of reality is tarnished. Being able to sustain one's own position with conviction is no longer a natural, albeit critical, time in the process of subjectivation but is experienced by the subject, who becomes entangled in it, as a betrayal with respect to the object. The feeling of guilt, all the more acute if the subject has fundamental ties to the object, can then work, unbeknownst to the subject's own awareness, as Freud (1907) seems to think when he speaks of the unconscious feeling of guilt. It can, however, be so powerful as to induce the subject to seek seemingly facilitating solutions, surrendering to maternal knowledge and its dictates. It is here that maternal love exerts corruptive power: the price to be paid for absolving guilt that is not there is the renunciation of exercising a judgement function on the perceptive traces, surrender of the ego, its agony. Alternatively, if a normal operation of translation is experienced as a betrayal, the subject, in order to evade feelings of guilt and silence the fury that agitates it, fury linked to the feeling of helplessness, will end up dividing itself: on the one hand, it will conform to the dictates of the maternal unconscious, on the other, it will seek pseudo-liberatory solutions. The subject's feeling of reality suffers.

We must therefore ask ourselves, when maternal love becomes corruptive, can betrayal be the only solution to get out of situations of *impasse*? At what price?

A recent issue of the review *Psyche* (*Dire di No*, 2014) explores this theme at different levels. In the Introduction to this issue, Maurizio Balsamo (2014) writes about how much work, both individual and collective, is necessary to say no as an existential affirmation, identity structure and refusal of an intrusion, but also as a space of dissent and conflict, of negativism. In the same issue, Vincenzo Bonaminio (2014) returns to the concept introduced by Anna Freud of *emotional surrender*: faced with the terror of a regression capable of causing dissolution of the personality, the individual, to avoid surrendering, entrenches themselves in a position of rejection. With just these brief hints, we are already faced with a wide range of *refusals*: before "no" can be said, pronounced, continuous work on a perceptive and emotional level is needed to ensure the subject its individuality. Before "I say", "I feel" must have space, the only guarantee for speech to be not only enunciated but also alive. Work on perception plays a fundamental role here. The bet is the acquisition of the subject's sense of reality: Margaret Mahler reminds us that the first perceptions concern the proprioceptive system, the state of being kept safe in the mother's arms even in moments of despondency or furious agitation. Traces of this can be found in the lullabies handed down for generations to comfort maternal exhaustion: "Ninna nanna ninna oh . . . questo bimbo a chi lo do, io lo do alla befana che lo tenga una settimana, io lo do all'uomo nero che lo tenga un anno intero . . . io lo do al lupo bianco che lo tenga di tanto in tanto".[1]

In order for mothers to hold their babies and take them to sleep and dream, they must be able to think about pushing them away: holding is not holding back. Mahler again (1981) illustrated how important it is for the mother to tolerate the baby's movements away. In Thomas Balmès' beautiful documentary *Babies* (2010) about the first year of growing up of children in different cultures, I was very struck by the child growing up in Mongolia with a mother, firm but calm, who lets him have his experiences even if they seem dangerous to an outside, stranger's view. The moment when this child stands with a look between trepidation and triumph is very moving. Standing up straight introduces into his world a three-dimensionality of which he seems to be as surprised as he is proud. Now he really has his feet on the ground, a phrase currently used to indicate the acquisition of a sense of reality, including what the reality of his own existence entails.

It is at this level, between adhering to another reality and acquiring a reality of one's own, that I felt I could reflect on betrayal and corruption, which I would like to place in antithesis here. Betrayal and corruption certainly intercept the theme of *No*, but before that they concern the holding of the self and the capacity to defend one's own reality: betrayal insofar as it opens up the possibility of differentiating oneself, corruption insofar as it constitutes a state of degradation and dissolution of what I am referring to here as the original nucleus and constitution of the Self, a possible object of corruptive phenomena by the care environment.

Is it possible to imagine what dilemmas the infant has to face and what solutions it can find to free itself from the absolute power of maternal love? The passage quoted from the book of *Proverbs* takes us to the heart of this debate, inaugurated by Freud in 1920 in *Beyond the Pleasure Principle*, when he introduced the two antagonistic drives of hate and love, of life and death. But even here, things are not, as we know, simple, since the declination of hatred goes from its destructive power to its imperative to differentiate itself before separating, and that of love goes from the capacity to welcome without question to a secret pact of alliances that gives no room for any individuation and, in this sense, ends up being corruptive.

I will therefore write about corruption and betrayal, phenomena that are often lumped together but which I would like to differentiate and even contrast here, especially with respect to the theme from which my considerations began: the process of subjectivation.

Betrayal between tradition and innovation

To better understand the philosophy of betrayal, I will now turn to other studies. In historical events, betrayal is not always linked to corruption – on the contrary, there is already the matter of the 30 denarii (a minimal sum for the time) with which the military allegedly convinced Judas to hand over Christ, which seemed to some to be a pretext hiding other, more complex motives. Borges embroiders on the subject in *Fictions* (1944) by scrutinising the texts of the three Versions of Judas and the related hypotheses proposed in the early 1900s by Nils Runeberg, a member of the Swedish Evangelical Union. According to this author, whose hypotheses, after Borges, have recently been revived, what need would Judas have had to hand over a man known to the multitudes for such a paltry sum? According to Runenberg, Judas was nothing more than a double of Christ, the invisible redeemer described in the third Version of Judas, a pawn in the fulfilment of the prophecies. In psychoanalysis, we would say that Judas, the richest and most cultured of the apostles, was the actor in a transgenerational mandate, a task assigned to his unconscious by the need to bring the ideals of previous generations to fulfilment.

The theme seems to be back *in vogue* in these times of uncertain or complacent identities. Benedict XVI wrote about it, commented on by Zagrebelsky (in the newspaper *La Repubblica, il Dibattito*, 6 September 2012), forcing us to reflect, and picking up on the themes addressed by Amos Oz in his recent novel *Judah* (2014). The young Shemuel's search for identity is set against the backdrop of the confrontation between two great characters, the real Ben Gurion and the fictional Abrabanel, on the problem of the origins of the state of Israel and its relationship with the Arab world: prophetic visions or betrayal? The dialogue is interrupted in the text by the violent death of a son, an extreme, destructive event that extinguishes every hope, every project, every word. Instead of the two discussants, an inaccessible refuge remains – a closed, empty room on one side and a man alone in his grief on the other. Here, too, a mental state appears that hangs over the betrayer and his torments, a painful state of splitting, of impossible dialogue not only between two men immersed in their respective beliefs but, we would say in psychoanalysis, between two incompatible states of the Ego, of the Self: one faithful to an ideal of origins at risk of turning into an ideology, the other projected into the future at risk of being subversive.

Betrayal thus appears as the result of a courageous act that opens the way to change and to life: "Anyone willing to change", Shmuel said, "will always be considered a traitor by those who cannot change and are scared to death of change and don't understand it and loathe change". In the novel, it is the young protagonist who reopens the room and questions the interrupted dialogue, to then set off again alone on life's journey in search of his own identity, with few certainties, a good dose of suffering, but much wisdom.

What use can be made of betrayal? What is at stake? The etymon of the verb, from the Latin *tradere*, leads us to deliver, but also to hand down. The concept has recently been revisited by Giulio Giorello (2012), who writes how, in the tension between tradition and innovation, the *betrayer*, who nonetheless delivers something to someone else, appears to be working primarily for the former, for tradition. Yet the innovative power of betrayal lies precisely in the narrow margin between handing over and handing down. We must therefore understand more clearly what is meant by tradition. The term *tradition* implies time and thus the succession of generations: tradition is not repetition, but rather creative acrobatics continually transforming and renewing what comes from the past with what is achievable here. In this sense, betrayal, meaning delivering but also handing down, appears as a state of tension watching over this passage – it is a bridge, a useful tension. It is the situation around this tension that I am interested in examining. In all times when tradition has lost the sense of a continuity capable of renewal and instead clothes itself in rituals of conformism or entrenches itself in ideological positions, the traitor – or who is considered as such – has been the one who has broken the chains to initiate a path of transformation and renewal, breaking with a pact that immobilises, offering a promise of freedom. Betrayal and corruption are antithetical here: corruption is deadly, betrayal is vital.

I was deeply moved when, in my reading, I came across Vidal-Naquet, the inspiration for an earlier and now distant reflection of mine on hiding, another borderland between surrender and innovation. In his essay *Du bon usage de la trahison* [*The Good Use of Betrayal*] (1977), Vidal-Naquet weaves his thesis around the betrayal of Josephus Flavius at the time of the Jewish War. With rich documentation of a terribly troubled period in Jewish history in the face of the Roman conquest, the author argues that Josephus, in taking sides with the Romans, was in fact guaranteeing the perpetuation of Jewish tradition, opposing an idealism that would bring death, represented in the text by Elazar's famous speech on the fortress of Masada, besieged by the Roman army. The Roman siege was *countered* here, following the speech, with a mass suicide of all the Jews barricaded inside.

It is not within my power, nor is it my intention, to enter into the merits of this highly cultured essay. It is, however, my conviction that betrayal can and should be put to good use whenever one finds oneself entangled in situations of *impasse*. I will now try to give reasons for these thoughts.

The origins of humanity and the good use of betrayal

I will now return to the process of subjectivation and the not only good, I believe, but inevitable use of betrayal. In the succession of generations, inner and outer worlds, ego and object, face each other continually. The process of subjectivation is at the centre of this encounter. We have seen how ambiguity, the ability to keep this encounter open, can initiate transformations – betrayal participates in this ambiguity. The individual is simultaneously the object of delivery and the subject of innovation. To be an agent of renewal over time, the individual must be able to transform the anguish of betrayal into an awareness of freedom. In order to do so, they must be well equipped to be able to read their emotions and the direction these emotions take: this is the task of early care; it is what shapes the primordial mind; it is what reappears in one of the most incisive moments of life – adolescence. If the mind is not able to carry out these operations, the betrayal is not absolved by the feeling of guilt that accompanies it, and the subject either remains inert or splits. It does not promote transformations in the conflict between the parts but continually oscillates, siding now with one side and then with the other. One cannot promote transformations if one surrenders to delivery, nor if one gets excited by triumphing over a state of dependence. The body is the theatre of this conflict, and this is where the possibility of becoming aware of the world of sensations and emotions and of transforming them comes into play – the good use of betrayal in favour of change, therefore, even if this entails the loss of presumed security that relies on solutions which are as facilitating as they are deceptive. If in the relationship with the other, the subject is carried away by convenience, time will stand still.

The problem is crucial and unavoidable in that coming into the world is originally overshadowed by ambiguity – every human being's arrival in the world involves an interweaving of innovation and continuity. Tradition cannot ignore the conflict between generations. The act of begetting *delivers* the unborn child to life with an ambiguous message: this new life is yours, but we, your parents, have begotten you, and through you we aim to perpetuate our continuity. What use will the unborn child make of this ambiguous message? At birth, the infant is already immersed in a great contradiction: "When we are born, we cry that we are come/To this great stage of fools" (Shakespeare, 1608).

The Hungarian psychoanalyst Ferenczi (1929) made us aware of the immense expenditure of energy required of parents to make up to their children for bringing them into the world without asking their permission. As psychoanalysts, we have often felt in patients a deep resentment for having been brought into the world *without their knowledge*. This resentment is all the more heated the more precarious the subject's sense of reality. The problem is therefore not the betrayal, but if anything, being able to perceive the betrayal as inevitable and even courageous in its effort, not as guilt that crushes and alienates. If birth is perceived as an authoritarian and violent act, with no possible opposition, violence will work in the subject – violence that is as secret as it is explosive, violence that we so often notice in patients caught between the obligation to survive and the impossibility of coping with the aspirations to live.

In dealing with how the identity of the subject is constructed, psychoanalysis has long taught us that there are transgenerational mandates, unconscious imperatives that weigh on the construction of the subject when the generation before it has not been able to resolve conflicts upstream, to unearth family secrets or to deal with disappointments. In this case, the conflicts of previous generations do indeed come – treacherously – into the constitution of the new identity. The individual lives laboriously burdened by an alien identity – it survives. However, the good use of betrayal does not only concern these extreme situations but is written from the beginning not only as a measure to confer originality on mental events but as a constant practice of every beginning, initiative and initiation.

Bion taught us to think of the mother–infant relationship as supported by two pillars: on the one hand, the *rêverie* function with which the mother takes in the raw sensory elements that the child transmits to her and makes them thinkable for the child; on the other hand, the negative capacity, which concerns the possibility of proceeding in uncertainty without rushing into action.

Much has been said and written about *rêverie*, at times at the risk of making it an infallible, decisive tool, but less has been said about the basis of negative capability and the useful tools for cultivating it. Thus I return to lullabies: in the age of motorisation, parents have got into the habit of putting recalcitrant children to sleep by putting them in the car and driving them around. We could say that they lull them to sleep by betrayal, deluding them about a possible family trip. The child who is about to fall asleep knows instead – and the parents know it too – that the problem is that of sustaining a separation: sleep also recalls the last sleep, from which one does not wake up. That is why the mother who continues to hold her baby, thinking she can, should and wants to push him or her away, is a mother who is doing a good exercise in negative capability: I am here to let you go. By accepting the loss of contact with the child and instead maintaining contact with herself, the mother proceeds in uncertainty, supported by her perceptions, her thoughts and her affections, and in so doing, conveys to her child that he or she can do the same, without fear. In these cases, betraying becomes a natural eventuality: *tradere*, handing over and handing down – handing over to another world, that of sleep and dreams, to begin a new day: "I have left, but I am still here, no one is offended". This is also what the analyst does in sessions, and it is this that made me think of the setting, with its times, its rhythms, its silences, as thinking arms. These are moments of great tension where the sign of *mission accomplished* is precisely the tonal relaxation of the child who has finally trusted that they can set off on the journey into the night with their own heritage of signs and dreams. It is those relaxed silences in analysis that indicate the work of free thought, which knows it can seek without necessarily finding and, above all, *without finding what the other expects.*

Note

1 A traditional lullaby which translates as "Ninna nanna ninna oh/Who will I give this child to?/I'll give him to the old witch who'll hold him a week/I'll give him to the bogeyman who'll hold him a year/I'll give him to the white wolf who'll hold him sometimes".

Bibliography

Badoni, M. (2014), "Corpo". In *Rivista di Psicoanalisi*, 60, pp. 917–932.

Balmès, T. (2010), *Babies*. Production companies: Chez Wam, Canal+, StudioCanal; distributed by: Focus Features, StudioCanal.

Balsamo, M. (2014), "Dire di no". In *Psiche. Rivista di cultura psicoanalitca*, 2, pp. 261–266.

Bonaminio, V. (2014), "Un articolo "fantasma" si aggira per l'Europa. Il "no" e gli "stati di negativismo" nella concezione di Anna Freud". In *Psiche. Rivista di cultura psicoanalitica*, 2, pp. 349–364.

Borges, J.L. (1962), *Fictions*. Grove Press, New York.

Cahn, R. (1991), "Du sujet". In *Revue Française de Psychanalyse*, 55, 6 pp. 1354–1490.

Ferenczi, S. (1929), "The Unwanted Child And His Death Instinct". In *Final Contributions to the Problems and Methods of Psychoanalysis*. Karnac, London, 1980.

Freud, S. (1907), *Obsessive Actions and Religious Practices*. SE, vol. IX, 1959.

Freud, S. (1911), *Formulations on the Two Principles of Mental Functioning*. SE, vol. XII, 1958.

Freud, S. (1920), *Beyond the pleasure principle*. SE, vol. XVIII, 1955.

Giorello, G. (2012), *Il tradimento. In politica, in amore e non solo*. Longanesi, Milano.

Green, A. (1993), *The Work of the Negative* (Trans. Weller, A.). Free Association Books, 1999.

Mahler, M.S. (1981), "Aggression in the Service of Separation-Individuation: Case Study of a Mother-Daughter Relationship". In *Psychoanalytic Quarterly*, 50, pp. 625–638.

Oz, A. (2014), *Judas* (Trans. de Lange, N.). Chatto & Windus, London, 2016.

Shakespeare, W. (1608), *King Lear* (Act 4 Scene 6).

Vidal-Naquet, P. (1977), *Du bon usage de la trahison*, preface to *Flavius Josephus, La Guerre des Juifs* (Trans. Savinel, P.). Minuit, Paris, pp. 30–32.

IX

A PROBLEM AT THE ORIGINS

Originality

In a previous work (Badoni, 2016), questioning the strength of maternal love and its enveloping power, I had wondered whether a *good use of betrayal* (Vidal-Naquet, 1977) might not temper its risk of corrupting.

In the following reflections, I would like to develop the theme starting from the succession of generations and the first vicissitudes, those that should allow the infant to sustain its otherness regarding the common matrix binding it to the mother and the family imprint. This involves complex mental work that, in the passage from one generation to the next, involves infants and caregivers and unfolds over time, finding in adolescence a fundamental junction point.

For some time, I have been wondering about situations of *impasse*, which, in the treatment of some young patients, I felt were difficult to overcome. In particular, I have noticed that when, for various reasons, the intimate workings of perception are obstructed, the feeling of existing can be threatened by a sort of disorientation or invalidated by deep feelings of guilt, as if *feeling otherwise* were equated with *feeling against*, a *dissent*. It is an experience that has deep roots, as if being able to find vitalising support in one's own perceptual system were tantamount to betrayal: *vita mea, mors tua*.

Could the etymology of the word *betray* mitigate the gloomy shadow that accompanies the word and offer a safe exit to otherwise suffocating situations?

DOI: 10.4324/9781003560647-15

The term "betray" comes from the Latin *tradere*, to deliver or hand over, as does the term "tradition". In the latter case, *tradere* means handing down memories, news and testimonies to another time, from one generation to another. It is therefore a term in tension between a gift, which is also a *prodigal* act (Ferenczi, 1929), the handing over to a living state, and a task, a transmission, with which the individual is burdened and assigned.

It would then be a question of finding a possible balance between the *physiological* burden that accompanies the passage of generations and an assignment tinged with violence. With this in mind, I have long since initiated a reflection on the possible *good use* of betrayal.

What arguments has psychoanalytic thought offered us – and still does so – in favour of a good use of betrayal? To address this issue, we need to dwell on the complexity of the passage between generations and its ambiguities.

Ambiguity in the passage between generations: handing over, handing down

The passage from one generation to the next calls us to witness a fact and commits us to taking on a task, as underlined by the etymology of the verb *tradere*, the source of both betrayal and tradition.

Here I would like to develop the nature of the movements that accompany the succession of generations: a handing over, but also a change of step. What is asked of the infant after handing it over to the world without its knowledge? (Ferenczi, 1929) The passage between generations harbours violence and foreshadows a destiny that can become a threat: in the myth, Oedipus is abandoned on Mount Cithaeron in the name of his father's survival and the continuity of paternal power, of maintaining the kingdom. Beyond this myth, parents – mothers in particular – know that bringing a child into the world thrusts them fatally into another generation and another time, inevitably closer to death.

What will parents ask for in return for the gift of life?

Given these premises, how can the originality of the infant be preserved? What use can the infant make of a message that, ignoring the caesura of birth, seems to take no account of the newborn's state of powerlessness and even less of the profound labour involved in the task of transmission? We know that the infant, the child still deprived of speech, although equipped to make contact with the surrounding world, is totally dependent on the care environment, as Freud had already emphasised by introducing the notion of *Hilflosigkeit*, then developed by Winnicott, considering the infant and the mother as a dual unity. How can the infant's originality be sustained with the task of handing down what has been acquired from the preceding generation?

The tension of the word "betray" allows us to range between the gratitude of a gift received and the gravity of a task such as transmission: can this tension really authorise us, as Riding's verses suggest, to be "original in innocence"? It would be a matter of being able to take one's own position, bargaining with anxieties, feelings of guilt and fears in support of the right to exist in freedom.

In the Victorian era, at a time of great change, when the society of the old landed gentry was strained by new powers and new initiatives, originality was considered a virtue (Graves, 1948, 513): being original meant having that "mental squint" that, by widening the field of vision, could include acquired rights and novelty. "Mental squint" brings to mind a gaze capable of keeping an eye on different fields, not to control them, but to have a third vision, a task that can become acrobatic, something that surprises and disorientates, and for this very reason is creative – a net that supports without, however, imprisoning can be useful.

How is the wisdom of living transmitted through life?

If the subject is hostage to a task assigned to them by the previous generation (Faimberg, 2005), they will be inhabited by a violence as secret as it is explosive, the one we so often feel in our patients caught, as Green (1999, 123) writes, "between the necessity to survive and the impossibility of facing their life aspirations". In adolescence, when a *new birth* has to complete the succession of generations, the issue is more pressing than ever: the *impasse* to which Green refers can confine the individual to a clandestine status (Badoni, 1994). It is here that, in *après-coup*, the failed betrayals of childhood, the failed conquest of one's own originality, are revealed.

Origins and originality: Freud's squint, Winnicott's arms, Bion and the primordial mind

"There is much more continuity between uterine life and early childhood than the impressive caesura of birth allows us to believe".
(Freud, 1926, 138)

This is a strong statement, in the background of which one glimpses Freud's need to distance himself from Rank's proposal (1924), which sees in the trauma of birth, hence in the caesura, the prototype of every subsequent situation of anguish. Disturbed by the question of the traumatic force of the caesura but attracted by the problem that it nonetheless poses, Freud oscillates in the following lines between a strong idea of continuity: "the child's biological situation as a foetus is replaced for it by a psychical object–relation to its mother", and an acrobatic leap: "But we must not forget that during its intra–uterine life the mother was not an object for the foetus, and that at that time there were no objects at all". On the one hand, the problem does not seem to arise; it is a matter of coordinating a biological situation with mental functioning, but immediately afterwards a fundamental question arises: how to jump from a *non-object* to an *object*, and what repercussions does this have on mental functioning?

Starting from these premises, Freud will elaborate (1926), in a central position in his work, a theory of anxiety that, without solving the problem, will be the premise of fundamental subsequent elaborations. The body, as a sentient instrument, plays a decisive role here.

A powerful mediator of this transit is, in fact, anxiety, which is "an affective state and, as such, can, of course, only be felt", writes Freud (1926, 140), an affect that can be devastating or valuable: devastating if it exceeds the mental apparatus's possibilities of tolerance, complicit in the breaking of the shield that protects against stimuli (Freud, 1926, 170); a signal, giving employment to the psyche, complicit in removal, in the relations between Ego, Id and Superego. An economic point of view, referring to the operations necessary to succour states of need and, on the other hand, an ordeal for the demands affecting the human psyche. It is anguish that creates removal, that mobilises the relations between demands, a stimulus for mental work as opposed to the regression that the Ego can use to extinguish, with the same drive motion, the mental work itself. And the caesura? It is not birth that is the trauma, but the lack of the mother, Freud writes. But how can it be articulated if the mother is not an object perceived as such?

Assuming that anxiety is "something that is felt", two qualities of anxiety are dealt with in the infant's cradle (Freud, 1926, 170): a vital but potentially traumatic anxiety aroused by a need that the mother should satisfy (and here the loss of perception is equivalent to the loss of the object) until "repeated situations of satisfaction have created an object out of the mother; and this object, whenever the infant feels a need, receives an intense cathexis which might be described as a 'longing' one". With this *longing*, the *non-object mother* seems to become an object in the form of *pre-conception*, but for this we will have to wait decades and Bion's thinking. For now, we can note that by looking at the *before* and *after* in an attempt to remove the traumatic value from the separation, to confer it instead on the object and the impelling need for the object, Freud opens up a debate on the caesura that is still ongoing.

For Freud, two paths present themselves: anxiety as an inappropriate automatic response, reproducing the anxious state of the origin and, if not rescued, submerging the Ego, or signal anxiety, which can be elaborated by the Ego: "a sort of inoculation, submitting to a slight attack of the illness in order to escape its full strength", Freud writes (Freud, 1926, 162).

Thus, after minimising the extent of the caesura, Freud returns to it, leaving us with valuable indications: anxiety, its modulations, something that is felt – thus the Ego/body plays a primary role. And the vaccine? It plays a decisive role in allowing us to contact each other without infection, so respecting originality. Without a separation, without a caesura, there can be no originality.

This is represented for us by Piero della Francesca, when in *La Madonna del parto*, he highlights not the child, but the caesura: a truly impressive cut traces a mark on the Madonna's belly that cannot escape our gaze. The two angels witnessing the event are striking for a clear difference in their gaze and in the colours of their robes, reflected in the colours of their magic wings – a magic touch by Piero. The dramatic gaze of the one reverberates in the confident gaze of the other: *she'll make it*, but fluctuations are to be reckoned with, as is the presence of someone who is not only not frightened by the contradictions but can be intrigued by them and support them. The child, on the other hand, in Piero's daring and absolutely original solution, is not there: it has not yet been seen; the game of resemblances that reappears each time over the new-borns' cradle has not yet been unleashed, today even more challenging, given new methods of procreation. Piero opens an abyss of possibilities on this caesura and an open challenge to the composition of the dilemma: origins and originality, suspended time and the beginning.

The first act is weighing, but, whether male or female, what will the weight be, and how much will their origins allow them their own originality, that *squinting* gaze that allows them to take in the past and venture into the future?

Going on being: **Winnicott**

Winnicott tells us that this infant must first of all be picked up, held and supported: once the floating in amniotic fluid is over, once the fulfilment of all needs through the organisation of the mother's body is over, other means will be needed (Freud, 1926, 138) to support the newborn's fragile subjectivity.

The weight will be felt, and it will be the mother's and partner's arms that will establish that *tonic dialogue* (de Ajuriaguerra, 1963) which will establish an initial, load-bearing link between the quality of the infant's tone and the caregivers' response. Winnicott describes this situation in terms of holding and handling: holding founds the integration process and protects the infant from a sense of annihilation; handling is a style of caring that includes a time (perhaps the acquisition of a rhythm) – a time for the infant to *process* – working through – and make their own the somatic events that for them are also the first mental events.

The proprioceptive sensibility, both conscious and unconscious, begins to weave its bonds. In this period, both intended care and misunderstandings will inevitably occur. If extremes, falls or screw-ups can be avoided, a three-dimensional space will be formed in which the infant can enjoy its time, support its needs and open up to desire.

The infant gradually feels that they are not only important to someone, but that they can be someone. According to Winnicott, this arouses the first feelings of guilt, the dark companion on the path to originality.

In the period of care, it will be up to the analyst, with the *thinking arms of the setting* (Badoni, 2008), to withstand old misunderstandings to try and re-establish continuity: going on being. Winnicott's fundamental thought as formulated in *being alone in the mother's presence* is fundamental to the problem with which we are dealing: originality. It would then be Bion who returned to the caesura and the origins, inviting us to new, fruitful investigations.

Beginnings and initiation:
Bion and the primordial mind

That corporeality required uncommon work from the infant was a great insight of Freud's, which, speaking of the drive, he defines "as a measure of the demand made upon the mind" (Freud, 1915, 122). The problem that Bion poses concerns the nature of the work of transforming raw sensory data, as manifested by the infant and as collected and transformed by the maternal psyche. Rather than underestimating the caesura, Bion allows himself to be impressed and investigates it, without forgetting Freud and perhaps without fully admitting his debt to Winnicott.

The new aspect on which Bion bases the quality of this work is the complex intrapsychic and interpsychic nature of these exchanges. The laws that regulate this collaboration have a highly complex construct. Bion calls this construct the *primordial mind*: it corresponds to a mental activity that has its roots in the body, a kind of thought, Bion would say, waiting for a thinker. Mental activity is articulated in several steps and is not to be confused with thinking. In commenting on Bion's work, Green (1998) emphasises the distinction between mental events, rooted in the body: thoughts without a thinker, corresponding to beta elements waiting to be transformed by the mother's alpha function, and thinking, which, as thought by a thinker, can at this point be transmitted. Elements remain, however, which will not be transformed and which nevertheless form an experiential basis.

Compared to other theorisations, the maternal function, given its negative capability, has a characteristic that I would call initiatory: it promotes transformations but does not hold them to account. In initiation rites, we know that there is a time when the initiate is left alone to test the experience (Badoni, 1994). It is less important here what one thinks than the capacity for thinking. In this perspective, guilt is less present in Bion's thought: the *good use of betrayal* is in the practice of negative capability, as of every transformative step. The mother does not transmit knowledge, she transmits a way of knowing, a wisdom – in the term "wisdom" there is tasting: in the Freudian binomial, I swallow/spit, and, with the experience of tasting, there appears the possibility of making one's own judgement. The child, therefore, has its own set of skills, abilities or competences that certainly need someone else to be seen, accepted, commented on and transformed, but, like every initiation, even in that to think-ing, there remains a self-managed experiential basis, a *hidden space of the Self*, we could say with Masud Khan, a free space (Golse, 2001), beyond maternal intervention – one's own very personal time.

The *good enough mother* is the one who has been able to renounce an ideal of perfection and the illusion of faultless knowledge. She transmits to the child not her intellectual acquisitions, but her knowledge, her way of having tasted (*sapio*) the world. In this exchange, which is written from the origins, no one is virgin land, not, of course, the mother, who presents herself at the appoint-ment with her own history and ties, but neither is the infant, who in any case has to manage an inheritance of legacies, previous experiences and potentialities of its own. Adolescence recalls and rekindles this conflict, but if the adolescent has not been initiated in childhood to learn from experience, they will not be able to do so now, when puberty revives the ancient grappling with their own body.

What about the institution?

It would be incorrect to conclude this consideration on the dilemma posed by the origins/originality juxtaposition without asking some questions about the responsibility the Institution has – or should have – to preserve its members' originality.

Thinking recently about the role that the Institution and the ana-lytic family have with respect to their members, I proposed (Badoni, 2020) that the best perspective for bringing new life and original-ity to psychoanalytic thought could lie, for those in the group of members, in the *capacity to be alone in the presence of the Institution*. By this I mean the ability, in the analytic family (Bolognini, 2008), to feel sufficiently oriented and guaranteed in one's own professional identity and at the same time be free bearers of one's own original thought.

Regarding the theme dealt with, it must be admitted that the ana-lytic family has been way ahead of its time, with respect to today's family, in programming its own family structure: not randomness, but selections; not education (it was only a few years ago that we began to think about group behaviour in the group), but training. As with today's parents, there is more interest in success than in succeeding.

Where, in the training itinerary, is the creative potential of the caesura and the wealth of developments that it proposes, in analytical training?

The long journey that precedes joining the association, despite the many efforts made, ends up weakening the driving force of this event. We have witnessed this in recent years as the presence of new associates proclaimed at the Annual General Meeting has been diminishing noticeably, as if the attainment of a *secure position* were being prioritised over an initial demanding passage into a group whose role should be to support creative play and be curious about its development.

What are the responsibilities in the *delivery room* where new "memberships" are decided? Who are the guarantors (Piero della Francesca's angels come to mind) who watch over this exciting moment of origin? And how much is the game of similarities, which also unfolds here, part of an inevitable recognition, and how much does it lead to idiosyncrasies?

Bibliography

Aulagnier, P. (1975), *The Violence of Interpretation. From Pictogram to Statement*. Routledge, Hove, 2001.

Badoni, M. (1994), "La clandestinità nella organizzazione sociale e nella relazione analitica". Atti del X Congresso Nazionale della Società Psicoanalitica Italiana *La risposta dell'analista e le trasformazioni del campo analitico*, Rimini.

Badoni, M. (2008), "Il corpo tra riconoscimento e alienazione". Relazione del Gruppo di Studio al Collegio, S. Carlo, Convegno *"Incontrare l'altro, evitare l'altro – emozioni e narrazioni"*, Milano, 12 aprile 2008.

Badoni, M. (2014), "Corpo". In *Rivista di Psicoanalisi*, 60, pp. 917–932.

Badoni, M. (2015), "Un corpo per pensare: dialogo tonico e dialogo analitico". Relazione tenuta al Congresso *Transiti corpo-mente*, Università degli Studi Milano-Bicocca, 24 ottobre 2015.

Badoni, M. (2016), "Tradimento e corruzione". In Ambrosiano, L., Sarno, M. (a cura di), *Corruzioni: perché si corrompe – perché si è corrotti. Ipotesi Psicoanalitiche*. Mimesis, Milano.

Badoni, M. (2020), "Il tempo dell'analisi, il tempo dell'analista". In Corsa, R., Fattori, L., Vandi, G. (a cura di), *Vecchiaia e psicoanalisi*. Alpes, Roma.

Bion, W.R. (1966), *Attention and Interpretation*. Tavistock, London, 1970.

Bolognini, S. (2008), "Freud's 'Objects'". In *Secret Passages. The Theory and Technique of Interpsychic Relations* (Trans. Atkinson, G.). Routledge, Hove, 2011.

de Ajuriaguerra, J. (1963), "Le corps comme relation". In *Revue Suisse de Psychologie Pure et Appliquée*, 21, 2, pp. 137–157.

Faimberg, H. (2005), *The Telescoping of Generations. Listening to the Narcissistic Linkes Between Generations.* Routledge, London.

Ferenczi, S. (1929), "The Unwanted Child And His Death Instinct". In *Final Contributions to the Problems and Methods of Psychoanalysis.* Karnac, London, 1980.

Freud, S. (1915), *Instincts and their Vicissitudes.* SE, vol. XIV.

Freud, S. (1926), *Inhibitions, Symptoms and Anxiety.* SE, vol. XX.

Golse, B. (2001), "De la différenciation à la séparation: it's a long way to go". In *Revue française de psychanalyse*, 65, pp. 369–380.

Graves, R. (1948), *The White Goddess.* Faber and Faber, London.

Green, A. (1993), *The Work of the Negative* (Trans. Weller, A.). Free Association Books, 1999.

Green, A. (1998), "The Primordial Mind and the Work of the Negative". In *The International Journal of Psychoanalysis*, 79, pp. 649–665.

Rank, O. (1924), *The Trauma Of Birth.* Kegan Paul, Trench, Trubner and Co., London, 1929.

Vidal-Naquet, P. (1977), *Du bon usage de la trahison*, preface to *Flavius Josephus, La Guerre des Juifs* (Trans. Savinel, P.). Minuit, Paris.

For Product Safety Concerns and Information please contact our EU
representative GPSR@taylorandfrancis.com
Taylor & Francis Verlag GmbH, Kaufingerstraße 24, 80331 München, Germany

www.ingramcontent.com/pod-product-compliance
Lightning Source LLC
Chambersburg PA
CBHW050648280326
41932CB00015B/2831